THE LEFT, THE RIGHT AND THE JEWS

THE LEFT, THE RIGHT AND THE JEWS

W.D. Rubinstein

UNIVERSE BOOKS
New York

Published in the United States of America in 1982
By Universe Books
381 Park Avenue South, New York, N.Y. 10016
© 1982 W.D. Rubinstein

82 83 84 85 86/10 9 8 7 6 5 4 3 2 1

Library of Congress Cataloging in Publication Data

Rubinstein, W.D.
    The left, the right, and the Jews.

    Includes index.
    1. Jews – Politics and government – 1948-.
2. Antisemitism.   3. Right and left (Political science)
4. Elite (Social sciences)   5. Israel and the Diaspora.
I. Title
DS143.R83   1982   909′.04924082   82–8614
ISBN 0–87663–400–5   AACR2

Printed in Great Britain

CONTENTS

To my friends and colleagues
in Canberra, Melbourne
and Geelong

INTRODUCTION

This is a book about the contemporary Jewish situation. It argues that the status of Jews in the Western world since 1945 has been different from that of Jews in any previous era because only since 1945 has virtually the whole of Western Jewry moved into the upper-middle class. This has occurred at a time when the conservative establishment throughout the Western world is largely pro-Israel and philo-semitic. Fringe neo-Nazi groups not-withstanding, significant anti-semitism is now almost exclusively a left-wing rather than a right-wing phenomenon. Jews have reacted to their changed socio-economic status and to the emergence of left-wing anti-Zionism and anti-semitism by a distinct move to the political and intellectual right throughout the Western world. The book examines these trends in the United States, Britain and Australia, while the Jewish situation in Israel and the Soviet Union is described by way of comparison.

These theses are bound to be controversial. Perhaps the most serious criticism they are likely to meet is that, in my frank description of contemporary Western Jewry as an 'elite', I am fanning the flames of anti-semitism. I can only state in defence that I fully appreciate this point and am well aware of how often the myth of a mysterious, all-powerful Jewish conspiracy has been used by anti-semites. I believe, however, that my use of this term, which is backed up by considerable objective evidence, is both factually accurate and sufficiently differentiated from the fictional depictions of anti-semites. Lord Macaulay said more than a century ago that 'bigotry never wants an excuse', and anyone who seizes on the evidence or opinions offered in this book to support anti-semitism is unlikely to respond to rational evidence or pleas for tolerance, however these are presented.

Although I alone am responsible for the opinions or facts in this book I owe a considerable debt of gratitude to many people for their assistance, advice or criticism. The most important of these are: (in Australia) Michael Danby, Dr Eva Halevy, Roy Hay, Dr Frank Knopfelmacher, Rabbi J. Levi, Sam Lipski, Pam Maclean, Dr Robert Manne, Chanan Reich, Professor T.H. Rigby, Dr Margaret Rose, Professor Robert Taft and Professor Francis West; (in the

United States) Professor Sidney Goldstein, Nathan Glazer, Marshall Sklare, Joel Carmichael, Milton Himmelfarb and Nathaniel Weyl; (in Britain) Alex Gerlis, John Reddaway, Malcolm Rifkind, MP, Harold Soref and Stanley Rubin. I owe a particular debt of gratitude to the invaluable services of Michael Danby and Sam Lipski of Australia – Israel Publications, Melbourne. My wife Hilary provided in every sense the original inspiration. It was Melbourne, and the virulence of left-wing anti-Zionism there, which caused me to put on paper the ideas which have been germinating for many years.

1 THE PATTERN OF MODERN JEWISH HISTORY

The most important single feature of modern Jewish history is the changing nature and size of the Jewish elite, and the relationship of that elite both to the mass of Jews and to the wider world. The essential features of this relationship have changed four times since the early nineteenth century.

In the first phase, lasting from 1815 to about 1870, a small Sephardic or German Ashkenazi elite within the Jewish community achieved great wealth and considerable influence in most Western countries.[1] In the second phase, 1870 to 1914, the influence of this elite continued to grow, although in an atmosphere of increasing anti-semitism, which was aimed at both the Yiddish-speaking 'horde' making its way West prompted by ever more intense pogroms in the East, and at the alleged power and influence of the Jewish financial elite. In the third period, 1918 to 1945 – the period of maximum danger in modern Jewish history – the power, wealth and leadership abilities of the old Jewish elite collapsed just before the eastern European migrants had begun to make their own social and economic ascent. Against a background of extreme anti-semitism and Fascism, and a general economic depression, the Jews at this time everywhere were in peril.

Since 1945 (and especially since about 1960) the formerly depressed eastern European migrants have moved *as a whole* into the upper-middle class and into the elites of most Western nations. This rise of the bulk of Western Jewry has taken place against a background of general abundance and a substantial diminution of anti-semitic movements; it has taken place, too, against the background of the birth of Israel and the continuing memory of the Holocaust. The general rise of Western Jewry to elite status has resulted in a realignment of the allies and enemies of the Jews, with the traditional 'right' and 'left' changing places in their regard for Jews and their interests.*

* The definition of 'elite' is extremely complex and, moreover, varies from society to society. Throughout this work the term 'elite' is used in its commonsense definition to mean the small minority of individuals who wield disproportionate influence or decision-making power in a society. This power may flow from many

It is perhaps modern British Jewry which has followed this development most closely, and it will be examined in most detail. Apart from its intrinsic interest as the world's fifth largest Jewish community, British Jewry is particularly interesting for two other reasons. First, as the largest European Jewish community not directly affected by the Holocaust, Britain serves as a bridge between the vanished or silenced communities of central and eastern Europe and the Jewish communities in America and other non-European democracies. Second, between 1918 and 1948 Britain was the colonial power in Palestine; the Balfour Declaration was issued by a British Foreign Secretary, and the struggle by Palestine's Jews for their independence was waged against British rather than German or Russian soldiers.

The Jewish Community in Britain

Although Jews were readmitted to Britain by Oliver Cromwell in 1653 (they had been expelled by Edward I in 1290), they only began to play an important role in British business life in the mid-eighteenth century. Since their numbers were still very small – there were only 25,000 Jews in Britain at the end of the eighteenth century – they were not the target of popular anti-semitism,[2] nor did theological anti-semitism figure prominently in the doctrines of any major religious group. On the contrary, much in British Protestant dissent disposed its adherents to look favourably upon the Jews. Many Protestants, especially those influenced by Calvinism, viewed themselves as the spiritual descendents of the Old Testament Jews; others viewed the settlement of Jews in Britain, and their prosperity there, as a sign of God's favour. Britain, too, was unique among European societies in the absolute rights given in law to property and possessions of all kinds, even those earned by 'usury'. Also, among the small, self-confident and immensely wealthy aristocracy there was a singular absence of any prejudice toward businessmen

and varied causes – the holding of political office, wealth or economic influence, status, charisma, the successful mobilisation of organised opinion or interest. Perhaps the most salient distinction, for our purposes, is between societies which are essentially capitalist and pluralist, and totalitarian regimes where economic power is subjugated to state, party, or dictatorial controls; where power in any of its manifestations is centralized in the state or party. Chapter 2 presents an extended analysis of the concepts of 'elites' and 'power', and, introduces the notion of a 'large' and 'small' elite in contemporary society.

or towards wealth earned in business life.[3]

In business life the small Jewish community of the time was overwhelmingly concentrated in the City of London as merchants, bankers, stockbrokers and financiers, and in other commercial and financial trades. Originally Sephardic, the nineteenth-century London Jewish elite became increasingly German Ashkenazi through migration from central Europe. Its leading families – among them the Rothschilds, Montefiores, Goldsmids, Samuels, Sterns, Beddingtons and Sassoons – became immensely wealthy, a self-contained and inter-married caste which has come to be known as the 'Cousinhood'.[4] Because these dynasties were centred in the capital-intensive commercial and financial trades of the City of London rather than in the labour-intensive northern manufacturing industries, they roused little popular anti-semitism in provincial England. As part of the backbone of Britain's commercial and 'invisible' links with the six continents when Britain was the 'clearing-house of the world', and largely situated in the City of London which had always been friendly to migrants and new arrivals, they attracted remarkably little elite prejudice. The rise of the Cousinhood fortuitously coincided with the increasing religious toleration characteristic of the Victorian 'age of reform'.

Until the late nineteenth century British Jews largely kept themselves to themselves. Practising Jews were barred from sitting in the House of Commons until 1858: Disraeli, who had, of course, been baptised as a teenager, was thus the only prominent Jew in British politics until the late nineteenth century. Practising Jews were also barred from Oxford and Cambridge until the middle of the nineteenth century. Perhaps as a result, British Jews played far less a role in British intellectual life than in the twentieth century. It is difficult to think of more than a handful of important British intellectual figures of the nineteenth century who were Jews: Disraeli and Ricardo (who was also a convert to Christianity) are perhaps the only names which come to mind. Instead, the Cousinhood remained an elite of wealth-making. Nathan Rothschild (*d*. 1833), founder of the English branch of the famous merchant bank, was probably the richest commoner of the first half of the nineteenth century; by the early twentieth century 20 per cent or more of all British millionaires were Jews.[5]

With disproportionate wealth went relatively easy *entrée* into Britain's political elite in the later nineteenth century. The case of the Sassoons illustrates what truly great wealth could do to even the newest family. The Sassoons were Baghdadi Jews who had never set foot in Europe, or even worn Western dress, until the mid-nineteenth century. As merchants and traders in the Far East (in, among other things, opium) the Sassoons accummulated a fortune that has been estimated at £20 million in the early part of this century. Settling in England only in the 1850s, they had become baronets and hereditary members of parliament for Hythe in rural Kent by 1910. The most successful politician in the family, Sir Philip (*d.* 1939), held ministerial office during the 1920s and 1930s, despite widespread underlying antipathy to him as a Jew.[6] According to Chaim Bermant, Sassoon 'tried to give the general impression that he was a Parsee' and was once, astonishingly, received by Hermann Goering at his country retreat.[7]

It can be argued that this halcyon period came to an end around the 1890s, as it did in the other Western societies where Jews had made similar gains. On the Continent the Dreyfus Affair and the waves of czarist pogroms produced modern Zionism. In the British context, the situation was altered by the sudden arrival of tens of thousands of desperately poor migrants from the Russian Pale to London's East End and, in lesser number, to provincial towns like Manchester, Glasgow and Leeds, thus creating the seeds of the 'alien horde' variety of anti-semitism. These immigrants were soon the target for significant right-wing political movements determined to restrict further immigration. The 1890s also witnessed the emergence of a new set of South African Jewish gold and diamond millionaires, the Beits, Joels and Barnatos who, along with such gentile South African millionaires as Wehrner and Rhodes, as well as many *nouveaux-riches* Americans, were the targets of much hostility on both the extreme left and right. This period – roughly 1890 to 1920 – coincided with a considerable growth of extreme right-wing and chauvinist movements in all Western countries. England escaped the more virulent anti-semitism of the Continent, but its right-wing ideologists plainly shared much the same political assumptions as those elsewhere.[8]

For the most part the wealthy and assimiliated British Jews were embarassed by the arrival of so many thousands of former *shtetl* dwellers. They were hostile to the newly-founded Zionist movement, which was supported mainly by the eastern European masses and their intellectuals. However, the effect of the marked increase in anti-semitism upon the Anglo-Jewish elite was minimal. On the contrary, it can be argued that the influence and prestige of the Cousinhood was never higher. On the political plane, practising Jews reaching British Cabinet rank for the first time in the great Liberal government of 1905–14, while in the economic sphere the great merchant banks and international finance houses were at the height of their wealth and influence in the golden age of 'finance capital'. The high position and social acceptability enjoyed by this portion of Anglo-Jewry was symbolised most strikingly by the friendship and patronage of King Edward VII. Even many Conservative politicians remained philo-semites; notably Arthur Balfour, Leader of the Conservative Party from 1902 to 1911. The sentiments underlining the Balfour Declaration, promulgated when Balfour was British Foreign Secretary in the years 1916–19, dated from long before.

Although anti-semitism increased from 1890 to 1920, anti-semitic movements and their leaders became much more powerful from 1920 to 1945, precisely at the time when the old Jewish elite had become too weak to resist.

A number of unfortunate and coincidental factors produced this period of maximum danger. As a result of the First World War, the old international cosmopolitan financial system in which the Jews had played so prominent a part was largely wrecked, seriously damaging the wealth of British Jewry's old elite. Many of the Cousinhood dynasties went into a period of decay with the advent of the grandsons and great-grandsons of the founding fathers. According to Chaim Bermant, by the inter-war period even

> The wealth of the English Rothschilds had not been Rothschildian for some time. During World War I Natty, Leo and Alfred [de Rothschild] died within a few years of each other and a large part of the family's wealth was swallowed up in death duties, and while the old money was being soaked up the New Court was in the doldrums and little new money was being made.[9]

In the inter-war British economy the growth areas were in cars, building, electricity and consumer goods in which Jews generally did not participate. These new areas relied upon domestic consumer demand rather than upon international trade and finance. The City of London became less important to Britain's overall economic position in the period 1920–45 than in the previous half-century. High finance itself now looked to the home market rather than overseas as before the First World War and the 'big five' discount banks, which had virtually no Jewish board members, became increasingly important. Those anti-semites who continued to point to a mysterious Jewish financial cabal controlling the British economy were unaware that history had passed the Jews by.

The political upheavals of the First World War and immediate post-war period had destroyed the Liberal Party – where most of the successful Jewish politicians of the period had situated themselves.[10] Furthermore, while for wealthy Jews the Conservative Party should thenceforth have become their natural home, the inter-war Conservative Party was by no means as friendly or eager to promote Jewish politicians as the Edwardian Liberal Party had been. Regarding nationalism, patriotism and imperial unity as the paramount virtues, the inter-war Conservative Party often ill-disguised its suspicion of Jews. The tone of this time is perhaps best illustrated by Austen Chamberlain's remark with reference to Edwin Montagu's conciliatory policies in India after the First World War, 'a Jew may be a loyal Englishman and passionately patriotic, but he is intellectually apart from us and will never be purely and simply English'.[11]

Such men as Chamberlain, Baldwin or Simon were not necessarily anti-semites – there were Jews among their Cabinet colleagues at this time, like Hore-Belisha – but their backgrounds weakened their sensitivity to the increase in anti-semitism in the world, whether over refugees from Nazi rule, seeking asylum in Palestine or during the Holocaust itself, as Bernard Wassenstein has recently demonstrated.[12] Conversely, the most forceful and effective opposition to the growing German menace came from old-style landed aristocrats like Churchill, Eden and Salisbury, or among other Conservatives from idiosyncratic right-wing politicians unattached to the Establishment like L.S. Amery.

However, Britain was not Germany, and the perils faced by British Jewry should not be exaggerated. If Churchill's romanticism and eccentricity made him a political failure during the 1930s, so did Sir Oswald Mosley's, and British Fascism received less popular electoral support than any European Fascist movement. It was the achievement of the Conservative and National governments of the inter-war period to keep the British middle-classes within the safe political confines of moderate politics.[13] The establishment right in Britain had surprisingly few links, political or economic, with Nazi

Germany,[14] and these grew fewer with each year that Hitler's intent became more evident. Britain's record of receiving Jewish refugees from Nazi Germany prior to 1939 was reasonably compassionate and generous. Britain admitted 60,000 Jewish refugees from Germany, Austria and Czechoslavakia between 1933 and 1939, thus increasing its Jewish population by one-quarter. This relative generosity must be viewed against Britain's own large-scale unemployment and the failure of better-placed countries like the United States to offer substantial assistance of any kind.[15] The balance sheet of the British establishment's attitude toward the Jews during the inter-war period would contain entries on both sides of the ledger: perhaps the only thing one can say with certainty is that it was less liberal and generous than either before 1914 or after 1945.[16]

The majority of British Jews at this time were not members of the Cousinhood but eastern European immigrants still resident in the East End of London and other underprivileged areas and suffering, in common with everyone else, from the economic effects of the Depression. When in employment, most of these Jews were engaged in unskilled or semi-skilled occupations or as small shopkeepers and traders; their standards of formal education were meagre.[17] In terms of the loss of Jewish influence and power during the inter-war period, this fact is critical, for while the old Sephardic-Ashkenazi elite was losing its influence, the Eastern European 'masses' had not yet risen to replace them.

For the Eastern European Jewish masses, allegiance to conservative politics would have been impossible, and only the Labour Party, or groups even further to the left, offered a viable political stance.[18] In the words of Geofffrey Alderman, 'socialism, in short seemed to provide the answers to the problems of Jews the world over. Many Jews joined the Labour and Communist parties, and many more supported these movements through the ballot box'.[19] It was, then, largely within the British Labour Party that Jewish political activity took place and Jewish politicians rose to positions of influence. This did not manifest itself until the 1945 General Election, when the overwhelming majority of Jewish members of parliament were Labour.[20] The number of Jewish Labour members of parliament continued to increase until the mid-1970s, totalling 30 or even 35 in most parliaments, more than ten per cent of all sitting Labour members. At the same time Jewish representation within the Conservative Party all but ceased. No

Jewish Conservative members of parliament were elected between 1945 and 1955, and only a handful thereafter until the late 1970s. At that point the number began to climb sharply, as did the influence of individual Jewish Members like Sir Keith Joseph and Leon Brittain.

From the point of view of Jewish influence the large Jewish Labour contingent was not particularly effective except perhaps in support for Israel. As politicians, they made very little national impact, and certainly never constituted ten per cent or more of all leading Labour politicians until, ironically, the 1970s. Yet the overwhelmingly pro-Labour loyalties of Jewish members of parliament probably reflected the political allegiances of the majority of British Jews in the late 1940s and early 1950s. However, during this period British Jews, and particularly Jewish Labour members of parliament, found their loyalty seriously strained. They were obliged to support Attlee's Labour government at a time when Britain, in the shape of Foreign Secretary, Ernest Bevin, worked actively against Zionist aspirations in Palestine. There are many Jews for whom Bevin occupies a high place in the twentieth century's role of infamy:

> once the full horror of the Nazi Holocaust had been revealed British Jews hoped that Foreign Secretary Ernest Bevin would lose no time in bringing the Jewish State into being. Instead came delay and (to Jewish eyes at least) pro-Arabism. In particular, Bevin's policy towards Jewish refugees and illegal immigrants in Palestine seemed nothing short of barbaric. The vast majority of British Jews regarded – and still regard – Bevin as an anti-semite.[21]

After two British soldiers were hanged in Palestine by the Irgun in July 1947, an unprecedented outbreak of anti-semitic acts occurred throughout Britain.[22] Nevertheless, although there is a lack of statistical evidence as to when the change of loyalties among British Jews occurred, this does not seem to have happened until the Attlee Labour government left office in 1951, despite the obvious fact that the Labour Party, in Alderman's words, 'should have lost Jewish votes as a result' of Bevin's policies.[23] At both the 1950 and 1951 general elections the heavily Jewish East End constituencies remained overwhelmingly Labour. As late as 1956 most Jewish Labour members of parliament backed Hugh Gaitskell's condemnation of the Suez invasion, despite Israel's involvement as an ally of Britain and France.[24] It is hardly conceivable that many Jewish members,even those on the extreme left, would have opposed an Israeli military action a decade later.

Since the 1950s, British Jews have enjoyed unparalleled affluence.[25] Although overwhelmingly a middle-class community, they probably retain a somewhat larger working-class sector than is the case among America's Jews. Among Britain's leading wealth-holders, it is likely that about 15–20 per cent of all contemporary British millionaires are Jews, a level not approached since the Edwardian period.[26] The Jewish presence in such post-1945 growth areas as property development, finance, retailing and entertainment has been substantial and disproportionate.[27] The fortunes of such famous Jewish tycoons as Wolfson, Weinstock, Clore, Hyams, Samuel of Wych Cross, the brothers Grade and Delfont, the Sieff and Marks families and Cohen (of Tesco) are legendary, and show clearly the extent to which the old Sephardic–German Ashkenazi families have been replaced by newer migrants from eastern Europe. Whether Jews have penetrated the corporate management of Britain's largest companies is a more open question.

It is clear, however, that their presence in other elite sectors has also increased in recent years. In politics, all recent British cabinets have included at least one Jew with many more at the junior ministerial level; again, these figures have not been bettered since the early part of the century.[28] The Jewish presence in the British scientific, cultural and educational elites is similarly disproportionate.[29]

On all fronts, the period since 1945 – especially since about 1960 – has been one of increasing Jewish participation in the British national elite in a manner reminiscent of the Edwardian era except that today's Jewish elite is of eastern European origin. Given that the elite segment of British Jewry is now drawn from the whole of the Anglo-Jewish community, it is perhaps not surprising that there should be a change in the political self-perception of Jews and the perception of Jews by the non-Jewish majority, especially at the elite level. It is clear that this realignment of Jewry has already occurred, and that the political allegiances of Anglo-Jewry have undergone profound changes over the past twenty years.

This four-part pattern which we believe best describes the course of modern Anglo-Jewish history is not unique. On the contrary, it is very similar to the movement of Jewish history in all other Western countries. The early Sephardic-Ashkenazi elite achieves prominence but assimiliates into the establishment. It is then replaced by a new vigorous upsurge from the second generation of eastern European immigrants. This group are the advance guard for the *whole* Jewish community which is soon able to move into the ranks of the upper-middle class. At this point the old leftist enthusiasms of the *shtetl* are abandoned for the warm security of the centre right.

The Jewish Community in the United States

As in Britain, before the turn of the century the American Jewish community was small, relatively successful and largely assimilated; it was a Sephardic-German Ashkenazi elite which met comparatively little hostility, even in regions like the Deep South, which would subsequently prove most bigoted and hostile to them.[30] A southern state like Florida elected a Jewish senator before the Civil War; the Secretary of State of the Confederacy, Judah P. Benjamin, was born a Jew; the first (1865–76) Ku Klux Klan was not anti-semitic, and had Jewish members, for instance Simon Baruch, the father of Bernard Baruch, a prominent South Carolina physician who had just served as Quartermaster-General of the Confederate Army.[31] On the other hand, no one could claim that the American Jewish community predominated in any sector of the American economy – a claim which could be seriously made of the international financial sector of the City of London by the 1860s – and in general Jews were entirely peripheral to the development of American history until this century. With the possible exception of Judah Benjamin and Haym Solomon, 'the financier of the American Revolution', no Jew is likely to be mentioned in a textbook dealing with America's history in its first century of independence.

The trends evident during the early phase of American history continued during the 'Gilded Age' following the Civil War. As economic power decisively shifted to the north-eastern industrial and financial plutocracy during the United States greatest period of economic expansion, Jews still comprised a small, though probably growing, portion of America's business elite.[32] Despite this the importance of the Jewish segment of America's leading business dynasties and leading wealth-holders cannot be compared with its equivalent proportion in Britain or elsewhere in Europe at the time. There were several reasons for this which lie deep in America's historical and economic structure. The United States was 'born free', without a surviving feudal or quasi-feudal aristocracy, and its national values and prevalent spirit were those of middle-class capitalism. Capitalists were not despised, and all white ethnic groups engaged in capitalist enterprise. There was nothing special about the Jews in the United States.[33] Unlike in Europe, Jews were not compelled to seek employment or opportunities in 'usury' or those forms of 'pariah capitalism' despised by the aristocracy. Although in the long run this would prove of inestimable benefit to American Jewry, it meant that, during the nineteenth century, Jews were in competition with all other white ethnic and sectional groups for entrepreneurial opportunities which in Europe would have been reserved exclusively for Jews. This competition was, furthermore, quite unequal, for these white ethnic and sectional groups had long been masters of the land and the state, and enjoyed immense economic and political advantages. As a result, by the late nineteenth century the term 'yankee' implied many of those values and modes of behaviour which in Europe were suggested by the abusive use of the term 'Jew'. Although America's liberal Constitution and Bill of Rights prohibited the establishment of a state religion or religious tests for office-holding, and made property-ownership virtually sacrosanct in law, until the Second World War, the American establishment remained white, Anglo-Saxon and Protestant.

However, the nature of American capitalism, as well as its prevalent values, also determined the relative unimportance of its Jewish elite at the time of America's greatest economic expansion. The financial and commercial trades in Britain carried on in the City of London were inherently more lucrative than the industrial and manufacturing occupations of northern England, and Jews were thus disproportionately numerous among Britain's leading wealth-holders because of their participation in the affairs of the City of London.[34] Although these differences in the inherent profitability of commercial versus industrial capitalism might well have existed in other European countries like France,[35] in the United States it is much more likely that the opposite was true: industrial capitalism was more lucrative and more productive of the greatest fortunes and biggest business concerns than was commercial or financial capitalism.[36] Certainly the greatest moguls of the Gilded Age were mainly industrial capitalists, men like Rockefeller, Carnegie, Mellon, Frick, Duke and Ford, while on the other side there were the Morgans and Crockers (with the numerous railway kings like Harriman, Vanderbilt and Gould occupying a somewhat ambiguous position). Jews would have been found, if anywhere, largely in the financial sectors of British life, as they were everywhere in the Western world. While American Jewry at this time produced its Kuhns, Loebs and Seligmans, important representatives of the United States' financial plutocracy, such men could not be compared in wealth or influence with the Protestant Morgans or other Anglo-Saxon financial dynasties.[37] The many anti-semitic diatribes of the early part of this century which suggested that a mysterious Jewish financial cabal led by the Kuhn–Loeb banking house wielded significant and illegitimate power were simply wrong.

The United States entered the twentieth century with a business-orientated Sephardic and German Ashkenazi elite, distinct from the American mainstream but having suffered no great disabilities, certainly much less than the Jewish elites in western and central Europe. The American situation was to be transformed in the forty-three years between 1881 and 1924 by the arrival of three million or more impoverished, ill-educated, Yiddish-speaking Jews from the Russian Pale, forced to move by czarist oppression and attracted by the opportunities provided by the United States' free society. In the space of a generation, the United States was transformed from the country whose Jewish minority was arguably the least significant and least central of that in any Western society to the undoubted capital of world Jewry. By 1940 the American Jewish community of four million was the largest in the world with the possible exception of the Soviet Union, where organised Jewish life was subject to the most severe persecution. Increasingly the United States came to be regarded as the key to the survival of the world's Jews, as eastern Europe went further down the road to Jewish annihilation.

This unequalled mass migration of Jews to the United States was accompanied by remarkably little anti-semitic backlash, although – as everywhere else in the Western world – anti-semitism at all levels increased. As only one among dozens of similarly undesirable ethnic groups entering the United States in large numbers at that time (and entering a society with a considerable and genuine tradition of religious toleration), the United States Jews did not encounter an anti-semitism as ferocious or single-minded as elsewhere. To most Americans, and not merely liberals or progressives, the czarist Russia which persecuted Jews represented everything which the United States – 'the last, best hope of man' – existed to overcome. The American establishment of the time genuinely abhorred this variety of brutal suppression, however much they may have acquiesced in more genteel anti-semitism at their university or their club. Open anti-semitism came from populist, relatively deprived elements in the south and west, who were also opposed to the north-eastern Protestant establishment and to blacks and Catholics.

The Yiddish-speaking masses proved a considerable embarrassment to the old assimilated American Jewish elite, and mutual hostility often resulted.[38] As elsewhere, it was the wealthy, assimilated, non-Orthodox elite which most vehemently opposed Zionism or any claims to a separate Jewish national identity. Despite the growing volume of anti-semitism, the old American Jewish elite produced some of its most prominent and distinguished figures during this period, men like Bernard Baruch, Louis Brandeis and Benjamin Cardozo, and its influence continued to be felt at the national elite level. Such men were, significantly, generally appointees or associates of Protestant establishment leaders of both parties, and seldom, if ever, themselves held major electoral office: Jews (in contrast to Catholics) rarely occupied important elected office at the Congressional or even the State level at this time, despite their considerable voting numbers in some states.

Whereas during the Depression Britain chose a Conservative-dominated 'National' government dedicated to rescuing orthodox capitalism, the United States turned to the progressive reformist capitalism of the 'New Deal'. To American minorities, and above all to American Jews, Franklin Roosevelt was a unique figure, who welded a powerful political coalition based in large part on minority and labour groups, and who opposed Nazism abroad in the name of democracy. American Jews voted for Roosevelt by majorities of 90 per cent or more; in the words of a Republican Congressman, Jonah J. Goldstein, 'The Jews have three *velten* (worlds): *die velt* (this world), *yene velt* (the next world), and Roosevelt.'[39] But although Roosevelt brought about a fundamental realignment in the voting habits of American Jews, specifically Jewish interests fared no better under Roosevelt than in the Britain of Stanley Baldwin and Neville Chamberlain: arguably they fared worse. The United

States' harsh, restrictive and deliberately anti-eastern European immigration laws were not relaxed, despite the urgency of the European situation and the inherently greater ability of the United States to absorb immigrants, even in times of recession Roosevelt was only luke-warm to the claims of Zionism, even after the reality of the Holocaust had become known. One of Roosevelt's last acts in international affairs, on the same trip which took him to meet Churchill and Stalin at Yalta, was a meeting with King Ibn Saud at Cairo. After this meeting Roosevelt declared that 'I learned more about the whole problem, the Moslem problem, the Jewish problem, by talking with Ibn Saud for five minutes than I could have learned in an exchange of two or three dozen letters.'[40] Worst of all was Roosevelt's attitude to the Holocaust in which he and his advisers all but acquiesced.[41] The chief State Department official responsible for Jewish refugees, Breckinridge Long, Jr, has been described by Urofsky, the most thorough historian of the matter, as 'extremely anti-semitic, [who] identified Jews as communists and shared Hitler's Jewish phobia.'[42] According to Urofsky,

After reading *Mein Kampf* [Long] declared it 'eloquent in opposition to Jewry and to Jews as exponents of Communism and Chaos.' His diary reveals a paranoid personality, one who believed himself destined to fight a long list of 'enemies', both of himself and of America. In his crusade against Jewish refugees, Long brought to bear a singleness of purpose, knowledge of the inner workings of government, and influential friends in both the White House and in Congress.[43]

But if the attitude of the Roosevelt administration towards the Holocaust was perverse, the attitude of the leadership of American Jewry defies belief. Their record of inaction, pusillanimity, fecklessness and what Urofsky describes as 'conflicting pressures within the Jewish community'[44] is beyond the understanding of a later generation. The American Jewish community could have threatened to direct its large voting strength *en bloc* to the Republican Party at the 1942 and 1944 elections if the Roosevelt administration was not prepared to take some determined action to rescue whatever portion of European Jewry it could. As today's Israelis often say of the efforts of Palestinian Jewry during the Holocaust, the American Jewish community was guilty of failing to go to any extremes to rescue Hitler's victims, and the prosperity of

American Jewry since 1945 has been coloured by this fact.

Perhaps the major reason for this inactivity was the political impotence and the precariousness of life for the American Jewish majority of eastern European descent. In the words of Hillel Goldberg, 'Recent East European immigrants to America . . . were unfamiliar with English, let alone with American political processes, through which massive rescue efforts could have been mounted. Many who could have mounted such efforts were themselves enlisted as soldiers', and he reminds us that 'One cannot project the image of the acculturated, economically secure, politically active, and Israel – and Soviet-Jewry – conscious American Jewry of the late 1970s onto the American Jewry of the 1940s, [and] find it wanting'.[45]

Despite this excuse for the inactivity of the eastern European masses, the attitude of American Jewry towards the Holocaust is typical of the Jewish leadership in all Western countries at the time. The old elite, which had in any case been less well represented in the American elite structure than in most other Western countries, was declining in influence in the wake of the Depression and the New Deal, while the impoverished masses of eastern European Jewry, who blindly voted for Roosevelt and his Democratic coalition had not yet risen to take their places. The direct representation of eastern European Jews in America's elite structure was limited; even in the House of Representatives, few Jews were to be found, and only one or two men, like Representatives Sol Bloom and Emmanuel Cellar, were of any real significance. America's major cultural and educational institutions continued to regard these Jews as pushy outsiders, an unpleasant intrusion and threat to the niceties of Anglo-Saxon culture, and discriminated against them in a variety of ways.[46]

American Jewish leadership institutions and representative bodies were split by this social division within the Jewish community, a division often, but not invariably, denoted by the split between Zionism and 'assimilationism'.[47] Urofsky terms the communal institutions and leadership of American Jewry 'a house divided', and claims that 'the community was actually on the verge of disintegration' by 1945.[48] At this time, according to another historian, Yehuda Bauer, 'Jewish political *power* [in the United States] . . . was indeed paltry, and in the liberal world toward which the great Republic was presumably progressing, ethnic or nationalistic power was expected to become superfluous, a deplorable remnant of a past age'.[49] Lacking cultural self-confidence and wishing to prove their 'Americanism', even institutions like Hollywood, where eastern European Jews were prominent to a very disproportionate extent, failed to assert their Jewishness or to rise to the perils of the hour: instead, either the Jew and his problems (in common with most other ethnic minorities) was ignored, or Hollywood-based Jewish writers produced the unflattering portraits, often verging on anti-semitic stereotype, of *What Makes Sammy Run?* and the early novels of Ben Hecht.

It is not easy to put a precise date on the transformation of the American Jewish community from relative powerlessness to their contemporary position of influence. More precisely, it is difficult to know whether the creation and maintenance of Israel was a consequence of American Jewish power or, in effect, an inspiration and central rallying-point for the gains which have been made since 1948. Yehuda Bauer, for instance, has recently queried

> Where and how did this political power begin to grow? A great deal more research is still needed into this vital topic. What appears clear today is that major strides were taken during the war, and that the Zionist movement in its various manifestations . . . was the prime mover . . . the Jewish vote began to be an effective instrument only in the later stages of World War II and beyond . . . The story of the Jewish emergence from powerlessness turned on the securing of a Jewish state.[50]

There have been two major consequences of the rise of the eastern European masses to middle-class status after 1945: first, the old Sephardic–German Ashkenazi leadership has been overwhelmed by the eastern European majority, and second, the birth of Israel has ensured that the residual anti-Zionism of the old Sephardic–German Ashkenazi elite, so common before 1939 or even 1948, has all but vanished. Though born in the Western world as a response by wealthy, assimilated establishment Jews to the nationalistic longings of the depressed eastern European masses, anti-Zionism has, since the 1960s, re-emerged almost exclusively among the Marxist or anarchist revolutionary left.

The German Jewish Community

Because everything concerning German Jewry is overshadowed by the Holocaust the German Jewish experience seemingly presents the sharpest contrast to Britain and the United States. In reality it fits the pattern quite well, with some obvious qualifications. Liberalism came fitfully to Germany; pre-modern and anti-modernist intellectual and social tendencies were highly characteristic of Germany from the time of Hegel onwards; the Hohenzollern monarchy forbade direct Jewish participation in political life, especially at the elite level, and hence Jewish participation in the German elite could only be in the economic or intellectual spheres, not the governmental.[51] Political anti-semitism received its modern beginnings, and most of its characteristic features in the Western world in Germany or the German-speaking areas of Austria.[52] Despite this, for the German Jews, the nineteenth century to 1873 was a Golden Age, carrying many from small-town ghettoes into the middle class. After moving in numbers to Germany's larger towns, especially Berlin, they were, as elsewhere, disproportionately prominent and successful in banking, finance and commerce, as well as in the liberal professions. Despite severe restrictions on Jewish academic appointments and promotion, the Jewish contribution to German science, technology and medicine is well known, as was the disproportionate Jewish contribution to German cultural and intellectual life.

Because Jews could not be ministers of the state, and were excluded from the elite institutions of the Imperial Government, Jewish penetration of the German elite was economic, especially through the great international banks like M.M. Warburg, Oppenheim or Rothschild's, or great individual financiers like Gerson von Bleichroder and Baron Hirsch.[53] The strange but potent friendship of Bismarck and Bleichröder, his confidant, private banker and secret agent, seemed to lend credibility to Disraeli's romantic notions of a mysterious Jewish presence operating behind the scenes and to the many cruder and more virulent formulations of this belief by anti-semites. Among 223 Prussian millionaires worth 10 million marks or more (about £500,000) in 1912 there were 46 Jews, around 21 per cent of the total and thus equivalent to the percentage of Jews among Britain's business millionaires at the time.[54] Naturally, the accounts given by anti-semites of Jewish 'power' in nineteenth-century Germany are exaggerated. Precisely because it operated, if at all, indirectly and vicariously, it was insecure; in the final analysis, the pre-1914 German establishment was unwilling to recognise German Jews as Germans, but left the issue unresolved.

As in Britain, the late nineteenth century and the end of the Imperial era saw an increasingly virulent and politically significant anti-semitism coincident with a German Jewish financial, commerical and cultural elite at the peak of its influence. Jewish society in Germany before 1914 presented many features which marked it as more successful and even self-confident than British Jewry. Far fewer Yiddish-speaking Jews came to Germany in the late nineteenth century than to Britain or the United States; its Jewish population was composed of long-established German-speaking natives. The socio-economic structure of German Jewry was disproportionately middle-class by 1900.[55] Fifty-six per cent of German Jews were engaged in commerce or transport in 1895, 16.7 per cent were self-employed, 6.1 per cent in the public services and professions but only 19.3 per cent in industry and trade – this at a time when perhaps one-half of Britain's Jews were living in poverty in the East End of London and in provincial slums. Consequently, too, Reform Judaism began in Germany while assimilationism was most marked there in all its aspects. As has often been pointed out, the Jewish population of Germany was in this period barely reproducing itself, and fell from 1.25 per cent of the total German population in 1871 to 0.95 per cent in 1910.[56]

As in Britain and the United States, the German economy and its economic elite were divided among themselves between landowners, industrialists and entrepreneurs of commerce and finance. As elsewhere, Jews were disproportionately successful in banking and commerce, and much Jewish influence in Imperial Germany, real or imagined, flowed from this fact. But the arrangement of economic power, ideological divisions and social loyalties characteristic of Germany were quite different from the situation in Britain or the United States and, in the long run, highly disadvantageous to German Jewry. In Germany, the landed aristocracy and the conservative elements generally were linked in alliance or quasi-alliance with heavy industry, which they regarded as innately more 'national', less 'cosmopolitan', more beneficial to Germany's military might and dreams of aggrandisement. In contrast to mid-Victorian Britain, where ideological spokesmen for manufacturing capitalism like Cobden and Bright demanded the abolition of the tariff on corn – the bulwark of the English landed classes – and 'free trade' was the motto of Manchester liberalism, in Germany, the Junkers (the landed gentry) were linked with major industrialists in their demands for tariffs to aid national economic development. The role of the state in Germany's industrial development was quite different from the British doctrine of *laissez-faire*. As the economic historian W. O. Henderson has put it, in Germany

> industrial progress was 'not hampered by any hard and fast adhesion to a definite line of policy in regard to the limits of public as compared with private enterprise'. The rulers of the German states were expected by their subjects to take an active part in fostering the economic growth of their territories. It was widely held that competent civil servants, dedicated to the public service, could run industrial enterprises in the national interest more efficiently than private entrepreneurs who were in business simply to make a profit.[57]

Late nineteenth-century German industrialism was marked by the growth of trusts and cartels throughout key sectors of heavy and manufacturing industry. This was very different from the situation in Britain, where large-scale heavy industrial firms were virtually unknown until much later, and it is more reminiscent of the business structure of the American economy.

Industrial capitalists, it may be argued, as in the United States, but unlike Britain, were more prominent among Germany's leading businessmen and wealthiest dynasties. Although the Jews were significant and powerful as financial and commercial capitalists they were not as central to the economy as in Britain, and, like the United States, Germany contained an inherently more dynamic industrial sector based on large-scale business units where Jewish participation was much more limited.

Although many ideologues of the German far right condemned both industrial and financial capital and although Nazism initially featured a radical wing which opposed factory capitalism, the historical alliance, unique to Germany, between the landed aristocracy and conservative orders on the one hand and industrial big business on the other was a persistent feature of modern German history.[58]

The Nazis regarded 'national' industrial capitalism in a more favourable light than 'cosmopolitan' finance. In the words of Valentin,

> The man in the street often imagines that industrialists, especially the chiefs of industry working for export, are national and beneficial to the State, while he has doubts of the great bankers in the former respect . . . In National-Socialist propaganda bank capital is described as unproductive, international, Jewish (*raffendes Kapital*) whereas industrial capital (and agricultural capital) is said to be productive, national and Aryan (*schaffendes Kapital*).[59]

Although the collapse of the Imperial order and the establishment of the Weimar Constitution gave Jews open access to all government positions for the first time, and therefore, at least initially, increased the Jewish presence in the government elite, this greater degree of elite-penetration was only illusory. The Weimar regime coincided with a severe decline in the demographic, social and economic position of German Jewry which probably made both Hitler's triumph and the success of his programme against the Jews that much easier. All of this was, of course, precisely contrary to Nazi propaganda, which depicted Germany as enslaved to, and controlled by, its Jews.[60]

Despite the opening of all political offices to the Jews in 1918 and the frequent electoral success of liberal and social democratic parties where they were chiefly to be found, Jews failed to penetrate the political or higher administrative elite of Weimar Germany to any real extent:

> In the twenty Cabinets that held office from [1918 to 1933], there were altogether two Jewish Ministers, Preuss and Rathenau, and four of Jewish descent. That is to say, out of about 250 Ministers all except six were pure 'Aryans'. Out of about 250 higher officials in the Ministries of the Reich, including Secretaries of State and members of Government boards, there were before Hitler's victory at most fifteen Jews or men of Jewish birth. The number of Jewish Secretaries of State in the administration between 1918 and 1933 was just two. Out of about 300 higher officials in the Prussian Ministries some ten were Jews or of Jewish birth. Out of Prussia's twelve *Ober-präsidente*, thirty-five

Regierungspräsidente, and over four hundred *Landräte*... there was not a single Jew . . . Of all Government officials in Germany [in 1925] 0.16 per cent were Jews; of the higher officials 0.29 per cent; of the intermediate and lower officials 0.17 per cent . . . between 1895 and 1925 the number of 'Aryan' officials in Prussia was multiplied by seven, that of Jewish by three . . .[61]

In other elite spheres where Jews had been permitted entry prior to 1918, the Jewish presence was actually declining. for instance, among students at German colleges and universities, Jews comprised 9.6 per cent of the total in 1886–7, 8 per cent in 1911, 5.08 per cent in 1930 and 4.71 per cent in 1932–3.[62] Similarly, Jewish participation in German economic life was also declining: if the First World War had harmed the role of the old merchant and international banks in Britain, in Weimar Germany, with its hyper-inflation and disruption of old trade links, the war proved fatal to such concerns. Soon even the prosperity of the mid-1920s gave way to the Great Depression.[63] The notion much propagated by the Nazis, that the Jews were 'war profiteers' who did well out of the First World War is thus the very opposite of the truth. Again, in Valentin's words

[T]he World war and the [1923] crisis had an extremely injurious effect economically upon Jewry . . . Those Jews who made money out of the War were far fewer than those who lost over it . . . It has been pointed out . . . how the War led to financial capital being outstripped by industrial capital. Both indeed were predominantly 'Aryan', but the latter far more than the former. thus the War meant a further decline for German–Jewish finance.[64]

The *weakening* of financial and commercial capital thus *reinforced* the ability of the Nazis, inherently unsympathetic to this type of capitalism, to attack and weaken it still further.

Only in the intellectual and cultural spheres did German Jews truly represent a disproportionate percentage of the Weimar elite. Yet here, too, a number of important qualifications must be made: Weimar Germany was bitterly divided between those who accepted the implications of the defeat of 1918 and the modernism this engendered (but who typically had no respect for the Weimar Republic itself), and those who rejected this entirely, draping themselves in a pre-modern or radically anti-modern intellectual framework.[65] To those who rejected modernity, any Jewish contribution to culture or the intellect, even in science,[66] was *a priori* illegitimate. Second, there was very little connection between the typical Jewish socio-cultural viewpoint and the politics of the left in Weimar, which were increasingly *judenrein* almost to the same extent as the far right. Not a single Jew sat as a Communist, for instance, in any Reichstag of the later Weimar regime.

There was a relative dearth of eastern European migrants among German Jewry: in 1933, only 76,000 of Germany's 560,000 Jews were aliens, that is, born abroad.[67] Germany thus largely lacked one significant element which everywhere else made for increased anti-semitism. Despite this demographic reality, talk of mass migration of hundreds of thousands of eastern European Jews into Germany was a stock-in-trade of anti-semites during the Weimar period. To no inconsiderable extent, the low regard in which the Yiddish-speaking 'horde' was held generally by the German right was widely shared by German Jews who harboured towards eastern European Jews an antipathy often indistinguishable from anti-semitism.

Although it is easy to depict Weimar Jewry as a doomed community,[68] this is not the argument of the chapter. Although it was far less powerful or significant than the usual view offered by Germany's anti-semites, and although it is contended here that this weakness helped to seal their doom, it is no part of this argument that they were in any sense responsible for the rise of Hitler or for the triumph of his policies. Rather, Hitler's rise can best be seen as the result of an extraordinarily unlucky and unlikely combination of fortuitous short-run political factors which had at their foundation Germany's defeat in the First World War and the abyss this opened up in national life. The destruction of German Jewry was not inevitable, and, even in 1928 or 1929, Hitler's eventual triumph would have seemed an inconceivably remote possibility, the Final Solution an utter impossibility. Nevertheless, the real weaknesses of German Jewry at the elite level can be seen as at least related to the strengths of the extreme right and of German anti-semitism. Had German Jewry been genuinely stronger and better represented in the channels of power, and above all in the country's elite structure, Hitler's victory, while not impossible, would have been more difficult and the execution of his plans for the Jews that much more complicated and troublesome.

The French Jewish Community

Although the history of modern French Jewry presents a similar chronology, it contains many important anomalous features. Prior to 1789, the Jewish community in France had been very small; its position was clarified, but in many ways deteriorated, under Napoleon.[69] Although French Jewry had many fears about the various regimes which held power between 1815 and 1870, these fears proved unfounded: 'The social rise of the French Jews which had begun under the Restoration also continued under the Second Empire . . . Practically every career, including the army, was open to Jews.'[70] As elsewhere in the Western world the period from 1815 to 1870 or slightly later was a golden age for the Jews, their entrepreneurial achievements meeting with relative tolerance.

As elsewhere in Europe, Jewish influence in nineteenth-century France was manifest, if it existed at all, in the financial sector of the business elite, although French Jewry, numbering 40,000 in 1788 and only 60,000 in 1880, never had the influence which a larger community might have possessed. Jews joined the inner circle of the banking elite in the mid-nineteenth century, although the greatest banking family (as elsewhere), the Rothschilds, began their ascent somewhat earlier. The first Jew to become a regent of the Bank of France did so in 1839; Fould was finance minister under Napoleon III. Many observers, for instance Marx, viewed the French bankers and the financial sector of the middle classes as holding disproportionate power and, indeed, running the country. 'The bankers,' wrote Stendahl, 'are at the heart of the State. The bourgeoisie has replaced the faubourg St Germain and the bankers are the nobility of the bourgeois class',[71] and the legend of France's '200 families' persisted to 1940 or even later. According to one modern French historian, for instance, the Paris Rothschild bank had subscribed over ten per cent of the total investment in France's seven leading railways constructed up to 1848;[72] it thus played a much greater role in key *domestic* finance than did London's merchant banks in the nineteenth century.

Yet there were a number of important reasons why the participation of French Jewry in France's business elite, despite the considerable myths which grew up around it, cannot in truth be compared with the role of the Jewish business community in Britain or Germany. France's industrial 'take-off' occurred later than Britain's (though before Germany's) and in a much more equivocal manner: indeed many economic historians now doubt whether a real 'industrial revolution' occurred in nineteenth-century France.[73] While superficially this implied that France's industrial and manufacturing sector was smaller and less lucrative than that of the United States or Germany, and hence did not represent an 'Aryan' challenge to finance capital, in reality both industrial and banking capital were weaker than elsewhere *vis-à-vis* the pre-industrial landed elite. France continued to be a rural-dominated peasant society until this century; its politics typically pitted small-town 'radicals' against rural conservatives (with urban, industrial forces weaker than elsewhere) and its wealth and elite structures have been more heavily weighted towards the landed aristocracy.

This continuing rural bias determined the nature of French anti-semitism, which was as virulent as anywhere else and which, in the 1890s, led to the most celebrated anti-semitic incident of the period, the Dreyfus Affair. The Dreyfus Affair in turn had the most profound importance for modern Jewry as it was the immediate influence upon Herzl's conversion to Zionism. Much of French anti-semitism was the pre-modern religious-based anti-semitism of a rural society.[74] Although Count Gobineau, the founder of modern racial anti-semitism, was a Frenchman, Jews were never quite so central to the heated imagination of the French ultra-right as they were elslewhere. Lucy Davidowicz's description of Hitler's anti-semitism – 'the Jews inhabited Hitler's mind. He believed that they were the source of all evil, misfortune, and tragedy, the single factor that, like some inexorable law of nature, explained the workings of the universe . . . The demonic hosts whom he had given a divine mission to destroy'[75] – cannot readily be applied to many Frenchmen. In the French ultra-right's pantheon of enemies, Jews always had to share undivided first place with Protestants, Freemasons and *métèques*, especially Germans.[76] The aims of the far right in France, even down to the inter-war period, focussed upon the pre-industrial goal of restoring a Catholic monarch, by divine right king of a Catholic France. Their world-view reflected a vision of society formed before the time when Jews became central to the modern state in any sense. A perfect understanding of the French establishment's view of the Jews may be obtained from Proust, in particular from his portrayal of Swann and Bloch.

The pre-industrial origins of the great split in French society moulded the views of the French left as well. Because, to them, the central event of French history was the overthrow of feudalism in

1789, a revolution carried out in a rural society, the revolutionary tradition continued to be defended by rural and small-town radicals who elsewhere would have been either complete reactionaries or radicals with a strong anti-modernist streak, as in the United States and Germany.[77] Thus we may see the crucial difference between the France of the Dreyfus period and Nazi Germany: whereas in Germany Nazi control was virtually uncontested, in France at least half the country – and, moreover, the victorious half – supported Dreyfus.

This in turn points to another important facet of the comparative unimportance of French Jewry, the fact that the French liberal and enlightenment tradition was virtually *judenrein*. Because so few of the classical figures of French liberal political thought were Jews, and because it was so widely believed among French conservatives that a small near-conspiratorial group of Enlightenment thinkers and their disciples 'made' the Revolution of 1789, it was that much more difficult to point to the Jews as central to all that had gone wrong with modern France.. It can, furthermore, be argued that demographic and political changes worked to make the situation of French Jewry less rather than more immediate and pressing. In 1871 one of the most heavily Jewish areas of France, Alsace-Lorraine, was ceded to Germany, immediately decreasing the Jewish population of France by nearly one-third. Many French Jews whose roots lay in Alsace-Lorraine, moreover, were as xenophoboic over this 'crime against France' as their gentile countrymen.[78] Furthermore, many of the demographic trends in mass migration of the period 1880–1914 largely passed France by – again, because the country was not perceived as a land of entrepreneurial opportunity in the same way as the United States or Britain. Only 25,000 Jewish immigrants arrived in France between 1880 and 1914 – much less than one per cent of the number arriving in the United States in the same period. Among them, Russian migrants were actually a minority among a disparate group which included many Sephardic Jews from Asia Minor.[79] Despite quite substantial migration of Jews from Nazi Germany after 1933, the Jewish population of France numbered only about 300,000 in 1940.[80] This ambiguity about the place of the Jews in French life continued during the Vichy period. It is generally estimated that 'only' about 80,000–85,000 French Jews perished at the hands of the Nazis, a lower percentage than in almost any other occupied country, and French Jews fared much better in the southern zone of

France where the Vichy government was sovereign.[81] In general – although the matter is hotly disputed – the Vichy government and its officials used their influence to moderate Nazi policy, although this became increasingly difficult as the Nazi programme became ever more extreme.

The post-1945 socio-economic and political history of French Jewry continues to differ from that of other Western Jewish communities, in part for reasons which stem from the development of French politics and society. France has since the 1950s caught up in economic terms with its rivals. It has urbanised and industrialised at a rate not seen before in French history. France still contains a conservative political half, dominant politically since the late 1940s, which has not 'caught up' but which continues to reflect in some measure the virtually pre-modern traditions of the French right as well as the national longing for *grandeur*. Given the continuing tradition and importance of *étatism* in the French economy and French society, with its elitist, bureaucratic, strongly nationalistic sentiment and style, one can draw a tentative comparison between post-war (and especially post-1958) France and one other regime we have discussed here: Imperial Germany. Contemporary France resembles Imperial Germany in the speed and suddenness of its industrialisation and urbanisation, its continuing nationalistic assertiveness and its strong tradition of state interference in, and direction of, the economy, within a capitalistic framework.

Virtually alone among European Jewish communites, French Jewry has increased enormously in size not merely since 1945 but since 1939. Moreover, this gain has come – again, most singularly – through migration from abroad. Some came from eastern Europe, but the bulk were North African Jews from France's former colonial empire. No fewer than 220,000 or more settled in France between 1954 and 1968.[82] The Jewish population of France is now generally estimated at 600,000–700,000 or even more, making it by far the largest continental European Jewish community, and twice as large as it was in the 1930s.

France stands in this matter where other countries did thirty or forty years before. It has a Jewish community with a still substantial working class. The antagonism of France's conservative governments to Jewish interests should, of course, not be exaggerated. France recognised Israel soon after its foundation; Jews have served prominently in most post-war French governments and have produced a remarkable gallery of leading politicians, including René Meyer, Pierre Mendès-France, Michel Debré and the first President of the European Parliament, the Auschwitz survivor, Mme Simone Weil. Obviously, too, French foreign policy is predicated on a variety of factors having nothing whatever to do with French Jewry, including the oil shortage and its perceptions of the weakness and vacillation of American policies; France has of course, taken a line independent of her Western allies over a wide variety of issues. Yet in 1967 only someone like General de Gaulle could describe the Jews as 'an elite people, self-assured and domineering' with all of the pejorative meaning that these words imply.

It remains to be seen whether the more overtly pro-Israeli stance adopted on taking office by the Socialist President Mitterrand will have a lasting effect on France's foreign policy which under successive right-wing presidencies has remained pro-Arab.[83] The French Communist Party, for instance, is highly antagonistic to Israel at all times. A majority of French Jews voted in March 1978 for the non-Communist left – 55 per cent for the Socialists and only 33 per cent for the Gaullist-Giscardian coalition.[84]

Conclusion

In the societies we have discussed (and elsewhere in the Western world [85]) the history of modern Jewry can be most usefully seen as conforming to the four-stage model which we have outlined. What is perhaps most interesting about this model is the way in which it parodies, yet differs from, the depiction of Jewish wealth, power and influence offered by gentiles – often motivated in their portrayal by anti-semitism – and many Jews alike. Those who have been aware of the fact that Jews have often enjoyed disproportionate influence and wealth have failed to observe that, historically, only a small part of the Jewish people have directly benefited from the success of a few; while those who deny that this disproportionate wealth and power exist seem simply to be historically inaccurate. But in the past, such power was always elusive, fragmentary and vicarious, and could generally be swept aside in a moment by a determined political force: after the Second World War, because of the absorption of the great part of Western society in the higher socio-economic groupings, such power and influence has become much more firmly based. Furthermore, the establishment of the state of Israel has increased the self-confidence of Jews everywhere. It has, for instance, removed the label of cosmopolitanism from the vocabulary of the Western establishment. For how can Jews be cosmopolitan when it is clear that they have an established homeland for which they are prepared to fight, and, perhaps more importantly, win? The establishment of Israel, and the upward movement into the top echelons of Western society by the Jews, may have been separately determined. Now the two issues are completely intertwined. Israel is the rallying-point and focus for Jewishness amongst the Jews of the diaspora and its existence makes it imperative that Jews everywhere should preserve their places in the elite: for thus they guarantee the continuation of their state and, coincidentally, help to minimise the likelihood of a recrudescence of anti-semitism.

Notes

1. This period was – from the Jewish point of view – largely an extension of the eighteenth-century and early modern world of the 'court Jew', who stood in relationship to the absolute monarchs of the time in a manner basically very similar to that of the great nineteenth-century Jewish banking houses and commercial leaders to the governments which they served; in many cases the families were the same. Significant, too, was the fact that the Yiddish-speaking mass of eastern Jews remained in the east (and were much less numerous). On the 'court Jews' see 'Court Jews' in *Encyclopedia Judaica* (Jerusalem, 1972), vol. 5, pp. 1006–11, and Selma Stern, *The Court Jews* (Philadelphia, 1950).

2. There were, however, widespread anti-Jewish riots in London in 1753 because of a proposed bill to liberalise the citizenship of Jews, and as a result it never became law.

3. This is a point on which Marxist and non-Marxist historians are agreed: see, e.g., Karl Marx, *Capital*, vol. 1 (1867), pp. 717–24, 728, 732, in H. Selsam, D. Goldway and H. Martel (eds.), *Dynamics of Social Change. A Reader in Marxist Social Science* (New York, 1970), pp. 241–5; Harold Perkin, *The Origins of Modern British Society, 1780–1870* (London, 1969).

4. Chaim Bermant, *The Cousinhood* (London, 1971) is the best guide to this group of families and their world.

5. W.R. Rubinstein, *Men of Property: The Very Wealthy in Britain Since the Industrial Revolution* (London, 1981), Ch. 5; Rubinstein, 'The Victorian Middle Classes: Wealth, Occupation, and Geography', *Economic History Review* (1977).

6. On the Sassoon family, see Bermant, *The Cousinhood*, Ch. 19, especially pp. 223–38.

7. Ibid. p. 234.

8. See B. Gainer, *The Alien Invasion* (London, 1972), and C.P. Gartner, *The Jewish Immigrant in England, 1870–1914* (London, 1960).

9. Bermant, *The Cousinhood*, p. 406. 'New Court' is the headquarters of the English Rothschilds' merchant bank in the City of London.

10. It should be noted that a majority of Jews in some Edwardian parliaments

(for instance that elected in 1900) were Conservatives rather than Liberals. Few of these, however, ever rose from back-bench status.

11. Cited in Sir Charles Petrie, *The Life and Letters of the Rt Hon. Sir Austen Chamberlain* (London, 1940), vol. II, p. 153.

12. Bernard Wasserstein, *Britain and the Jews of Europe, 1939–1945* (Oxford, 1979).

13. See John Ramsden, *The Age of Balfour and Baldwin, 1902–1940* (London, 1978), Chs. 13–14.

14. Ibid., pp. 348–9.

15. Britain also admitted another 110,000–120,000 refugee Jews during the Second World War or afterwards as displaced persons. See *The Jewish Year Book. 1975* (London, 1974), p. 188, and A.J. Sherman, *Island Refuge. Britain and Refugees from the Third Reich, 1933–1939* (Berkeley, 1973), pp. 264 and 269–72. Sherman summarises the 'balance sheet' as 'in the context of the pre-war period . . . comparatively compassionate, even generous' (ibid., p. 267).

16. Compare, for instance, the circle around Edward VIII while he was Prince of Wales with the associates of Edward VII only a generation before: both were similar in being composed disproportionately of foreigners and *nouveaux-riches*. But while Edward VII openly welcomed Jews, Edward VIII's circle always had a pro-German bias.

17. Dividing British Jewry into a Sephardic-German elite and an underprivileged community is an oversimplification. It does not take into account, for instance, the 60,000 refugees from the Reich, most of whom were middle-class professionals and businessmen. These refugees, however, had arrived too recently to play any part in British public life. It is also probable that many eastern European Jews had, as in the United States, already begun their ascent into middle-class status.

18. On socialism in the East End of London, see William J. Fishman, *Jewish Radicals. From Czarist Shtetl to London Ghetto* (New York, 1974).

19. Geoffrey Alderman, 'Not Quite British: The Political Attitudes of Anglo-Jewry', *British Sociology Yearbook*, vol. 2 (London, 1975), p. 195.

20. Ibid.

21. Ibid., p. 197.

22. See David Leitch, 'Explosion at the King David Hotel', in Michael Sissons and Philip French, *The Age of Austerity 1945–51* (London, 1963).

23. Alderman, 'Not Quite British'. The Labour government did, after all, grant independence to Israel, albeit with infinitely bad grace; more importantly, perhaps, it recognised its existence soon after independene. The new-born state of Israel based many of its institutions, including its parliamentary system and its currency, on British models.

24. Ibid., p. 199.

25. See Ernest Krausz, 'The Edgware Survey: Occupation and Social Class', *Jewish Journal of Sociology*, vol. 11 (1969).

26. See Rubinstein, *Men of Property*, Ch. 8.

27. See, e.g., the list of new property development millionaires in Oliver Marriott, *The Property Boom* (London, 1967), at least half of whom are Jewish.

28. It should also be made clear that today's prominent Jewish politicians represent all shades of the political spectrum, including most certainly the right. Indeed, perhaps the most interesting feature of today's Jewish presence in the British political elite is its ideological broadening to include very prominent Conservatives, a very different political distribution from even twenty years ago.

29. Specific evidence for this claim will be provided in Chapter 2.

30. Probably the most comprehensive introductions to the histories of individual American Jewish communities are to be found in the relevant articles in

Encyclopedia Judaica.
   31. 'Baruch family', *Encyclopedia Judaica*, vol. 4; Margaret L. Coit, *Mr. Baruch* (New York, 1957).
   32. See, e.g., the well-known essays in William Miller (ed.), *Men In Business* (New York, 1952).
   33. On American 'exceptionalism' (a matter much-debated by American historians and sociologists) see, e.g., Louis Hartz, *The Liberal Tradition in America* (New York, 1962).
   34. On this matter, see Rubinstein, *Men of Property*, Chs. 3 and 5. 'The Victorian Middle Classes'.
   35. See the essays in W.R. Rubinstein (ed.), *Wealth and the Wealthy in the Modern World* (London, 1980), especially the Introduction and the essay on France by Adeline Daumard.
   36. See ibid., and the essay on post-1865 America by Frederic C. Jaher.
   37. An important exception were the Guggenheims, who earned their wealth as copper kings (American Smelting and Refinery Co.). Most great industrialists eventually moved to New York City, which became their headquarters. This would have further diminished the influence of Jews, so heavily centred in New York after 1880.
   38. On this, and on the American Jewish elite, see Stephen Birmingham, *Our Crowd* (New York, 1967), and André Manners, *Poor Cousins* (New York, 1972).
   39. Cited in Melvin I. Urofsky, *We Are One! American Jewry and Israel* (Garden City, New York, 1978), p. 46.
   40. *New York Times*, 2 March 1945, cited in Urofsky, p. 62. Urofsky declares that this statement 'fell like a bombshell' on the American Jewish community.
   41. On Roosevelt and the Holocaust, see Urofsky, pp. 40–64; James MacGregor Burns, *Roosevelt: The Soldier of Freedom 1940–1945* (London, 1971), pp. 395–8; Arthur D. Morse, *While Six Million Died* (New York, 1968); and Henry L. Feingold, *The Politics of Rescue: The Roosevelt Administration and the Holocaust, 1938–1945* (New Brunswick, New Jersey, 1970).
   42. Urofsky, *We Are One!*, p. 49.
   43. Ibid. Urofsky also cites the 'passive attitude' of Secretary of State Cordell Hull as significant.
   44. Ibid.
   45. Review of Yehuda Bauer, *The Holocaust in Historical Perspective*, in *Congress Monthly*, January 1980, p. 21. However, not all America's Jewish leaders were eastern Europeans, and surely such structures are justified when speaking only of the inactivity of the old Jewish elite.
   46. See the autobiographies of New York Jews of eastern European origin who attended college at this time or even later; e.g., Isaac Asimov, *In Memory Yet Green* (Garden City, New York, 1978), Norman Podhoretz, *Making It* (New York, 1967), Alfred Kazin, *New York Jew* (New York, 1976).
   47. See Urofsky, *We Are One!*, pp. 17–93, and his *American Zionism From Herzl to the Holocaust* (Garden City, New York, 1975).
   48. Urofsky, *We Are One!* p. 65.
   49. Yehuda Bauer, *The Jewish Emergence From Powerlessness* (Toronto, 1979), p. 58.
   50. Ibid., pp. 59, 60, 60–1. It would be interesting to know exactly when the concept of a 'Jewish vote' in the United States became an accepted political notion.
   51. Writings on modern Germany are legion, as are writings on Jewish life in Germany. See, e.g., the bibliography in the *Encyclopedia Judaica*, vol. 4, pp. 502–4. Well-known studies of some important aspects of this topic include Fritz Stern, *The Politics of Cultural Despair* (Berkeley, 1961); P.G.J. Pulzer, *The Rise of*

Political Antisemitism in Germany and Austria (New York, 1964); George Mosse, *Germans and Jews* (New York, 1970). A good recent general history of Germany is Gordon A. Craig, *Germany, 1866–1945* (Oxford, 1978), which contains a lengthy and up-to-date bibliography.

52. See Pulzer, *The Rise of Political Antisemitism*, and Craig, *Germany, 1866–1945*, pp. 84ff, and 153–5.

53. *See, e.g., E. Rosenbaum and A.J. Sherman, M.M. Warburg & Co, 1798–1938. Merchant Bankers of Hamburg* (London, 1979); and Fritz Stern, *Gold and Iron. Bismarck, Bleichroder and The Building of the German Empire* (New York, 1977).

54. Cited in Hugo Valentin, *Antisemitism Historically and Critically Examined* (London, 1936), p. 223. Prussia published named lists of its wealthiest inhabitants at the time. Valentin's book is one of the best and most detailed accounts of the decline of German Jewry in this period, especially at the elite level. Many of his statistics do not seem to have been published elsewhere.

55. See the table in *Encyclopedia Judaica*, p. 481.

56. Ibid.

57. W.O. Henderson, *The Rise of German Industrial Power 1834–1914* (Berkeley, 1975), pp. 71–2. The words in quotation are by W.H. Dawson.

58. Kenneth D. Barkin, *The Controversy Over German Industrialization, 1890–1902* (Chicago, 1970), pp. 201–2.

59. Valentin, *Antisemitism*, p. 212.

60. Ibid., Chs. XI–XIII.

61. Ibid., pp. 198–9.

62. Ibid., p. 199.

63. See, e.g., Rosenbaum and Sherman, *M.M. Warburg & Co. 1798–1938*, Chs. 7–9; Valentin, *Antisemitism*, Ch. XII.

64. Ibid., pp. 218–19.

65. See Walter Laqueur, *Weimar Culture* (London, 1974).

66. Cf., for instance, the astonishing degree of opposition to Einstein and the theory of relativity for its alleged 'radical' and 'Jewish' origins.

67. Valentin, *Antisemitism*, p. 111.

68. As, demographically, it probably was, because of its low birth rate and high incidence of inter-marriage and conversion or apathy.

69. 'France', in *Encyclopedia Judaica*, vol. 7, pp. 19–25; M. Roblin, *Les Juifs de France* (Paris, 1952).

70. 'France', *Encyclopedia Judaica*, pp. 26–7.

71. Cited in Theodore Zeldin, *France 1848–1945*, vol. 1 (Oxford, 1973), p. 77.

72. B. Gille, *Historie de la Maison Rothschild*, vol. 1 (Geneva, 1965), p. 374, cited in Roger Price, *The French Second Republic. A Social History* (London, 1972), p. 42.

73. See, e.g., Patrick O'Brien and Calgar Keydor, *Economic Growth in Britain and France 1780–1914. Two Paths to the Twentieth Century* (London, 1978).

74. See 'France', *Encyclopedia Judaica*, pp. 28–30.

75. Lucy S. Davidowicz, *The War Against the Jews 1933–1945* (New York, 1975), p. 21.

76. Whether Jews are absolutely central to the far right is probably a good test of general anti-semitism: in general the second Ku Klux Klan, for example, considered blacks and Catholics much more adversely, probably reflecting wider American values.

77. It is true that from 1871 a new myth defined the extreme left in France, that of the Paris Commune. But its appeal was limited by the social structure of France.

78. See, e.g., Stephen Lukes, *Emile Durkheim. His Life and Work* (London, 1973), Part One.

79. 'France', *Encyclopedia Judaica*, p. 31.

80. Ibid. In the period 1900–40 the Jewish contribution to French culture became very pronounced. Durkheim, Bergson, Proust, Maurois, Chagall, Pisarro, Modigliani and Sarah Bernhardt are only the most outstanding French cultural figures of Jewish descent in this period.

81. Ibid., p. 33; see also 'Holocaust' in ibid., vol. 8, p. 889.

82. Ibid., p. 36.

83. President Giscard d'Estaing on a trip to the Middle East in early 1980 'particularly shocked French Jews by peering through binoculars at Israeli territory from neighboring Jordan. This was interpreted by people like Baron Guy [de Rothschild, a leader of the Jewish community in France] as a way of recognizing the hostility of Israel's neighbors as legitimate' (*Melbourne Age*, 12 May 1980, reprinted from the *Washington Post*). Interestingly, the same report stated that 'an attempt to organise the Jews of France to counteract the French Government's anti-Israeli policies has developed into a bitter dispute over the continued leadership of the French Jewish community by the Rothschild banking family', and that an Israeli diplomat, Avi Primor, 'is accused by members of the French Jewish establishment of encouraging a revolt against the Rothschilds for allegedly acting as if poorer, less well-connected French Jews need the family's aristocratic protection . . . supposedly to preserve access to Mr Giscard and his entourage' (ibid.). It is difficult to imagine such a dispute in any other Western Jewish community. The synagogue bombing at rue Copernic in 1980, and the other recent manifestations of virulent French anti-semitism, must surely be seen in the context of the anomalous history and structure of French Jewry (and of the socio-economic development of contemporary France) which has been outlined here.

84. One per cent voted for the French Communist Party. (J.R. Frears and Jean-Luc Paroidi, *War Will Not Take Place. The French Parliamentary Elections March 1978* (London, 1979). p. 81).

85. Later we shall briefly examine the history of the smaller Australian Jewish community. The histories of Russian/Soviet Jewry, and of Israel, which will also be discussed later, do not readily fit this model.

2 POWER, ELITES AND THE JEWS IN THE POST-WAR WORLD

Power and Modern Society

No issue in the social sciences is more complex and less amenable to an academic consensus than political power, which is an ideological rather than a descriptive concept. Yet without an informed discussion of this most basic concern, no far-reaching conclusions about the nature of Jewish influence in the modern world are possible.

Social scientists have, broadly speaking, evolved three models of the nature of power in modern society: the pluralist, the elitist and the Marxist. The pluralists contend that political power has become increasingly fragmented and diffused in Western society.[1] They perceive democratic societies as intricately balanced between competing interest groups of all kinds so that no single interest group can predominate. However, the elitists argue the opposite: in all societies there must be a small group which rules and a vast majority which does not and cannot. Curiously, the elitist view has been held both by extreme conservatives like Pareto, and by radicals like Mills, who have much in common with the Marxists, especially the 'vulgar Marxism' which particularises political actors according to their economic interests.

Although the Marxist view of political power has often been taken as mirroring the elitist views of Mills and his school, it has evolved in the recent past. For the Marxists, what matters is the nature of ruling: cultural and intellectual as well as political and economic. In capitalist societies, individual actors are only the embodiment of the capitalist class, which rules by virtue of the hegemonic position it enjoys in all spheres of life. Although socialist parties may win elections these victories are basically irrelevant to the question of who *rules*: capitalism continues to rule, though it may not always 'govern'.

Who, then, is right? It is our belief that the most accurate conceptual model of power in modern Western democracies is one which includes features of both the elitist and pluralist schemas and in which these societies are viewed as possessing, as it were,

43

a bicamerality of power, divided between an elitist 'upper house' and a pluralist 'lower house'.[2] In most societies 'the upper house' – which we shall henceforth term the 'small elite' – comprises about 1,000 people, although it may range from several hundred to 5,000 or more.[3] It includes such obvious figures as the President or Prime Minister and the Cabinet, the major opposition figures, the most important (or possibly all) members of the national legislature, the high court, the chairmen or managing directors of the largest business enterprises, the heads of the major trade unions, leading civil servants, media and communication leaders and editors, major religious leaders and spokesmen for the most influential lobbying and interest groups. It also encompasses a nation's 200–300 wealthiest men and women, the presidents or vice-chancellors of the leading colleges and universities, the most distinguished scientists and thinkers and the most important opinion-makers, however defined. The small elite probably also includes important *éminences grises* or advisers influential behind the scenes. It is this small elite which decides both policy outcomes and the more basic and elusive question of which items reach the 'agenda' at all.

The 'lower' house of the 'parliament of power' is plurally-based. Various interest groups can get their way even in the face of opposition by the small elite.[4] However, the real nature of this pluralist 'house' must be carefully delineated. At election time, 'democracy' prevails; this is the ultimate sanction of the political process in Western societies.[5] At all other times, it does not. Between elections, organised interest groups are the real voices of the 'lower house', and, by definition, they rarely represent the poor or powerless.[6] Instead, they are usually organised by what we shall henceforth term the 'large' elite – the top 10–20 per cent of the population measured in terms of income, wealth, occupational importance and education. This leading 10–20 per cent of society is also the most advantaged group, accounting for anything up to two-thirds of all consumer demand and holding anything up to 90 per cent or more of all significant private assets. This group is both the manufacturer and consumer (and hence, generally the arbiter) of virtually all important sources of knowledge and opinion, especially in the field of public affairs. Moreover, it is from the large elite that most members of the small elite emerge. The importance of the large elite is therefore crucial; but – equally – it is not a united or cohesive group. No stratum of society which in the United States would number more than 20 million people could possibly be.

Even the large elite embodies only a relatively small minority of the population: nearly 80 per cent do not belong to the large elite on our definition. It follows that any individual member of a group represented in the large elite is considerably magnified in weight and influence *vis-à-vis* the general population. It is quite possible for a group of individuals to achieve greater power than their numbers in the total population would imply by their systematic over-representation in either the large or small elites.

This contemporary structure of power, common throughout the Western world, differs very markedly from the structure of power and influence implied in our previous discussion of the history of the Jews in Britain, the United States, Germany and France. Prior to 1945, it is doubtful whether an 'affluent society' existed anywhere in the world, even in the United States. Higher education was confined to a tiny majority; interest groups and lobbies, though they obviously existed, were less demonstrative and less successful. However, in the last thirty years the very bases of power seem to have changed. Knowledge and technical skills have, it is argued, replaced capital and wealth as the principal source of power in the modern world.[7] It is much more difficult today to define the divisions between landed, commercial and industrial capitalism. The importance of the large elite has grown considerably since 1945 in the Western world, certainly when compared with its size or weight before 1939, and relative to the small elite.

Change, too, has come to the small elites of all Western nations. Since 1945 there has been a broadening of the types of persons or position-holders represented in the small elite, and a very considerable diminution of national differences and idiosyncracies. Trade union leaders, leaders of major interest groups and lobbies and intellectual, academic and scientific figures are only the most obvious types of elite position-holders who would be included as significant members in the contemporary small elite, whose equivalents a century ago, or even fifty years ago, would be numbered among a nation's small elite with much less certainty. This is obviously an important issue when discussing the nature of the power structure prevalent throughout the Western world, for although 'capitalism' may still be an accurate designation of our economic system, the small elite of all Western democracies may have become much less dependent upon capitalists or upon the debate over capitalism or the distribution of material wealth.[8]

All Western societies, furthermore, resemble each other much more today than they did in the past, and this is indicative of the international dimension of the structure of power. There is a definite hierarchy of national influence in the Western world. At present, the United States is still the leader of the Western nations. The United States still dominates all the salient spheres of international power and influence. Japan may export cars to the United States, but she does not export ideas. Britain's quality press, its non-commercial television or its intellegentsia may keep alive that nation's distinguished cultural heritage, but its manufacturing industry is increasingly dominated by American-owned corporations. In fact, 'America' is, in many ways, not so much a nation but a mode of thought and a hierarchy of values, a mental frame of reference and behaviour. To many foreigners, 'America' seems an extraordinary place because it is there that their material dreams seem to come true, however tarnished it may be by its manifold problems and excesses. The United States enjoys its dominant position today because, from 1776 onwards, its national ideals and values have been those which are now universal: it has had 200 years to practise what other Western nations have adopted only over the past thirty-five.

The adoption of the American outlook throughout all Western nations has assisted in the homogenisation of national elites. Each national elite today more or less mirrors the rational, highly-educated capitalistic elite found in the United States despite the very different national histories and evolutionary patterns characteristic of each nation down to the Second World War.[9]

The United States (and, more significantly, the ideals it unconsciously denotes and embodies) enjoys a supreme position in the contemporary Western world. Both because of the power and dominance of the United States, and of the successful imposition of American values in all other Western societies, American elites are intrinsically more important than those of other Western nations. A member of the American large or, still more, small elite is 'twice blessed' and is in two separate ways 'more equal' than others: as an elite figure and as an American. In perhaps no field is this international hierarchy so important as the cultural and intellectual. Because of the powers of publicity and advertisement which the United States academic, publishing and media worlds have at their disposal, ideas and attitudes which are taken up in the United States quickly gain common currency the world over. Seldom does it work in the other direction, except in limited spheres. A Peruvian poet, a Norwegian school of philosophy, an Australian or even a Canadian political or social commentator might for all practical purposes not exist, unless he has access to the American stage. The major exceptions to this are for the most part limited to those ancient, and hence acceptable, seats of European culture and learning such as Oxford and Cambridge, London or Paris, where a Sartre, a Leavis or a Bertrand Russell might gain international fame.

This concept is an oversimplification if taken at face value. National differences and idiosyncracies are still important. In several key respects, indeed, the social and political structure of the United States differs markedly from those of most other Western nations. In the political sphere America differs from almost all other Western nations in not possessing a socialist party of any real significance: still less does America have a socialist party which is capable of forming a government. America's trade union structure is different from elsewhere, with – for the most part – no hostility to capitalist affluence. However, in most of the key sectors of Western life the American experience is typical.

The economic elite is almost as important. Economic power resides in the Western world to a considerable extent in large and impersonal corporations, often multinational. These corporations are owned and managed in some cases by wealthy individuals and families but increasingly now by institutional investors, finance corporations such as insurance companies and by pension funds. But wealthy individuals have another role in the present matrix of power. Because of their wealth *and for no other reason*, they are generally able to influence policy outcomes to a greater degree than men who are not wealthy: we have defined the top 10–20 per cent of income-earners and wealth-holders as belonging automatically to a large elite. Precisely because corporate managers, though themselves well rewarded and powerful, are not normally 'wealthy' in the sense that asset-owning tycoons are wealthy (or as very successful members of the most lucrative professions – medicine, the law, engineering – are wealthy), they are such men *as individuals* inherently less influential. *Time* magazine noted that 'most of America's real money – the *big* money – goes to its small businessmen, entrepreneurs, and professionals'. In contrast, 'a lot of bank Vice-

Presidents and middle managers in heavy manufacturing are lucky to crack $35,000; they commonly get a title in lieu of money'.[10] Corporate managers do enjoy a sufficiently high income to place most of them within a nation's large elite. But as individual income-earners they constitute only a fraction of the millions of members of a nation's large elite; any especial power in influence accrues to them by virtue of their corporate control rather than their wealth or status.

There is an important sense in which corporate managers are more limited in their ability to influence or control events than wealthy independent asset-owners or even successful members of the best-rewarded professions. As employees of large corporations, corporate managers cannot, as a rule, direct the profits of their corporations into concerns of interest only to themselves. This is especially so if that concern is overtly political or is controversial: on the contrary, large corporations will take considerable pains to avoid such controversy, especially given the formidable economic and political powers of those other sections of the large elite who might be most offended.[11] Except for those at the very top, managers are normally expected to conform to a life-style which punishes eccentricity, let alone political controversy. But independent businessmen and very successful professionals are under no such restraint. They can be as eccentric and controversial as they wish;[12] they can even devote half a lifetime's work to giving away the fortune which they laboured to build in the years before, as did Andrew Carnegie, John D. Rockfeller, the Ford family and numerous American multi-millionaires. They can finance a political cause or candidacy (occasionally of themselves or members of their families) in a way which corporations or corporate managers can seldom do directly, and for which corporate managers below the highest level lack the resources. Independent wealth remains a most significant advantage for those seeking to enhance their own power or interests.

The limitations upon multinational corporations should be clear. They work for their own aggrandisement, but in a very circumscribed and constrained way. They have no ideological interest other than an interest in the maintenance of capitalism, and have no reason to support or oppose the particular interests which individuals might wish to support.[13] They are, moreover, a target increasingly attacked by the political left everywhere in the Western world. As large-scale investors and employers of labour in developing countries, they are doubly vulnerable to attack or confiscation in these countries, as well as to charges that they are failing in their duties of employment and investment at home. Their profits and the power they undoubtedly exercise is not without its considerable costs or risks.

As well as the economic sector of the elite structure, another segment might be suggested as disproportionately important, especially in its ability to mould opinions. This is the world of media and communications. Few would deny that television and, to a lesser extent, radio and films, confer upon their controllers incalculable power to mould public opinion.[14] Perhaps paradoxically, because of their non-literate content and form, the electronic and visual media are inherently much more influential among the majority of the population outside the elite than among the elite minority. Among the large elite the influence of the visual media is less important, while the influence of the 'literate' media – publishing, journalism and academic and semi-academic productions of every kind – rises accordingly. Although the writers for the Western world's intellectual magazines and journals often seem to be speaking exclusively to each other, they are addressing an audience whose importance is heightened because it consists of members of the large – and of the small – elite. The readership of journals like *Commentary*, *Encounter* or *Quadrant* might be very small, but their influence is out of all proportion to what the circulation figures might suggest; similarly the readership of *Business Week* or *Scientific American*, *The New York Times* or the London *Times* is of high status. 'Ideas have consequences', if only because they influence the men and women who make up the decision-making elite.

This system of power and influence exists throughout the Western world. Its most salient single feature is its inegalitarianism: the power of certain individuals is systematically enhanced by their wealth, status, education or occupation. Equally important is its inegalitarianism in national terms. The United States is the most powerful nation, and therefore American modes of thought, behaviour and organisation are accepted, perhaps to the fury of some nations like the French, as both the norm and goal of modern life. This system of power and influence is more benign than any which has prevailed in the past; were this not so, it could not last for very long without resort to brute force and, whatever the faults of the system, brutality is not one of them. It succeeds in the final analysis because it is a somewhat flawed version of the system which most people would have chosen anyway, had they been given the choice.

The Jews as an Elite

In suggesting that Jews are an elite and disproportionately over-represented at the national elite level it is not implied that Jews constitute some mysterious and secretive cabal which manipulates governments, nations and finance on a world scale. This concept of an 'international Jewish conspiracy', from which Jews have so often suffered in the past, is not the point of this book. The historical discussion in the previous chapter demonstrated how fallacious and misleading this concept was even in the period between about 1880 and 1925, when it was offered most regularly by anti-semites and superficially bore the closest resemblance to reality.

First, and perhaps most importantly, there is nothing either improper or mysterious about 'Jewish influence' in today's world: we live in democracies, and Jews, like any other group, have a perfect right to lobby for any goals they wish. The aims of most Jewish lobbying are, moreover, unusually limited and visible, centring around the maintenance of Israel. When Jews have as a group lobbied for ends further afield, they have often quite gratuitously aided and assisted other groups perceived as victims of racial discrimination, most notably blacks in the United States during the initial phase of the civil rights period from the late 1940s to the late 1960s.

There is, furthermore, all the difference in the world between disproportionate power, which it can sensibly be claimed the Jews do possess, and omnipotence, the ability to make or unmake governments, wars and nations, to control all the major actors on the world scene from Wall Street to Moscow.

Jews are not omnipotent in today's world, and are often distinct losers in the corridors of power, even in places where their influence is apparently strongest. In the past ten years the energy crisis and the power of the OPEC states may well have shifted the world balance if not decisively against Jews, at least significantly against them. Except perhaps over Israel's existence, Jews do not act in concert over any issue: it may well be that Jews are more divided among themselves at present than at any time since the Second World War, especially in the United States, where there is no Jewish consensus on their future relationship with left-liberalism, the ideological position taken by the majority of American Jews since the New Deal. Finally, Jewish influence since 1945 could not have existed without a fundamental change in the nature of capitalism and of the establishment right in most Western nations.

Since 1945 things in the Western world have, perhaps for the first time in history, gone well for the majority of Jews. Why this has been so is a valid question for inquiry, and it is disingenuous to pretend that since the end of the war there has not been a fundamental change in the status of Western Jewry. Examinations of Jewish history in this century have focused on two events which are generally taken as the most significant of the modern period, the Holocaust and the establishment of Israel. While there can be no question of the fundamental importance of these events, overconcentration on them, together with understandable reluctance to discuss Jewish socio-economic advantages in an explicit fashion, has led to the neglect of another important trend: the steady rise of Western Jewry into the upper-middle class, together with the broadening of Jewish membership in the institutional elites of most Western countries. Conversely, the rise of Western Jewry into the upper-middle class, together with the broadening of Jewish membership in the institutional elites of most Western countries. Conversely, the rise of Western Jewry to unparalleled affluence and high status has led to the near-disappearance of a Jewish proletariat of any size: indeed, the Jews may become the first ethnic group in history without a working class of any size. This latter phenomenon has had two significant consequences. It has rendered obsolete (and rarely heard) the type of anti-semitism which has its basis in fears of the swamping of the native population by a limitless horde of Yiddish-speaking aliens, and it has made Marxism, and other radical doctrines, irrelevant to the socio-economic bases of Western Jewry, and increasingly unattractive to most Jews.

While there have been many wealthy and powerful Jewish individuals and dynasties throughout modern history, only since the 1950s has Western Jewry *as a whole* risen into the upper-middle class, and the Jewish proletariat transformed itself into a near-universal Jewish bourgeoisie. As recently as, say, 1948 – the year of the establishment of the State of Israel – it is likely that more than one-half of the Western world's adult Jews were employed in working-class or low clerical trades. In contrast, at the present time it is probable that under 20 per cent of the Western world's Jews (and possibly much under 20 per cent) remain in the working class; those who do are mainly elderly.[15]

The present socio-economic structure of Western Jewry in a sense confirms the striking image postulated at the beginning of the century by the Jewish socialist Ber Borochov of the Jewish social structure of his day: an 'inverted pyramid'.[16] Borochov did not, needless to say, mean that the world's Jews of *c*. 1920 consisted of hundreds of Einsteins, Rothschilds and Trotskys supported at the base by a small Jewish working class. Rather, in Ernest Germain's words,

> Borochov maintained that the Jewish question was rooted in the fact that Jews, and above all Jewish workers, played no important role in the vital sectors of the economy (heavy industry, metallurgy, coal, and so on), but instead occupied important positions solely in the peripheral spheres of economic life. The social composition of other peoples resembled a pyramid having at its base hundreds of thousands of miners, metal workers, railway workers, etc., and then passing through large layers of handicraftsmen, topped off by ever thinner strata of businessmen, industrialists, and bankers. But the social composition of the Jewish people resembled an 'inverted pyramid' in which large handicraft strata rested on narrow layers of workers – who moreover engaged in non-vital sectors of industry – and had to bear the full weight of an enormous mass of businessmen.[17]

Borochov was a Zionist socialist who believed (again in the words of Ernest Germain) that

> It was first of all necessary to 'reverse the inverted pyramid,' i.e., to create a 'normal' Jewish society like those of other peoples; until this was done the Jewish proletariat could not seriously undertake revolutionary struggle; and such a society could be created only in Palestine.[18]

Borochov's fascinating views of Jewish social structure are worth some examination, for they seem to rest upon a number of premises which were either false or questionable. The Jewish representation in the various national elites of the time, though strong in some respects, was not broadly-based and was highly vulnerable to anti-semitic pressures. Furthermore, Borochov's metaphor is quite misleading as a description of the prevalent socio-economic condition of world Jewry at the time. Certainly there was not, relatively speaking, an 'enormous' mass of Jewish businessmen at the time; rather a social structure in which the Jewish working class predominated heavily. Writing of the vast Russian 'Pale of Settlement' where the majority of the Western world's Jews lived until the late nineteenth century,[19] Uriah Z. Engelman has noted:

The appalling poverty among Jews in the first half of the nineteenth century is also attested to by their occupational composition. Of the Jewish population of Poland in 1843, 10.8% had some 'claim' to a gainful occupation. Of this group unskilled workers and artisans supplied the largest part, 53.9% of all gainfully employed; small traders and shopkeepers was the second largest occupational class, 21.19%; innkeepers and tavern owners comprised 11.4%; 6.7% were engaged in agriculture as tenants, independent farmers, and agricultural workers; and *1.5% were classed as capitalists, bankers and manufacturers.* The last term, it must be understood, is not intended to describe a modern industrialist. The 'manufacturers' were small ink-makers, candle-makers, and wax-makers, whose 'bedrooms were factories, who peddled their own wares, and whose profits rarely exceeded the meagre wages of an unskilled labourer. The rest of the population, almost 90%, were classed as dependents . . .'[20]

Again, according to Engelman,

Economically, also, the Jewish population of Eastern Europe was homogeneous in a very high degree. Poverty was general, and the difference in the degree of affluence between members of the commercial and artisan classes not very large. As a result there was little antagonism between economic groups which was not easily bridged.[21]

Although these conditions changed somewhat during the second half of the nineteenth century, the basic economic condition of the Jews in the Pale did not alter. By 1898, about 44 per cent of all employed Russian Jews were skilled craftsmen who worked for their immediate consumer (Engleman's phrase). Most of these were employed in clothing, wearing apparel and related trades, including those who worked in small factories.

The wages of the artisans and of the factory workers were very small, ranging from 50 to over 500 roubles ($25–$250) per annum, with the vast majority earning yearly about 100–175 roubles ($50–$87.50). This was considerably below the minimum required to feed and shelter a Jewish family in a small town. The hours of labour were very long, from sixteen to eighteen hours per day.[22]

Of the remaining gainfully employed portion of Russian and Polish Jewry at this time, 31.6 per cent worked in commercial trades. Most of these were small merchants and traders, or even pedlars (who formed a prominent and typical section of the *shtetl* community) – and their employees – rather than substantial businessmen. Most of the other Jewish workers were depressed to a still further degree: the third largest group were – rather surprisingly – domestics and others rendering personal service, who accounted for 11.6 per cent of all employed Jews. The next largest category consisted of *unskilled* workers (7 per cent), including cabmen, teamsters, diggers, stonebreakers, long-shoremen and water-carriers.[23]

In contrast, the other end of the occupational scale was extraordinarily small. The Russian Jewish professional class, including rabbis, teachers, musicians and entertainers, doctors and nurses, civil servants and writers, numbered five per cent of all employed Jewish males in 1887. However, if minor employees in the synagogues and primary schools – whose economic status was often lower than artisans and factory workers – are excluded from these figures, only *1.5 per cent* of all employed male Russian and Polish Jews (22,574 out of 5,216,000 Jews resident in the Russian Empire in 1897) were professionals in the ordinary meaning of the term in Russia at the end of the nineteenth century.[24]

From these statistics it is evident that the Jewish population of Russia [and Poland] was predominantly a labouring one with skilled workers, unskilled labourers and domestics comprising over 62% of the gainfully employed. Judging from the large number of artisans, their very low earnings – a natural result of the overcrowding and intense competition in the trades – and from the large class of Jewish unskilled workers who had to compete with non-Jewish unskilled labourers for wages below a level of subsistence, one must conclude that the Jews flocked into any avenue that offered employment and a chance to earn a living, no matter how meagre that living might have been.[25]

Because Russian and Polish Jews, with only a limited number of exceptions, were legally confined to the Pale of Settlement they were faced by the classical 'Malthusian trap' as their population outstripped available resources. The Jewish population rose at an extremely rapid rate: orthodox Jews married very young and did not practise birth control; the Jewish death rate, particularly among infants, was unusually low. As a result, the Jewish population of Europe rose from 2.7 million in 1825 to 8.7 million in 1900, despite very substantial emigration to North America and elsewhere.[26]

It is important to keep in perspective the socio-economic circumstances of the *bulk* of Western Jewry at this time. The overwhelming majority of the Western world's Jews in 1900 (and for many years thereafter) were exceedingly poor and socially, economically and culturally depressed and persecuted. Although the Russian Pale was both the numerical centre of Jewry as well as the most impoverished and backward region of Jewish settlement, most other areas in eastern Europe were of a similar nature – in Galicia (part of Austria), Romania and Hungary. When Jews did emigrate in large numbers, it was initially to areas as depressed and impoverished as those which they left. This impoverished mass of Jews was culturally distinct, palpably alien and visibly differentiated from the host community wherever they lived. They were strangers and outsiders, arousing suspicion and mistrust wherever they settled. In addition they had to bear the entire historical weight of anti-semitism, of virulent hostility to Jews which was nearly everywhere so ancient a tradition as to seem immutable. Thus was born the type of anti-semitism which had as its target the Yiddish-speaking 'horde' of migrants and the 'dangers' they presented. This *type* of anti-semitism is essentially different from anti-semitism aimed at the Jewish elite, particularly the financial elite. Despite this, both types of anti-semitism copied each other, just as the socio-economic and political structure of both sides of Jewry had certain definite links. Both the Jewish elite and the Yiddish-speaking 'horde' were, first and foremost, aliens wherever they settled: to the anti-semite this applied equally to the Rothschild or the Einstein as to the poorest-paid Jewish factory-worker. Both sides of the Jewish social structure, moreover, were characterised as 'middlemen': the activities of the Rothschilds, Sasoons or Warburgs were, no doubt, on a larger scale than those of Yiddish ribbon-pedlars but both were, in the final analysis, 'parasites' who produced nothing, exploiting the native population for the exclusive benefit of Jewry. Both sides of the Jewish social structure laboured to produce the domination of overthrow of their host governments: the elite through its forging of financial chains and backstairs manipulations, the masses through their perpetually radical politics, disease, criminal activities and rivalry with the native population for employment. This logic, the stock-in-trade of anti-semitism for three-quarters of a century after about 1870, linked both sides of the Jewish social structure in a symbiosis of malignity and evil.

The great increase in the size of the European Jewish proletariat during the nineteenth century brought about many far-reaching results in other spheres. One was the rise of Zionism as a solution for the endemic anti-semitism aimed at the Yiddish 'horde'. The second was, of course, the great migration of eastern European Jewry to the United States, Britain, South Africa, Argentina, Australia and elsewhere. Fully *one-half* of the total number of Jews living in eastern Europe – just under four million people – migrated elsewhere in the period 1881–1929. The majority went to the United States, whose Jewish population increased from only 10,000 in 1825 to 250,000 in 1880, to perhaps four million by 1939.[27] But initially, little or nothing had changed; New York's Lower East Side might be the 'golden door' to equality and prosperity, but all that was for a future generation. Even by the First World War, the socio-economic profile of Western Jewry had hardly altered at all, despite its relocation in lands of opportunity.

There is some evidence that this situation began to alter during the inter-war period. Some detailed evidence, for example, exists for Jewish fathers and sons in Detroit in 1935.[28] Among Jewish sons – then aged between sixteen and twenty-five, and hence born between 1909 and 1919 – in this sample, 12.3 per cent were already in the professional and proprietary occupational classes, compared with only 4.2 per cent of a sample of non-Jews in Detroit born in the same period.[29] At the other end of the social scale, 33.5 per cent of Jewish sons in this sample were engaged in semi-skilled or unskilled trades, compared with 59.4 per cent of non-Jews.[30]

During the post-1945 period, with its twenty-five or more years of affluence, with the ready availability of free or inexpensive tertiary education and the decline of much old-style anti-semitism, the trends first glimpsed in the inter-war period rapidly became the norm, especially in the United States. After only ten years of steady upward mobility, the chance which had come over American Jewry was evident for all to see. In the perceptive words of the eminent sociologist Nathan Glazer, himself an example of this upward rise,

> In the 1930s about half of those American Jews who were immigrants were still workers; only a slightly larger proportion of the second generation were clerks, office workers, salesmen and the like. However, the fifteen years of prosperity from the end of the thirties to the mid-fifties have wrought great chances, and created the Jewish community we know today. The effect of these changes has been to raise the East European Jews – the immigrants of 1880–1924, their children and grandchildren – more or less to the level previously achieved by the German Jews . . . In these fifteen years, the older generation of East European Jewish immigrants, with its large proportion of workers, has been further reduced by the natural effect of age, while the younger generation has risen in the social scale. Perhaps a majority of the younger generation is now composed of businessmen and professional men.

Moreover, even by the mid-1950s

> This community of businessmen and professional men is better educated and wealthier than most of the population – probably as well educated and as wealthy as some of the oldest and longest established elements in the United States.[31]

Since the 1950s, the many studies of the socio-economic and

educational status of American Jews have confirmed this picture.[32] In the 1950s the average income of American Jewish families was higher than that of the general population,[33] and this situation continued into the 1960s.[34] More evidence on this matter was provided by *A Profile of the Jewish Freshman*.[36] A very large sample – nearly 11,000 Jews and 150,000 adherents of other religions – among the freshman class at more than 100 representative colleges and universities completed extended questionnaires revealing a wide variety of personal data, including estimated parental income.[36] The findings revealed a considerable difference between Jews and non-Jews. A more recent study with similar results was that undertaken in April 1978 by Geraldine Rosenfield for the American Jewish Committee on Contemporary Jewish Concerns. In this study a total of 1,100 questionnaires were completed by members of Jewish groups in nine large American cities and urban areas.[37] The educational, political and religious affiliations of the respondents were sufficiently normal for the author of this *Report* to state that 'we note that the respondents in this survey are the Jews we recognize'.[38] Finally, from a somewhat different realm, there is the evidence on the income of Jewish political activists and leaders. Obviously, such evidence cannot be random in a statistical sense, but it is highly significant in providing an economic profile of one of the most influential segments of the American Jewish community.[39]

The evidence from other Western countries is less sound. There are fewer studies and these almost invariably measure occupation rather than the more pertinent (and personal) area of income. In Britain, it seems that no scientific study of Anglo-Jewry has been made more recently than 1964. In Ernest Krausz's study of Jews in Edgware – a heavily Jewish area of north-west London – undertaken in 1964, the occupational distribution of a sample of 403 adult males was: 16.2 per cent professionals, 40.8 per cent employers or managers and 32.1 per cent foremen, skilled manual or 'own account' (unfortunately the three categories were grouped together). 'Non-manual workers' accounted for a further 6.9 per cent, while only 4.0 per cent of the sample were engaged in semi- or unskilled trades or in personal service.[40] Interesting data exist as well for contemporary Australia. The findings here are more comprehensive and well-grounded than elsewhere, for they are based upon the statistics of the Australian Census (which is taken every five, rather than ten years). This requires each inhabitant to declare his religious affiliation which can be cross-tabulated with the variety of socio-economic data which is also polled by the Census such as education, occupation, residence, etc. The Australian findings are interesting for another important reason: somewhere between one-third and one-half of all of Australia's 70,000 Jews are Holocaust survivors or their children, and the Census findings thus measure the progress of a community whose roots, to a disproportionate extent, lie in the economically impoverished, now-vanished world of Continental Jewry, and who as individuals, bear an indelible psychic scar from the events of that period. Although most of this segment of Australian Jewry arrived there as penniless refugees, by 1971 fully 46.1 per cent of *all* occupied Jewish males in Australia were employed in the professional and managerial occupational categories, with 21.2 per cent in the small business and clerical trades. Only 6.7 per cent remained in semi- or unskilled occupations.[41]

What should be clear from these and other similar studies is the transformation of the socio-economic profile of Western Jewry in less than forty years. In a real sense, Borochov's description of the Jewish social structure of his day – 'an inverted pyramid' – is now an accurate one; in particular, the impoverished mass of Yiddish-speaking working-class Jews has all but disappeared.

The formation of disproportionate Jewish presence in the large and small elites – and the near-disappearance of a Jewish prolerariat – have had many consequences of central importance to the situation of contemporary Jewry, and are entirely novel in modern Jewish history.

The primary vehicle of this dramatic upward rise has been the relatively open educational system, particularly at the tertiary level, provided by all Western governments.[42] In most Western nations between 80 and 90 per cent of all Jews aged 18-22 engage in some form of tertiary education, that is, virtually every qualified Jew of appropriate age. Such a level of attendance has had two far-reaching effects upon the Jewish people and their membership in the large elite. First it has transformed the socio-economic profile of Western Jewry, as tertiary education has generally been an automatic ticket of admission into the upper-middle class. Thirty-five unbroken years of this – as has occurred since 1945 – will affect, and has affected the occupational and income structure of Western Jewry. Second, it has substantially increased the *relative* Jewish proportion of all tertiary graduates and of all undergraduates, since non-Jews attend college or university in lower proportions than Jews. Since there are more Jews at elite colleges and universities than at mediocre ones, it will enhance the Jewish proportion of graduates at elite institutions to a greater degree. In the 1969 study of Jewish freshmen quoted above it was found, for instance, that in 1967, while Jews comprised 5.4 per cent of all tertiary freshmen, they accounted for 9.9 per cent of all university freshmen enrolled at four-year colleges.[43] The Jewish rate of attendance at the better American colleges was considerably in excess of their percentage in the American population.[44] Such a disproportionate rate of entry into the upper-middle class and into the upper percentiles of the population as measured by years (and quality) of education – and, presumably, income and occupational status – will, if maintained continuously over a generation, raise the Jewish percentage of America's (and other Western countries') large elite to a level considerably in excess of their tiny percentage in the overall population. It is, naturally, difficult to estimate what percentage of the large elites of today's Western nations are Jews. A reasonable estimate would be that about 10–15 per cent of America's, 5–10 per cent of Britain's and 3–5 per cent of Australia's large elites are Jews, compared with the overall percentage of Jews in the population of these countries of, respectively, 3, 1 and 0.5. The ability of Jews to function as a well-organised interest group within the large elite is further enhanced by two other factors: their geographical residence in important urban centres and their common viewpoints, especially on the maintenance of security of the State of Israel.

It is thus in the Jewish proportion of the large elite that the position of Jews in the structure of power has changed most decisively in this century. Half a century ago the Jewish proportion of the various national elites was much smaller – in all likelihood smaller than their overall proportion in the general population, since the bulk of Jews in most Western countries were situated in the workn; class or very close to it. This movement of Jews into the large elite on a wide scale has coincided with two other closely related phenomena. One is the rise of America to pre-eminence in the Western world and the other is the dramatic change in the *nature* of elites, the elite structure and the structure of power in the West since 1945. The atavistic, nationally idiosyncratic, differentiated relationships of forces which we examined for the period 1815–1945 in four Western countries has been replaced by a more broadly-based, rational-capitalistic power structure near-uniform throughout the Western world, where the large elite is *intrinsically* more important to the power structure than hitherto, because its membership has become more open.

The Jews have also moved into the small elite of most Western countries. Paradoxically, this movement is less novel than the increase in the proportion of Jews in the large elite, for throughout modern history, as we have seen, there has always been a Jewish component in the small economic, intellectual and even political elites in most Western countries. Since the Second World War, and especially since 1960, two changes have come over the participation of Jews in the small elite. First, there has been an increase in the *overall* Jewish level of participation in the small elite; second, there has occurred a considerable *broadening* of the areas of Jewish participation in the small elite beyond the stereotyped areas of Jewish elite membership – for instance, as millionaire merchant bankers or retailers, or as leading scientists – although Jewish participation in these areas is still strong.

Statistical evidence about Jewish participation in the small elites of most Western nations is fairly good, although in general (Britain is an exception) such studies suffer from a lack of historical evidence with which to compare them. For the all-important American small elite, however, there apparently exists only the American leadership study carried out by Allen Barton of Columbia University and Charles Kadushin of the City University of New York. Identifying the 545 national leaders in government, business, labour unions, the media and other important spheres of American life in the mid-1970s, they discovered that 57 out of the 500 national leaders whose original religion was known were Jewish by origin – 11.4 per cent. The highest Jewish proportion found in any elite was among media leaders, where Jews accounted for 25.8 per cent of the known total.[45] Since a study of only 545 leaders in the United States certainly excludes many other very important elite figures in other areas, it is unfortunate that no other wide-ranging American study of the elite seems to have investigated this question.[46]

In Britain, as in the United States, there exist fairly accurate figures about the Jewish representation in the small elite. Moreover, there is data here of an historical as well as a contemporary nature. Harold Perkin of the University of Lancaster investigated the social origins of twenty-six British elite groups for the period between 1880 and 1970. These include groups not typically found in studies of this kind, such as millionaires (identified from probate records), major landowners, heads of the leading professional societies and newly-created peers. A total of 951 men and women belonged to one or another of these elite groups between 1960 and 1970.[47] Of this total, 58 (6.1 per cent) were Jews. This figure probably understates the true position of Jews in the British small elite, for in general the more peripheral elites like the large landowners and the heads of professional societies demonstrate the least Jewish representation. The Jewish percentage among the British small elite is highest among millionaires, cabinet ministers and newly-created peers, many of whom (like Lord Goodman) are skilful operators behind the scenes. Then, too, most of the elite figures of the 1960s would have been born in the period 1900–20, when opportunities for Jews, particularly those of an eastern European background, were much more limited than subsequently. It is therefore likely that a similar survey of the British small elite in the 1970s and 1980s would reveal a higher rate of Jewish participation; conversely, during the Edwardian period – supposedly the 'golden age' of British Jewry – the Jewish percentage of the small elite was much lower, probably around 1–2 per cent of the total small elite, and highly concentrated in the economic sphere. Moreover, the Jewish elite figures of this period would have emerged exclusively from the Sephardic-German Ashkenazi Cousinhood; few, if any, would have sprung from an eastern European background, as have the majority of today's elite Jews.

Among other Western societies there is a particularly good study on the Australian small elite, carried out in 1974–5 by John Higley and his colleagues at the Australian National University.[48] Higley's study revealed that five per cent of the 370 leading Australian elite figures surveyed were Jews: 2–5 per cent were leaders in politics, the media and voluntary associations, 12 per cent were senior civil servants and 15 per cent leading academics. Six per cent of the business sector (which included trade union leaders) was Jewish.[49] Unfortunately, very little recent data appear to be available on other Western societies like France, Canada or South Africa, where there are substantial numbers of Jews.[50]

In the United States, academic studies of the small elite suggest that the Jewish participation rate is around 10–15 per cent of the total, with 5–10 per cent in Britain and five per cent in Australia being a likely order of magnitude in these countries. Moreover, it seems equally likely that the percentage of Jews has risen sharply since 1945, as Jews of eastern European background have risen and as anti-semitism has generally decreased.

The Jewish percentage of the small elite is not strictly proportional to the overall Jewish percentage in the populations of the three countries we surveyed. In the United States, where Jews are proportionately six times as numerous as in Australia (and nearly ninety times as numerous in absolute terms), Jews are not six times as numerous in the American small elite but only two to three times. A number of explanations for this may be offered. First, the level of anti-semitic discrimination may be lower in societies where there are proportionately fewer Jews.[51] Alternatively, societies like the United States, which have attracted proportionately more Jews, may be animated by a more dynamic ethos throughout.

If Jews are over-represented in both the large and small elites of the United States and other Western nations, it is equally true both that they are still a very small minority and that there are definite limits to their permeation into the national elite structure. However, in some fields, the degree of Jewish achievement at the very highest levels is phenomenal. For instance, 27 per cent of all American-educated Nobel Prize winners in science were Jews,[52] a figure which takes no account of numerous Jewish refugees from Hitler and other sources of persecution. About 19 per cent of all 286 Nobel prize-winners in science between 1901 and 1972 were Jews, compared with their 1–2 per cent (or less) of the total population of Europe and North America.[53] During much of the period, too, this degree of over-representation was achieved despite the discrimination which worked against Jewish enrolment in tertiary institutions and, later, prevented them from teaching. The American Jewish Nobel Laureate ratio is also significant, for it is considerably in excess of the proportion of Jews employed as college and university teachers in the United States: 9.3 per cent of all academics who came from one of the three principal religious backgrounds (Protestant, Catholic, Jewish) in 1968 were Jews.[54] Again, the percentage of Jews employed as faculty members at 'elite' American colleges and universities was higher still – 20.9 per cent of those from any of the three main religions.[55] In Britain, where Jews account for about one per cent of the total population, in 1965 they comprised

3.5 per cent of all British university lecturers, but in 1971 made up seven per cent of the membership of the Royal Society.[56]

Such a ratio of over-representation is also found in other fields of intellectual achievement. It has been frequently said that three of the four most influential intellectual figures of the past century and a quarter were Jews – Marx, Freud and Einstein (the fourth was Darwin[57]). Among what might be termed the contemporary American public intelligentsia – that sector of intellectuals who publish widely, in the most respected journals of opinion, on public issues of the day – the Jewish over-representation is so remarkable that it was stated to the author of one academic study that 'everyone is Jewish'.[58] About 45 per cent of the American intellectual elite (totalling 172 individuals) identified by the author of this study was Jewish, although this rises to 56 per cent of all elite academics in the social sciences and 61 per cent in the humanities. Of the 20 most prestigious American intellectuals in 1970 – as ranked by other intellectuals – at least 15 were Jews.[59] The most widely-read American journals like *Commentary*, *The Public Interest*, *The New York Review of Books*, *New Republic* and *Partisan Review* are either explicitly Jewish or contain a disproportionately Jewish input. Such examples again conform with Lipset and Ladd's detailed study of over 50,000 American faculty members in 1969. While only 25.2 per cent of Jewish faculty members (compared with 50.6 per cent of the Catholics and 43.8 per cent of the Protestants) had published *no* articles in academic or professional journals, 20.8 per cent of the Jews, compared with 6.2 per cent of the Catholics and 9.1 per cent of the Protestants, had published more than 20 such scholarly articles, despite the fact that the Jews, on the whole, were considerably younger than their gentile colleagues.[60] It might be worth making the point that Jewish academics earned substantially more than their colleagues, with 16 per cent of Jewish academics earning $20,000 or more in 1969 compared with 6.9 per cent of Protestants and 4.3 per cent of Catholics.[61]

Power and the Problem of the Jews

The contemporary structure of power in the Western world is, it would seem, tailor-made to enhance the influence of Western Jewry. The enhancement has been to a large extent the consequence of a number of historical accidents: the dominance of the United States and American modes of thought and the disappearance of competing cultural power centres elsewhere, coincident with an upwardly mobile Jewry whose principal diaspora locus is the United States. Most of all, however, that the influence of Jews has been enhanced by their over-representation in the large and small elites of the Western world, thereby producing the crucial gap between numbers and their performance.

Elites in one form or another must obviously exist in any society; it is their nature and composition which must change. The crucial 'gap' between numbers and power – productive of the enhancement of Jewish influence on the issues which Jews regard as vital – probably exists exclusively under modern capitalism, because captialism is inegalitarian but pluralistic. It is the structured *inequality* (and pluralism) of the Western world, particularly given the historical form assumed by its elite structures since 1945, which for the Jews is its most redeeming feature, for it presents them with the opportunity to magnify the importance of their small numbers. If one wished to see an accurate foretaste of what 'equality' in the abstract would mean for the Jews one need but turn to the voting decisions of the United Nations General Assembly and other United Nations bodies during the past ten years. During this period the Communist and Third World nations have formed a voting majority. In consequence, Israel has become virtually an international outlaw. Were it not for the support provided by the United States and other Western nations, Israel would certainly perish overnight. So long as Jews are able to take advantage of the system of inequality provided by the structure of power prevalent in the Western world, Israel will continue to exist despite the power of the forces ranged against her. Let the Jewish portion of the diaspora elite structure markedly decline, and this is less likely.

The converse of this is true as well. Any levelling doctrine *per se* is likely to be harmful to the Jews of the Western world; in particular, this is true of socialism. In so far as socialism in practice brings about the equality of wealth and income, and the nationalisation of the means of production it is inimical to the interests of Western Jewry, and more so than for any other people. It would reduce or eliminate the gap between the Jews' level of achievement and their small numbers. It would eliminate the possibility of Jews (or any other group) establishing alternate or

competing modes of power apart from those directly sanctioned
by the government, and would thus leave the suppression of anti-
semitism fully at the mercy of the non-Jewish majority. It would,
furthermore, mean the inevitable triumph of anti-Zionism in
foreign policy. Socialism can surely be acceptable to Western Jewry
in its present circumstances only in so far as it is social democracy
– reformist, moderate and pluralistic – whose modes of thought
are modified by capitalism and by the goals and ideals common
to the post-war Western world.

Elites and Jewish Self-perception

Four major arguments can be advanced against the thesis presented
here, each originating in a different perspective – two from within
the mainstream Jewish community and two from without. There
is, first, the Marxist or quasi-Marxist point of view. Focusing on
the importance of the 'military-industrial complex' of 'monopoly
capital' and the multinational corporations, which are virtually
free of Jewish influence, the Marxist would view the Jews, despite
their apparent wealth and high status, as essentially outside of
the true locus of decision-making, whose interests would readily
be sacrificed by monopoly capital should the occasion arise.[62] In
the words of Peter Camejo, US presidential candidate of the small
Socialist Labour Party: 'That [i.e., American support for Israel]
doesn't mean there isn't anti-semitism. Right now the army of
the United States is run by an anti-semite. We've got Nixon –
did you hear the [Watergate] tapes? Nixon was all for Israel.
General Ky, who said we need seven Hitlers in South Vietnam,
liked Israel too.'[63] Capitalism, according to the Marxist viewpoint,
is inherently racist; anti-semitism is a product of capitalism, and
will disappear, together with all other forms of ethnic oppression,
only under socialism, the one social system under which Jews
and other minorities would be truly secure.[64]

The Marxist left, in other words, denies that Jews are truly
an elite in the contemporary Western world; their position is at
best highly precarious and probably far worse. It is difficult to
refute this perspective because the concepts of power employed
in this book are evidently so different from those of Marxism.
The best refutation is the historical evidence of the rise of Western
Jewry in the post-war period. There is surely a set of phenomena

to be explained – the seeming rise to affluence and power of Western Jewry along with an historically unprecedented diminution in anti-semitism and the establishment of Israel – which this viewpoint simply fails to explain. To claim that the 'true' monopoly capital-based ruling class is 'really' anti-semitic (even though it seems to be the opposite) is designed to salvage an ideology against countervailing empirical evidence. Such claims are, moreover, curiously linked with contentions from the same sources that Zionism is the ideology of the Jewish bourgeoisie and that Israel was established as a military outpost of 'imperialism'.[65] As for the 'security' which Jews would enjoy under socialism, the record of the Soviet Union speaks for itself.

The second expected criticism of our viewpoint originates from the radical but non-Marxist anti-Zionist left, and is frequently met with among the small but rather vocal minority of Jewish anti-Zionists. The argument of this school is that Jewish powerlessness was a virtue rather than a tragedy and that, in particular, the method of establishing and maintaining Israel has been a moral disaster for Jewry, turning Jews into latter-day imitators of their czarist and even Nazi oppressors.[66] Morally contaminated, Zionist-centred Judaism has also raised its political visibility, producing a (just and natural) Arab backlash which has made Israel and its Jewish supporters in the diaspora more determined and which threatens Israel's very existence. In the words of Moshe Menuhin, one of the most outspoken advocates of this viewpoint,

> '[T]he new specimen of fighting Jew' was . . . a specimen completely unknown to the world for over eighteen hundred years . . . During the long Talmudic era presided over by the nonprofessional rabbis (great scholars who, on principle, supported themselves as woodchoppers, blacksmiths, tailors, tanners, watercarriers) and later in the ghettoes of Europe, the Jews constantly hoped and prayed for one thing: the realization of the prophetic ideals in the entire world. That was the essence of evolved Judaism-Jewishness. [*sic*] . . . [U]ntil the nineteenth century there was no 'Jewish' political nationalism (Zionism) because there were no such rabid ideals as general political nationalism . . . Alas, the 'Jewish' political nationalists (the Zionists) have swallowed the whole hog of the prevailing secular nationalism of their nineteenth century

persecutors, and, like them, have become inspired and obsessed by the 'sacred egoism' of a grasping, expanding, conquering political nationalism.[67]

Menuhin also links his opposition to Zionism with the tradition of Prophetic Judaism: 'Jews', in his words, 'were destined to be a kingdom not of this earth'.[68]

The radical Jewish anti-Zionist position thus accepts that Jews have achieved greater power than ever in the past, but denies that this has been at all beneficial to Jewry; in particular, it sees Israel as a perversion of Judaistic ideals. The overwhelming majority of the world's Jews would, needless to say, reject this moral and political viewpoint. They would rightly see any reduction in Jewish power as self-castration and effort which would place the destiny of the Jews in the hands of others. While one may reasonably criticise Israel's policies on a variety of grounds, to condemn its existence root and branch, without analysing the reasons for its foundation, is obviously unbalanced and unfair.[69] This viewpoint does have one considerable merit: its proponents typically pay far more attention to diaspora Jewry than do many Zionists. In the words of Everett Gendler, an American anti-Zionist rabbi,

There has been in recent years a tendency to undervalue Diaspora Jewish experiences and to over-value Israeli Jewish experiences and this has worked out badly both for Israeli and for Diaspora Jews. Israeli Jews often complain that Diaspora Jews expect too much of Israel and its Jews, and in many cases that is true. But that should come as no surprise given the present mood.[70]

To that extent, one might expect a more balanced overall picture of world Jewry and its current situation which might parallel that presented here. But this analysis of diaspora Jewry is partisan, and the crucial point, that the rise to status and influence of Western Jewry has occurred independently of Israel's existence (and would have occurred had it never existed), is not clearly seen.

Within the mainstream Jewish community in the Western world it is likely that objections to the thesis presented here will take two forms. The first of these is that Zionist standpoint, which views the creation of Israel as the central historical event of contemporary Jewry and which defines Jewish power and influence almost exclusively by reference to Israel rather than to the structure of power in the Western world. As Professor Abba Lessing, a notable American Jewish philosopher, has said,

> The State of Israel signifies the end of Jewish powerlessness. Jews are today once more defined as at least *potential* citizens of a sovereign Jewish State which itself is defined by national legitimacy, communal will, and supported by historical and natural rights. In spite of its difficulties, its very existence proclaims Jewish power. Once more, Jews have an actual government and a land of their own in which they can recover their original peoplehood. It is my firm conviction that only as actual citizens of an actual political State can Jews shake off the burden of degradation and injustice.[71]

Although the paramount importance of Israel for contemporary Jewry is unquestionable, and although Israel's very existence, indeed, 'proclaims Jewish power', there is in this interpretation a hint of the denigration of the circumstances of diaspora Jewry. But surely without an influential and united diaspora community, Israel's existence would have been infinitely less likely. In the words of the distinguished Israeli scholar Yehuda Bauer in his discussion of the Jewish emergence from powerlessness in the modern world:

> How was the emergence from powerlessness achieved? . . . The decisive influence was American pressure which prevented Britain from implementing her anti-Zionist policy . . . So the establishment of the State of Israel and the consequent achievement of a political power base for the Jewish people was made possible, to a large degree, by the Jews in the Diaspora . . . This corrects the impression that the main factor leading to statehood was the activity of the Jewish underground movements in Palestine . . .[72]

Objectively speaking, the welfare of diaspora Jews is at least as important to Jewish survival and to Jewish power as the welfare of Israel. Because of the failure of Israel's Jews to attain the elite socio-economic status common to much of Western Jewry the paths taken by Israeli and diaspora Jewry have to a certain extent diverged, while Israel is crucially dependent on the political and socio-economic circumstances of Western Jewry.

Finally, there is the reaction of the ordinary upper middle-class, informed, involved Western Jew. Many such will look at the chronic and seemingly insurmountable problems facing the Jews today, from the maintenance of Israel through 'reverse discrimination' (in the United States) to rampant inflation and the threat of oil blackmail, to the low birth rate and high incidence of intermarriage and indifference within the Jewish community, and find the portrayal of Western Jewry as an elite rather exaggerated. But the status and socio-economic position of the Jews in the Western world has objectively changed in the past forty years in a way which is quite new in modern history. What must be explained is how and why the circumstances of the Jews have altered for the better in the past thirty-five (or fewer) years. It is to understand these changes that the socio-economic circumstances of the Jews have been discussed. Jews may be an elite today, but they are seldom supremely self-confident in their status: one of the major hallmarks of the contemporary mood of Western Jewry is the self-perception by Jews of the precariousness of their status and the dangers which beset them. To a large extent, these doubts are well founded in political and social reality. They also reflect the novelty of the situation as well as the cultural and characteristic attitudes of Jews, unused as they are to genuine status achievement and permanent power and security. There is (especially in the United States) a gap between the influence and status of Jews and the manner in which they behave which is *so* striking that it must be discussed at length. Today's Western Jews may thus best be characterised as objectively rather than subjectively an elite.

Notes

1. Much of this discussion is derived from the analysis in Eva Etzioni-Halevy's (Australian National University) book, *Social Change. The Advent and Maturation of Modern Society*, (London, 1980) and especially Ch. Seven, 'The Advent and Maturation of the Modern Polity: The Power of Government and Ruling Elites'. I am most grateful to Dr Etzioni-Halevy for allowing me to see her work.

2. This is not to dispense with the very valuable, though misunderstood, notion of 'hegemony', which has a wide relevance to understanding modern society. However, the notion of hegemony in contemporary Western society is often confused with two other notions, the 'logic of the system' (i.e., capitalism) and post-

Renaissance Western modes of thought (in particular the distinction between the public/political and the private (personal) which are essentially unrelated to the idea of a hegemonic 'ruling class'). In terms of the current discussion, the notion of 'hegemony' is most relevant to the exploration of the role of intellectuals and the power of the media discussed below.

3. It is significant that the size of the 'small' elite does not vary with the population, wealth or complexity of a particular society. The number of individuals included in the most plausibly-designed study of elites in nations of widely differing size (as, say, the United States and Australia) would be of the same order of magnitude; elite position-holders in the 'small' elite are thus more densely distributed *per capita* in less populous or politically significant nations, although the 'power' potentially commanded by key position-holders in nations of the first or second rank is, of course, greater than in other societies seen from a worldwide perspective.

4. The consumer and ecology movements of the past ten to fifteen years, as well as the various 'liberation' movements (women's, homosexuals'), seem to represent genuine and at least partially successful lobbies initiated from below whose programmes are either costly to the small elite and its interests or which the small elite would rather have left off the 'agenda' indefinitely. For a discussion of this see, e.g. J. Hewitt, 'Elites and the Distribution of Power in British Society', in P. Stanworth and A. Giddens (eds.), *Elites and Power in British Society* (Cambridge, 1974). It is also true that most (but not all, e.g. the movement for civil rights in the United States from the 1940s onwards) such successful lobbies comprise men and women of the 'large' elite (on which, see below).

5. Although the electorate divides along class, occupational, ethnic and sectional lines in coherent and predictable patterns, while organised interest groups can alter the result of many elections.

6. The major exceptions are, of course, the trade unions. But trade union *leaders* most obviously belong to the 'large' elite if not indeed to the 'small' elite.

7. See Daniel Bell, *The Coming of Post-Industrial Society* (New York, 1973).

8. This, or a rather similar point, is the central argument in Ralf Dahrendorf's *Class and Class Conflict in Industrial Society* (London, 1959), although its implications for elite theory have perhaps not been classified.

9. There are two other important manifestations of America's role which ought to be stressed. One is the central importance of the English language as the virtual *lingua franca* of the second half of the twentieth century throughout the world. The second is the importance in today's world of another language (or set of languages) – computer language – which originated in the United States and which is a typical artefact of the American way of thinking.

10. Marshall Loeb, 'Where Big Money is Made', *Time*, 30 Apr. 1979.

11. However, American (and other) corporations commonly devote a small percentage of their resources to assisting community-aid projects, hospitals, scholarships, support for educational and charitable groups, etc. Such assistance is almost invariably non-controversial and non-political.

12. Though no doubt the behavioural code, official and unofficial, of many professions (and particularly the law) works to limit and restrain the controversial.

13. On multinational capitalism see, e.g., Richard J. Barnet and Ronald E. Miller, *Global Reach. The Power of the Multinational Corporations* (London, 1975); Louis Turner, *Invisible Empires* (New York, 1970); Christopher Tugendhat, *The Multinationals* (London, 1971).

14. See, e.g., Ben Stein, *The View from Sunset Boulevard* (New York, 1979) on how America's image of itself is created by television, as well as the political attitudes of television's leading figures. On other aspects of this subject see Stanley Cohen and Jack Young (eds.), *The Manufacture of News A Reader* (Beverley Hills, California, 1973).

15. France, as we have seen, may be an exception to this trend. In studies of Jewish occupational structure carried out in several American cities in the late 1950s and early 1960s it was found that the percentage of Jewish males engaged in working-class trades varied from 5.2% (Trenton, 1961) to 13.0% (Camden, 1965), compared with 52.2% of all urban US males in 1960. The percentage of Jews employed as clerical and sales workers ranged from 13.4% to 25.4% (compared with 17.2% for all urban US males). Among professionals, the Jewish percentage ranged from 27.4% to 37.8% (compared with 12.9% for US males); among managers and proprietors from 24.5% to 54.0% (compared with 13.3%).

16. On Borochov's theories see Ernest Germain, 'A Biographical Sketch of Abram Leon', in Abram Leon, *The Jewish Question. A Marxist Interpretation* (New York, 1974), especially pp. 16ff.

17. Ibid., p. 16.

18. Ibid.

19. The 'Pale of Settlement' was the portion of western Russia, mainly in Poland, the Ukraine and the Baltic areas, to which Russian Jews were restricted in residence from 1772 to 1915.

20. Uriah Z. Engelman, *The Rise of the Jew in the Western World* (New York, 1944), pp. 120–1. The statistics mentioned here are derived from *Schriften für Wirtschaft und Statistik* (Berlin, 1928) I, p. 30.

21. Ibid., pp. 122–3.

22. Ibid., p.27.

23. Ibid.

24. Ibid.

25. Ibid., p. 128.

26. Ibid., p. 103.

27. Ibid., pp. 103, 109. See 'United States' in *Encyclopedia Judaica*.

28. S. Joseph Fauman, 'Occupational Selection Among Detroit Jews', originally *Jewish Social Studies*, 14 (1952) and reprinted in Marshall Sklare (ed.), *The Jews. Social Patterns of an American Group* (Westport, Conn., 1958), pp. 119–37. 'Sons' were 'all sons who were living at home, had completed their education [and] were working or seeking work . . .' (ibid., p. 122). This definition would eliminate 'sons' away at college and hence probably understates the status-attainments of this generation.

29. Ibid., p. 123.

30. Ibid. The Jewish and non-Jewish percentages of remaining occupational classes measured here were: clerical-Jewish 45.6%, non-Jewish, 21.4%; skilled-Jewish 8.6%, non-Jewish 15.0%.

31. Nathan Glazer, 'The American Jew and the Attainment of Middle-class Rank: Some Trends and Explanations', in Sklare (ed.), *The Jews*, p. 138. (Originally published in *American Jewish Year Book*, 56 (1955)).

32. See, e.g., Miriam K. Slater, 'My Son the Doctor: Aspects of Mobility Among American Jews', *American Sociological Review*, (1969); Sidney Goldstein, 'Socio-economic Differentials Among Religious Groups in the United States', *American Journal of Sociology*, (1969); G.I. Gockel, 'Income and Religious Affiliation: A Regression Analysis', *American Journal of Sociology*, (1969); D.L. Featherman, 'The Socio-Economic Achievement of White Religio-Ethnic Subgroups: Social and Psychological Explanations', *American Sociological Review*, (1971); Sidney Goldstein and Calvin Goldscheider, *Jewish Americans* (Englewood Cliffs, New Jersey, 1968); Norval D. Glenn and Ruth Hyland, 'Religious Reference and Worldly Success: Some Evidence from National Surveys', *American Sociological Review*, (1967); Sidney Goldstein, 'American Jewry, 1970: A Demographic Profile', *American Jewish Year Book*, 1971.

The best recent survey of the American Jewish occupational and income structure is probably Fred Massarik and Alvin Chenkin, 'United States National Jewish Population Study: A First Report', *American Jewish Year Book, 1973* (New York, 1973), pp. 264–89, esp. pp. 283–9. This essay contains detailed breakdowns of Jewish household and individual income by age, size of family, etc., for 1971, and revealed that among householders in the 30–59 age category, only 5% reported incomes of less than $6,000, while 60% in this age-group reported incomes of $16,000 or more (ibid., pp. 286–7). Seventy per cent of *all* Jewish males over 25 were employed in the professional, technical, managerial and administrative categories, while only 11.0% were to be found as craftsmen, operatives, service workers or labourers (ibid., p. 284).

33. In 1956, 42% of American Jewish families received incomes of $7,500 or more, compared with only 19% of the general population. See Bernard Lazerwitz, 'A Comparison of Major United States Religious Groups', *Journal of The American Statistical Association*, Sept. 1961.

34. In 1966 the median income of Jews among a random sample of 1,013 Americans was $14,688. The Jewish median income was thus very considerably higher than that of Protestants polled in the same sample ($10,117), Catholics ($9,999) or of any single Protestant denomination surveyed except for Congregationalists ($17,500), whose total number (only ten individuals) in this sample was probably too small to be statistically significant. (See Edward O. Lauman, 'The Social Structure of Religious and Ethnoreligious Groups in the Metropolitan Community', *American Sociological Review*, 34 (1969), quoted in Daniel W. Rossides, *The American Class System. An Introduction* (Boston, 1976), p. 170.). In this sample, Jews had completed a median total of 15.7 years of schooling, compared with 12.0 years for Protestants and Catholics alike.

35. This was a study of first-year Jewish undergraduates compiled in the autumn of 1969 by David E. Drew for the American Council on Education's Office of Research. Since the parental income figures given here are only *estimates* offered by the sampled freshmen, they are not precise, although it is difficult to see why their accuracy should be religiously biased. 'Freshmen' included both men and women. The distribution of the total sample in each income class was:

	Jews (%)	Other Religions (%)
Less than $4,000	1.7	5.4
$4,000–$5,999	3.5	9.1
$6,000–$7,999	6.1	13.7
$8,000–$9,999	9.9	17.0
$10,000–$14,999	24.5	29.1
$15,000–$19,999	16.5	12.4
$20,000–$24,999	11.7	6.0
$25,000–$29,999	7.4	2.6
$30,000 or more	18.6	4.7

Perhaps the most remarkable feature of this study will not be obvious at first glance. Since 85–90% of *all* American Jews enter college or university, compared with about 50% of other Americans, these figures substantially *overstate* the family incomes of non-Jews, since they take only half of the total gentile population into account – and that, by and large, is the *wealthier* half.

36. *ACE Research Reports*, vol. 15, no. 4 (June 1970). The exact wording of the question was: 'What is your *best estimate* of the total income last year of your parental family (not your own family if you are married)? Consider annual income from all sources before marriage' (ibid., p. 46).

37. This report was careful to note that it was not a scientific sample of American Jewry, and was 'short on young Jews, sparsely representative of non-affiliated Jews,

unevenly representative of the various geographical areas'. Equally, however, it was stressed that 'the variety of the population interviewed . . . and the large number of total answers provide the substance for some very useful observations'.

38. Two-thirds of the sample surveyed gave their political allegiance as Democratic. The sample was polled as to its income, and the results by percentage and income level were:

Under $7,500	12%
$7,500–$9,999	8%
$10,000–$14,999	13%
$15,000–$24,999	24%
$25,000–$34,000	11%
$35,000–$49,000	11%
$50,000 or more	21%

39. Jeanne Kirkpatrick, *The New Presidential Elite* (New York, 1976), p. 87. This surveyed the delegates to the 1972 Democratic and Republican nominating conventions, and revealed that nearly one-third of all Jewish delegates – who comprised 11% of all delegates – had incomes of $50,000 or more, while 71% earned $20,000 or more compared, respectively, with 14% and 40% of all other delegates. The great majority of all Jewish delegates were pro-McGovern at the Democratic convention, thus lending weight to the idea that rich and affluent Jews are further to the *left* than less affluent ones.

40. Ernest Krausz, 'The Edgware Survey. Occupation and Social Class', *Jewish Journal of Sociology*, II (1969), p. 75. See also Krausz's 'The Economic and Social Structure of Anglo-Jewry', in Julius Gould and Shaul Esh (eds.), *Jewish Life in Modern Britain* (London, 1964), pp. 27-40.

41. Walter Lippman, 'Demography of Australian Jewry' (Melbourne, 1974). The figures here are, of course, far in excess of high-status attainment among all Australian males.

42. One particularly striking example will suffice to illustrate the implications of this process. It is, of course, known to everyone that Henry Kissinger was a Jewish refugee from Hitler who emigrated from Germany in the 1930s. What is certainly less well known is that Kissinger was far from having advantages in his rise from obscurity to world leadership, and just how narrow was the boundary which separated success from failure in his case. Although he was a straight-A student in high school, his thick accent and disrupted childhood caused him to be withdrawn in personality. After his high-school graduation in 1941 Kissinger *took a job in a shaving brush factory* and began courses at City College in New York *in the hope of becoming an accountant*. Only after his army career did he win a New York State Scholarship which enabled him to enter Harvard University, where his distinguished academic career began his road to world leadership. (Thomas R. Dye, *Who's Running America? Institutional Leadership in the United States* (Englewood Cliffs, New Jersey, 1976), p. 59.).

43. Drew, *Profile*, p. 11.

44. The Jewish population of the United States (around six million) was about 3% of the American population of 195–200 million in 1967. But it is likely that Jews amounted to a somewhat lower percentage of all Americans of freshman age (17–19) because of the notably lower Jewish birth rate, even during the peak 'baby boom' years following the Second World War.

45. *American Leadership Study Codebook*, table, p. 109. (The author is most grateful to Dr John Higley for allowing him to see these data.)

46. See, e.g., Dye, *Who's Running America?*, in which 5416 elite position-holders are studied. Unfortunately – and most curiously – there is no analysis of

ethnic or religious background, perhaps because the reference sources (*Who's Who*, etc.) which provided most of the biographical information do not generally give such data. As good a guide as any to the literature of this subject in the United States is Norman L. Crockett (ed.), *The Power Elite in America* (Lexington, Mass., 1970).

47. Information provided by Professor Perkin. The author acted as Research Associate on this project, which is currently being updated to include elite position-holders of the period 1970–80.

48. This has been published as John Higley, Desley Deacon and Don Smart, *The Australian Elite* (London, 1979).

49. Data supplied to the author by Dr John Higley and Desley Deacon.

50. For the Canadian elite, there are data for the 1957–61 period in John Porter, *The Vertical Mosaic. An Analysis of Social Class and Power In Canada* (Toronto, 1965).

51. This was suggested to the author by Dr Frank Knopfelmacher.

52. Harriet Zuckerman, *Scientific Elite* (New York, 1977), p. 68. Only 1% of all American Nobel Laureates were Catholics, compared with their 25% of the total population.

53. Ibid.

54. Ibid., p. 27, quoting Seymour Martin Lipset and Everett C. Ladd, Jr, 'Jewish Academics in the United States: Their Achievements, Culture and Politics', *American Jewish Year Book 1971*. Jews constituted 8.7% of *all* American academics, including those from the religious categories of 'any other' and 'none'. (Lipset and Ladd, ibid., p. 92.).

55. Zuckerman, *Scientific Elite*.

56. Lipset and Ladd, 'Jewish Academics in the United States', p. 98; A.H. Halsey and Martin Trow, *A Study of British University Teachers* (unpublished, 1967); and private information from Professor Julius Gould (University of Nottingham).

57. If one were to add a fifth name to the list it might be Keynes, a fellow-member, with Darwin, of the extremely distinguished and closely-linked Cambridge intellectual aristocracy, on which see Noel Annan, 'The Intellectual Aristocracy', in G. Kitson Clark (ed.), *Studies in Social History* (London, 1955).

58. Charles Kadushin, *The American Intellectual Elite* (Boston, 1974), p. 24.

59. Ibid., p. 30.

60. Lipset and Ladd, 'Jewish Academics in the United States', pp. 92, 101.

61. Ibid., p. 102.

62. See Arthur Liebman, *Jews and the Left* (New York, 1979), pp. 588–99. This is an important historical study of the involvement of American Jewry with the left which argues that American Jews will inevitably return to their 'natural home' on the political left.

63. Michael Harrington *et al.*, *The Lesser Evil? The Left Debates the Democratic Party and Social Change* (New York, 1977), p. 39.

64. We shall discuss more of the left's view of the Jewish question in Chapter 3.

65. E.g., Peter Camejo's remarks: 'After the war ended Jewish refugees wanted to come to the United States. The United States refused to let them in . . . Instead, the Democrats and all the anti-Semites in the world said, "Well, the Nazis weren't able to kill all the Jews, but we've got a new plan. Let's force them into the Middle East to be a beachhead for European and American imperialist interests"' (Harrington, *The Lesser Evil?*).

66. On the historical virtues of Jewish powerlessness, see the essay by Michael Walzer in Gary V. Smith (ed.), *Zionism: The Dream and the Reality* (New York, 1974) and Eliezer Berkovits, *Faith After the Holocaust* (New York, 1973). See also the essays on the 'Western Jewish Diaspora' in Uri Davis, Andrew Mack and Niva Yuval-Davis (eds.), *Israel and the Palestinians* (London, 1975), pp. 215–42.

67. Moshe Menuhin, *Jewish Critics of Zionism. A Testamentary Essay With the Stifling and Smearing of a Dissenter* [*sic*] (New York, n.d.(*c* 1973)), pp. 6–8. This pamphlet was published by the Arab Information Centre of The League of Arab States. Menuhin, who grew up in Palestine prior to the First World War, is the father of Yehudi Menuhin, the celebrated violinist, and has been an outspoken critic of Zionism for decades.

68. Ibid., p. 1. Historically this is false, as ancient Israel was an independent state for centuries.

69. See, e.g., the writings of Reinhold Niebuhr on the notion of power.

70. Rabbi Everett Gendler, 'To Be a Jew in the Diaspora', in Davis, Mack and Yuval-Davis, *Israel and the Palestinians*, p. 27.

71. Abba Lessing, 'Jewish Impotence and Power', *Midstream*, Oct. 1976, p. 58. Much of this article is a valuable discussion of Jewish powerlessness with which this author does not disagree.

72. Yehuda Bauer, *The Jewish Emergence from Powerlessness* (Toronto, 1978), p. 76. Bauer also contends – somewhat surprisingly – that 'There is no doubt that the influence of organized Holocaust survivors . . . set the stage for the Zionists' diplomatic triumph'.

3 THE REALIGNMENT OF ANTI-SEMITISM

No matter what the power or influence of Jews in the modern world might be or how great their elite over-representation, they are still a minority, even at the elite level. If the non-Jewish majority of a nation's elite is anti-semitic – as in Nazi Germany and in the Soviet Union today – there is ultimately little that Jews can do about it. Yet since the Second World War there has been a fundamental transformation in the attitudes of non-Jewish elites towards the Jews throughout the Western world, of a nature at least as significant as the increased wealth and status of Western Jewry: the sources of anti-semitism have been realigned.

In recent years anti-semitism of the extreme right has virtually disappeared except among small fringe groups like the National Front in Britain or the American Nazi Party. The old animosity of conservative groups and forces towards Jews has declined to the point where the establishment right is now the most actively philo-semitic and pro-Israeli section of the elite in most Western nations. Jews and Israel are perceived as fellow-members of the elite and of the pro-American pro-capitalist Western bloc threatened by the Third World, terrorism and Communism.

A revolution just as significant has occurred on the political left. Today, the main enemies of the Jews and Israel are almost exclusively on the left, most obviously the Communist states, the radical Third World anti-Zionist nations and their sympathisers in the West. Within the Western democracies the main danger to contemporary Jewish interests comes from left-socialist anti-Zionists, especially if they can wrest control of the social democratic parties from their moderate colleagues. For, with very few exceptions, it is a general rule that the further left along the political spectrum one goes, the greater the degree of anti-Zionism, until, among Trotskyite and assorted Marxist fringe groupings, anti-Zionism takes on the appearance of a pathological obsession.

This chapter will discuss the post-war realignment of anti-semitism under four general areas: the nature of anti-semitism and philo-semitism, both before and after 1945; the shift of the establishment right to a generally philo-semitic and pro-Israeli position; the historical development of the attitude of the political

77

left, both Marxist and social democratic, to the Jews and Zionism; and the disposition of the political left toward Jews and Israel in today's world. (Some of these topics will be explored in more detail in later chapters, and one all-important consequence of these changes – and of those discussed in the last chapter – the shift of most Western Jews to a conservative position, will form the subject-matter of Chapter 4.)

Anti-semitism and Philo-semitism

The phenomenon of anti-semitism is complex and no brief discussion of it can do it justice.[1] It is possible, however, to distinguish six *major* sources of anti-semitism in modern times; there are many others. First, there is religious anti-semitism: Jews as 'Christ-killers' are a pariah people, perpetually damned wherever they go. Second, there is the explicitly racist anti-semitism which arose during the nineteenth century in the wake of Gobineau and the other advocates of Aryan racial superiority. Third, politically close to this (and often indistinguishable from it) is the widespread dislike of Jews as a powerful and mysterious elite – the 'international Jewish conspiracy' – which formed so formidable a component of late nineteenth and twentieth century anti-semitism. Related to this is a fourth stream in modern anti-semitism: dislike of Jews for their invariable urbanism and cultural modernism.[2] These four secular variants of anti-semitism regularly appeared together, especially in continental Europe which had undergone sudden profound social and political change. The anti-semitism of the Nazis, for instance, combined a hatred of Jews as racially inferior, as a powerful elite, as corrupt and depraved purveyors of cultural degeneration and as the epitome of the Bolshevik menace. A short distance away – and despite the anti-semitism which depicted Jews as a mysterious elite – is the fifth form of anti-semitism: dislike of Jews as radicals and revolutionaries. Finally, we may perceive a sixth stream in modern anti-semitism: dislike of Jews as an alien proletariat horde, threatening employment and the ethnic purity of the host population through the mass migration of the poor and dispossessed. The combination of this last variety of anti-semitism, aimed at the Jewish masses, with those variants of anti-semitism aimed at the Jewish elite may have lent to European anti-semitism its peculiar virulence: while other groups have been resented as either elites or as masses; perhaps only the Jews were resented as both simultaneously.

Several points are worth making about these varieties of traditional anti-semitism. First, all (except possibly the first variety) arose out of the anomalous political, economic and social structure of the Jews in modern Europe, and in particular out of the absence in Western Jewry of four features possessed by every other people[3] – a territorial nation-state, a military, an aristocracy and a peasantry. It was the absence of these particular features of Jewish society which determined the shape of all European anti-semitism and directed it into the characteristic channels it assumed. The anti-semitic case revolved around their aberrant and deviant socio-economic and political structure. It was a case with a good deal of factual basis. Jews did not possess a nation-state, a military, a hereditary aristocracy or a peasantry. Second, European anti-semitism was strongly associated with the political right, because the European right drew its support from, and existed to defend, just those four institutions and characteristics which the Jews so notably lacked. This should not, of course, be exaggerated. Not all European conservatives were anti-semites nor were all anti-semites conservatives.[4] Even the early Fascist movements (except, of course, in Germany) included Jewish followers and many scholars have debated whether these movements were anti-semitic in any sense.[5] Conversely, the Marxist left evolved its own brand of anti-semitism. Nevertheless, the history of modern European anti-semitism marks it as a right-wing response to the presence of a politically, economically and socially deviant Jewry in a world of rapid change and transformation. Consequently, prior to 1945 the more right-wing the regime, party or movement the more likely was it to be anti-semitic, and the most odious and pervasive outbreaks of anti-semitism from czarist pogrom to Nazism emanated from the political right.

Finally, anti-semitism has changed in the post-war world for three main reasons: the nature of conservatism itself has altered in the manner outlined in Chapter 2; the Jews have moved *en bloc* into the middle class; the Holocaust and the subsequent creation of Israel have taken place.

Perhaps the most important reason for the decline of anti-semitism has been the Holocaust, which generated a sense of sympathy for the Jews tinged with guilt among gentiles around the world. To many gentiles the mass murder of millions of Jews in occupied Europe, sometimes recorded on film, is perceived not as involving the deaths of some remote people but of their own kith and kin. Because the Holocaust was the first instance in history of the scientifically-organised destruction of a people and a civilisation its significance is seen as universal. Many Jewish (and other) writers now use such terms as 'the central experience of the modern world' to describe the Holocaust.[6] As one Jewish writer recently said, 'the Holocaust is the beginning of a new historical consciousness for the Jewish people. As did the destruction of the Second Temple, it begins a new epoch'.[7] Some Jewish theologians believe there is a serious danger that the Holocaust will replace the Old Testament as the centre of contemporary Jewish life, to the detriment of Judaism as a religion.[8] But to Jew and gentile alike, the Holocaust has acquired a symbolic importance which has made direct expression of anti-semitism much less common than before 1939. It is also responsible for making explicitly racist doctrines unpresentable in any serious forum. Interest in all aspects of the Holocaust has increased in recent years as it recedes into the past.

Israel's creation and maintenance have had a profound effect upon the image of Jews in the eyes of gentiles. If European anti-semitism was essentially derived from the anomalous political and socio-economic structure of Western Jewry, and in particular from the absence of a Jewish nation-state, a military, an aristocracy and a peasantry, it is not difficult to see why this should be so. Israel is a nation-state which has been maintained by military force and success on the battlefield. She possesses a social structure much like that of any other country and its most celebrated domestic achievements have been agricultural. Thus in so far as the popular image of all Jews has been transformed by the creation and success of Israel, this change has been most effective on the political right, among those former right-wing anti-semites most impervious to pleas for humanity, brotherhood or tolerance in the abstract. Would right-wing anti-semitism have disappeared to the same degree if Israel had lived peacefully with its Arab neighbours as a haven of social democracy?

Because the image of the new fighting Israeli Jew is so far removed from that of the clannish, alien, 'cosmopolitan' financiers of the anti-semitic stereotype, it is doubtful whether Israelis are even perceived as 'Jews' in the traditional defamatory sense by extreme right-wing anti-semites. Some evidence for this was found by the social psychologist Michael Billig, who interviewed many rank-and-file members of the neo-Nazi British National Front. The National Front's ideology heavily attacks 'Zionism' and the 'power' of 'cosmopolitan finance capital' in the manner of yesterday's anti-semites, and its *leaders* are certainly strongly hostile to Israel as well as to British Jews. Yet Billig found that among the National Front's rank-and-file members

> The interviewees who believed in the [Jewish] conspiracy theory used the concept of 'Zionism' almost exclusively in its conspiracy tradition sense . . . The word was seldom used in its customary mainstream sense of the movement designed to create, and now maintain, the Jewish State of Israel. When Israel was mentioned, it was done so perfunctorily . . . The abstraction of the concept of 'Zionism' from the reality of Israel into the half-digested conspiracy mythology of the interviewees produced some bizarre statements. K [an interviewee] . . . expressed himself as being anti-Zionist [in the 'Jewish conspiracy' sense] . . . [but] also expressed praise for Israel: 'I've got a lot of sympathy for the Israeli people. I do feel strongly for them. I think they're a great nation, I really do. I think they've come a long way and whatever they've wanted they've stood up and fought for. I really do respect them.' For him then Israel was not a focal point of Zionism [i.e., as used by anti-semites as synonymous with an 'international Jewish conspiracy'].[9]

This positive attitude toward Israel is often projected backward upon Western Jews in a manner which counteracts the old negative stereotypes formerly held by anti-semites.

Moreover, the geopolitical realities of the contemporary political scene have meant that Zionists and gentile conservatives throughout the Western world (particularly in America) have increasingly found themselves in a tacit alliance. To a large extent their interests coincide; each recognises in the other an important and historically most unusual ally. In the wake of the Holocaust, conservatives must take great pains to demonstrate their freedom from anti-semitism; what could be better proof of this than their quasi-alliance with the Jews? Yet this process takes on a life of its own, and it is likely that active co-operation with the Jews and their interests would breed admiration and understanding.

This alliance between Zionists and conservatives throughout much of the Western world has another important consequence. It increases understanding for the Jews in the very areas of elite life where Jews are least well represented, the military and defence contracting areas. In recent years an important part of the American military establishment has been allied with right-wing Jews in an effort to increase America's defence capability to meet the rising Soviet threat. The March 1979 issue of *Midstream*, a leading Jewish monthly published by the Theodore Herzl Foundation of New York, published an 'open letter to the President' from more than fifty retired army generals, bewailing the state of American military preparedness in the face of the Soviet Union's recent military build-up.[10] It seems unlikely that such a letter could have appeared in an intellectual American Jewish journal even twenty yars ago.

For reasons relating to the originality of the Israeli achievement in the context of Western Jewish history, it is wrong to link today's attacks on Israel with the earlier anti-semitism, especially when such attacks emanate from the political right (as they do only infrequently). An example of such an erroneous reading of the situation might be found in these remarks by Edward W. Shapiro:

> Although overt anti-Semitism in the U.S. has dramatically declined since the Second World War, one can still see the images [of the Jew] at work in the public's perception of Israel and the Middle East conflict. The Israelis, some Americans claim, don't know their place (they are pushy). They refuse to come to terms with their neighbors and become a Levantine people (they refuse to assimilate). American Jews are the chief financial and political mainstays of Israel (Israel is a product of a world Jewish conspiracy). The Israelis are militarists and commit atrocities against the Palestinians (they are criminals). The American taxpayers are paying for Israeli obduracy (Israelis are Shylocks). The Israelis should internationalize the holy city of Jerusalem (Jews are enemies of Christianity). Israel should repeal the Law of Return (Israel considers Diaspora Jews as eternal aliens). Israel is an outpost of Western technology and economic interests . . . (Israelis are capitalists). Israelis have introduced modern social values in a traditional part of the globe (Israelis are radicals).[11]

Although some characterisations of the kind Shapiro describes are made, it would be wrong to link them to old-style anti-semitism.

Who, for example, has ever claimed that Israelis are 'pushy' in the sense implied by the stock description of Jews in stereotyped anti-semitism? Israelis are rather criticised for their military prowess and, by their enemies, for their deadly efficiency at meeting terrorist threats to their country's existence. Such attacks emanate from the 'revolutionary' left and cannot be likened to yesterday's image of the Jew without basically distorting the import of these attacks.

Another factor which has affected the old-style anti-semitism has been the virtual disappearance of a Jewish proletariat. Few gentiles in the Western world can fear the mass migration of hundreds of thousands of alien Yiddish-speaking Jews, a stock-in-trade image of European anti-semitism only fifty years ago. With the passing of this fear has come a diminution of the old image of Jews as perpetual radicals, although many Jews, especially in America, are radicals. The leadership of the Western world's radical fringe has largely passed to Third World-oriented Marxists who are almost invariably bitterly hostile to Israel, Zionism and even to Jews as such, and who advocate the overthrow of the capitalist system from which Jews benefit so strikingly.

It will be a long time before Jews accept that the political right is no longer hostile to them and their interests. In the United States, where there is no mainstream anti-Zionist socialist left and where Jewish commitment to left-liberalism remains strongest, many Jews are unable to believe that on most counts American conservatism now serves the interests of American Jews better than left-liberalism. As Henry Siegman, Executive Director of the American Jewish Congress, one of the most important of mainstream American Jewish organisations recently wrote,

> That our Jewish neoconservatives experience even minor disappointments with liberals as betrayal seems to me tacit acknowledgment of the higher expectations they continue to have of liberalism. And for good reason, for 'in their hearts they know' that the principal antagonists of Israel and the Jews are still on the Right – the oil cartels, old-line Wasp conservatives, and neo-Nazi groups.[12]

Siegman represents a lingering view among today's Jews, especially in the United States.

Upper-class social anti-semitism continues, though in an ever-diminishing way. It is clear that the large oil companies and other international businesses are responsive – though perhaps not very responsive – to Arab pressures. But in the political sphere the extreme anti-semitic right like the National Front in Britain[13] and the neo-Nazi groups in the United States mentioned by Harry Siegman have no real influence whatever. This cannot be said of the extreme anti-Zionist left. Although it is true that political extremes do meet it is contended here that they *do not* in the case of Western Jewry today. Specifically, although left-socialist anti-Zionists can obtain important positions of power and influence within the mainstream left parties of the Western world, the anti-semitic extreme right cannot obtain power within the mainstream right-wing parties except in the most unusual circumstances. This principle is probably true of right and left in a far broader sense: while every important Western socialist party contains within it important factions which desire and work for a fundamental change in the nature of society, and which are occasionally opposed to political democracy in the sense in which this term is commonly used in the Western world, mainstream conservative parties *do not* contain an equivalent neo-Fascist element on their extreme right. Moreover, in Italy and France, Communist parties, at least theoretically committed to bringing about the 'dictatorship of the proletariat', obtain up to one-third of the seats in parliament, while the representation of the extreme right in all Western European countries is very small.

Economically and socially, the sources of right-wing anti-semitism are entirely different from the socio-economic bases of the establishment right, typically deriving from a working or lower-middle class milieu. But this is true conceptually at a deeper level, for, in so far as the right exists to protect capitalism, it automatically serves the interests of Jews in the Western world today as a prosperous elite, and ceases to do so only when it enacts a programme of right-wing collectivism like the 'national socialism' of Nazi Germany. The establishment right has become hostile to any such right-wing collectivist schemes in the past generation. Fascism and quasi-Fascist programmes are much more associated with the period of scarcity prior to 1939 than with the time of relative prosperity since, and show remarkably few signs of re-emerging, despite the economic troubles of the 1970s and 1980s. On the contrary, the response of the establishment right to the breakdown of the social-democratic consensus has been the rediscovery of *laissez-faire* liberalism (in the form of Friedmanite monetarism) rather than any reassertion of either a quasi-collectivist or corporatist solution reminiscent of the response of the extreme right during the inter-war period.

There is another sense, too, in which the left and right are not equivalent. While the establishment right has been growing steadily more philo-semitic during the past generation, the extreme left has been growing more anti-Zionist, and this appears closely related to age and generation. Some statistical evidence of this is available from a recent important survey of American attitudes towards Jews and Israel carried out by William Schneider for the American Jewish Congress. It found that

> There is a little evidence of anti-Semitic backlash from the political right. However, there is evidence of anti-Semitic backlash from an unanticipated direction, namely, the political left . . . Evidence from a 1974 survey indicates that political liberals were less pro-Israel than political conservatives, but only among those under forty. Among older respondents, there was no consistent difference between liberals and conservatives in their support for Israel. Thus, disaffection with Israel seems to be more characteristic of younger liberals than of older liberals . . . The reverse is true for anti-Semitism: older conservatives in 1974 were more anti-Semitic than older liberals, but there was no difference in anti-Semitism between younger conservatives and younger liberals.[14]

Schneider notes that his statistical findings

> suggest a generational interpretation – that anti-Semitism is an 'old' ideological difference between right and left which has tended to fade away among younger voters. But Israel and antimilitarism are 'new' ideological issues that split right and left only among the younger generation. All this suggests that disaffection with Israel is more characteristic of younger liberals . . . than of older liberals . . . [who] grew up convinced that support of Israel was a legitimately liberal policy, given the experience of the Holocaust and the predominance of the socialist movement in Israeli politics. Younger liberals tend to doubt the legitimacy of Israel's liberal credentials.[15]

In other Western societies where there is a mainstream socialist left this pattern exists in a much stronger form. Throughout the Western world many young, committed left-socialists are anti-Zionists, and anti-Zionism forms a major component of today's typical left-socialist programme. While the younger socialists form the backbone of anti-Zionism throughout the Western world, the equally younger mainstream conservatives are at present most friendly to Jewish interests.[16]

The ultra-right still exists and, for a variety of economic and social reasons, has increased in significance during the past ten years. Perhaps the most electorally significant party of the ultra-right is the British National Front, but there are clear limits to their growth potential, and they have never exceeded 1 per cent of the national vote at a general election. Ideologically the National Front and similar movements are a continuation of the pre-war ultra-right with a correspondingly pre-war view of Jewish 'power'. According to one scholar who has studied this movement in detail,

> It is alleged that 'the twin evils of International Finance and International Communism' are 'perhaps better described as International Zionism' . . . – the creation of a world state is 'the Big Idea' of political Zionism. The connection of this use of the word 'Zionism with *The Protocols*[17] tradition, rather than with the present reality of Israel, is shown by the contention that the name 'Israel' was 'probably used to help confuse naive Christians about the reality of Political Zionism'.[18]

Similarly, and in order to avoid a direct charge of anti-semitism, the National Front

> frequently uses attributes which anti-Semites have traditionally applied to Jews to apply to unnamed conspirators . . . [who] are frequently described as 'cosmopolitan', 'alien', 'rootless', 'shifty', 'sinister', 'money-lenders', 'usurers', etc.[19]

These terms are, of course, all stereotyped characterisations of Jews by right-wing anti-semites. More significantly, they are also the same terms frequently used for precisely the same purpose by left-wing anti-Zionists, especially the vituperative anti-'Zionist' tracts emanating from the Soviet Union. Indeed, in most respects the attitude of the National Front toward 'Zionism' is rhetorically almost identical to the virulence of the anti-Zionist ultra-left.

In the recent past the ultra-right has adopted another, more novel approach in its attitude to the Jews. This is the growing tendency to deny that the Holocaust occurred. Such a suggestion, contrary to all historical evidence, has been made several times before during the past twenty-five years, most notably by a Frenchman, Paul Rassinier, who argues by means of some exceedingly dubious demographic statistics that the number of Jewish victims of the Nazi Holocaust has been greatly exaggerated.[20] In Britain in 1974 a booklet was written by Richard Harwood (the pseudonym of Richard Verrall, an official of the National Front) entitled *Did Six Million Really Die?* All these works were, however, but a prelude to A.R. Butz's *The Hoax of the Twentieth Century*, which appeared in 1976. This book takes the work of Rassinier and Harwood to its logical conclusion. The thesis of this book is that the Holocaust did not occur. It was a gigantic hoax created by 'Zionists' and 'Marxists', operating through the Allied wartime and post-war governments. The Nazis had no programme of extermination; Auschwitz and the other extermination centres were chemical factories; the corpses seen in Holocaust photographs are typhoid victims. But why has no leading Nazi ever denied that the Holocaust occurred? And where are the six million Jews of occupied Europe who vanished off the face of the earth? According to Butz, the Nazis admitted to the 'Holocaust legend' at the Nuremberg and later war crimes trials as a form of 'plea-bargaining' and the trials themselves were conducted amidst torture, the mass forgery of documents and general hysteria.[21] The people are living as illegal immigrants in the United States, the Soviet Union, Israel and elsewhere. The Jewish population of the United States is not 5.5–6 million as demographers believe, but probably nine million, of whom 'at least 4,000,000 [live] in the New York City area alone'.[22] Most of the 'record Jewish movement' to the United States came during the years 1937–49 when the United States had a 'very open immigration policy'.[23] Just why did the Jews concoct this incredible legend? Butz provides two reasons: the first

> naturally relates to Palestine. The 'justification' that Zionists invariably give for driving the Arabs out of Palestine always involves the six million legend to a great extent . . . When, in November 1975, an overwhelming majority at the United Nations . . . endorsed a resolution declaring Zionism to be a

form of racism (a truth as inescapable as $2 + 2 = 4$), the U.S. representative . . . was reduced in astonishing short order to hysterical yapping about the six million.[24]

The second reason is a financial one. The Holocaust legend was devised in large part so that Jews could obtain large amounts of money from the West German government by fraud, as 'compensation' for murders which did not occur:

As of 1975, the Bonn Government had paid Jews about $2 billion worth of restitution . . . Since this [book] has shown that . . . [the Holocaust is] a hoax, and, specifically, a Zionist hoax, it then develops (*sic*) that Israel owes Germany a lot of money, since the proposed justification for the reparations has been invalidated.[25]

The basis for the Holocaust legend was, however, laid by Jews long before, specifically by the ancient rabbis who compiled the Talmud. Their claims of the mass murders of Jews by the Romans

seems remarkably similar to the spirit of our century's hoax [i.e., the Holocaust]. In this connection it may be noted that it is not really anomalous that a Talmudic scholar like Rabbi Wiessmandel plays a significant part in the hoax. Also Rabbi [Stephen] Wise . . . may also have some claim to being a Talmudic scholar. One suspects that such scholars might have been exactly the type required to give birth to the hoax.[26]

Despite the crudity of these extracts *The Hoax of the Twentieth Century* is not a clumsy work of racial literature but a closely-written book of apparently deep scholarship containing many footnote references to German and Allied sources, whilst the author is an Associate Professor of Electrical Engineering at Northwestern University near Chicago. Second, the work is at the centre of a growing worldwide network of Holocaust-denial 'scholarship'. In July 1979 in Los Angeles was held the first international convention devoted specifically to 'proving' that the Holocaust was a hoax. It attracted seventy delegates from several foreign countries, including Britain, France and Australia, as well as those from the United States.[27] Proponents of this strange view of history have aroused bitter controversy, particularly in France and Australia.

No Jew can read *The Hoax of the Twentieth Century*, without the most profound sense of shock. When it received wide publicity in Australia in 1979 through a letter to a local newspaper which restated its central thesis, Yehuda Svoray, an Israeli journalist living in Melbourne wrote

> I read the letter twice and I didn't know whether to scream out loud, to bang my head against the wall, or whether to laugh insanely . . . My grandmother, my aunt, my uncle and dozens of my friends and acquaintances were killed in Nazi extermination camps during World War 2. I feel personally affronted, slapped in the face, spat upon . . .[28]

Butz and his associates have this effect wherever they go; one can readily infer this by the increasing and widespread references to his work in recent Jewish writings.[29] The private and unending grief of the Holocaust survivors has been transformed into their public guilt.

Of course, mainstream newspapers and journals refuse to give publicity of any kind to Butz and his school.[30] It is inconceivable that the old image of the Jew so frequently portrayed in popular fiction down to the Second World War could appear in any legitimate mainstream publication, partly because of the large number of Jews working in the media and partly because of the historical changes that we have discussed.

Despite everything, the change which has taken place in the gentile's perception of the Jews seems only partly explained by the new circumstances surrounding Jewry since the Second World War. One of the most important of these changes, their upward socio-economic rise, might seem to reinforce the old stereotype of Jews as a powerful and mysterious international elite. Why, for example, has this change not resulted in an increase in anti-semitism? An explanation must take into account *philo-semitism*, both at the elite and mass levels.

At its base, philo-semitism consists of sympathy or admiration for the Jews because they are a unique people in many ways, including their liability to suffering. This is not the same as the biblical claim that Jews were elected by God, although it is related to it and may be a secularisation of it. The religious notion that Jews are in some sense the 'chosen people' is also an important one, and rather more widespread than Jews believe; it is an element, above all, in Protestant thinking, especially in those strands of Protestantism which derive from Calvinism or are fundamentalist in character.

One of the most widespread manifestations of contemporary philo-semitism is the admiration felt for Jewish intellectual achievements. This might be christened the 'Einstein effect', because it was Einstein who did more than anyone else to give to Jews the reputation for intellectual genius. Einstein, the best-known of all Jewish refugees from Hitler, also typifies another component of philo-semitism, a sense of sympathy for Jews derived from a perception of their vulnerability to anti-semitism.

Although this phenomenon doubtless exists at the elite level, it is, perhaps surprisingly, at the popular level that it exists in its clearest form. Writing of his experiences as an army draftee in the mid-1950s, shortly after graduating from Columbia and Cambridge, Norman Podhoretz has, in his description of the attitude of his platoon sergeant, caught this sympathy perfectly.

> The truth was that this sergeant – like almost everyone, regular or conscript, officer or enlisted man I met in the Army after Basic Training – was as humble before people better educated than he as I had felt in relation to the platoon sergeants at Fort Dixon. The only instances of that famous American ˙ 'anti-intellectualism' I ever came upon in the army were either justified in being directed against college graduates who affected a prissy superiority but were in reality neither intelligent nor good for *anything*, or else derived from feelings of intimidation toward the idea of education so touchingly great as to border on superstition. The more common response was a frank and self-abasing respect. Thus everywhere I went in the army I would find myself being treated with deference and becoming the barracks adviser on everything from sex to religion. . . It was no tribute to *me* that my commanding officer in Kassel took me out of the category of enlisted man and gave me an officer's job along with many of the perquisites thereof: he did it because my record said that I was a graduate of 'Harvard and Oxford' and because of that fact alone, *even in the army* – even, by 1954, in the *American* army – meant that I properly belonged to the upper (i.e. officer) class and so too with my fellow enlisted men.[31]

The non-elite majority may retain frames of reference *more* philo-semitic than a part of the elite. The decline of what social psychologists term the 'authoritarian personality' type since' the Second World War – especially among the working class – due chiefly to greater affluence and mobility, the widening effects of television, greater education and more permissive sexual attitudes. may have augmented this trend. Can it be that the non-elite is not now, in essence, more predisposed towards anti-semitism than the elite?

Such a perspective might be extended to include another, at first surprising, source of popular philo-semitism: fundamentalist and Calvinist Protestantism. It has been noted that, historically, those countries with the least anti-semitism, like Scotland, the Netherlands and the United States, have a common origin in Calvinism and in the type of Protestantism which sees today's protestant believers as spiritual descendants of the biblical Hebrews.[32] In the past, such a nexus has also existed to the benefit of Jews: one thinks, for instance, of Cromwell's deliberate re-admission of Jews to Britain in 1653.[33] An interesting article by David Rauch, 'American Evangelicals and the Jews', has drawn attention to the affinity of fundamentalist Protestantism for the Jews and their friendliness towards Israel:

> Fundamentalist-Evangelicals consistently supported the restoration of the Jewish people to Palestine. The support of Israel as a national homeland for the Jewish people is today a key concern of Fundamentalist Evangelical dogma. Professor Michael Harrison . . . points out: 'Protestants leaning to the direction of Fundamentalism, like [Jimmy] Carter, are likely to be impressed by the notion of the miracle of modern Israel as are the Jews, and perhaps more so.[34]

Rauch notes:

> Do the Jewish people have anything to fear from Protestant Fundamentalist-Evangelicals? I think not. Rather, in our modern period of history it is liberal theology that seems to be the nemesis of the Jewish people. Fundamentalist religion since its inception in the nineteenth century has consistently supported the Jewish people and their right to the 'Promised Land', while the record of liberal theology is marred by camouflaged anti-

semitism that is perceived clearly only on occasion. While disaffirming the Jews' 'Jewishness' it has dehumanized the Jewish people in an effort to obliterate them in the melting-pot of mankind at large. When they refused to be conquered the Jewish people met with extreme antagonism.[35]

In 1977 a number of leading American Protestant Evangelicals, including Arnold Olson, Co-ordinator and President-Emeritus of the Evangelical Free Church of America, and Harold Lasswell, Editor of *Christianity Today*, placed a full-page advertisement in *The New York Times* and other American newspapers expressing their concern at 'the erosion of American governmental support for Israel'. They noted that

> while the exact boundaries of the land of promise are open to discussion, we, along with most evangelicals, understand the Jewish homeland generally to include the territory west of the Jordan River.

They also expressed their 'grave concern' over any effort 'to carve out of the historic Jewish homeland another nation or political entity, particularly one which would be governed by terrorists whose stated goal is the destruction of the Jewish state.[36] Recently, too, the best-known American Evangelical leader, the Reverend Billy Graham, has stated that 'the vast majority of evangelical Christians in this country and abroad support the State of Israel's right to existence . . . In Biblical history and in secular history, Israel has every right to exist – as does Syria, or Egypt, or Russia, or the United States'.[37]

Arthur Hertzberg has noted that 'the political and religious left of today did not invent the rhetoric of anti-Zionism; it was to be found in the *Christian Century* of the 1930s and 1940s, against which Reinhold Niebuhr fought'.[38] Such an attitude continues among liberal Protestants today. An interesting example of this has recently been described by Dr Marvin Maurer, that of the opposition of American Quakers to Israel and their friendliness to the PLO.[39] The Society of Friends is generally as ultra-liberal in politics as in its religious beliefs. During the 1960s American Jews and Quakers co-operated over such issues as civil rights for blacks and ending the war in Vietnam. In February 1977 the American Friends Service Committee (AFSC), the best-known social activist group among the Quakers, held a conference in Maryland on the subject of 'The New Imperatives for Israeli-Palestinian Peace', with Jews, Arabs and Quakers in attendance. In Dr Maurer's words:

> At the public level the A.F.S.C. sought to keep a balance between its support for the PLO and Israel. However, any such pretense was abandoned in the panel meetings and special workshops. At this level of discourse the conference was designed to mobilize action against Israel and the Jewish community . . . During the meeting of the mass media workshop abuse of the term 'Jewish Zionist' became so pronounced the A.F.S.C. moderator imposed a minute's silence in order to restore 'harmony'. The workshop dealt with the techniques aimed at 'crushing the Jewish monoliths'' control over news output in this country.[40]

After noting that 'the Quaker apparatus is committed to third world totalitarianism . . .' Maurer concludes that 'if the Jews became a downtrodden people again the Quakers would reveal their eleemosynary hand'.[41]

A similar dichotomy may be perceived among some strands in Western Roman Catholicism, although here the picture is much more complicated because of the Catholic tradition of religious anti-semitism tempered by the protection of Jews.

Since 1962, Catholicism has officially removed much of the more flagrant anti-semitic relics from the Catholic liturgy in the face of 'right-wing' opposition.[42] Yet liberal Catholics, like liberal Protestants, are increasingly critical of Israel and supportive of Palestinian claims.[43]

The Western Establishment and the Jews

Throughout the post-Second World War era the conservative segment of the establishment in most Western nations has become more philo-semitic and pro-Israel. Since 1973 there has been some evidence of a weakening in this pro-Israeli position. A closer examination of conservative aims in the Middle East will reveal that claims for such a weakening are exaggerated, especially when placed in the context of the political spectrum.

The positions we wish to analyse in this section are two: that the gentile establishment right[44] (with certain deviant exceptions) is now actively philo-semitic and pro-Israeli. Furthermore, that establishment right figures who are motivated by explicitly 'conservative' ideology are more likely to be philo-semites and pro-Israeli than those who are less explicitly committed to such ideas.

Today's sympathy of the establishment right for the Jews and Israel has three dimensions:

(1) The shift in conservative values to those defined by the United States;
(2) The movement of Jews *en bloc* into the large elite; and
(3) The perception of Israel as a beleaguered Western nation threatened by Marxist terrorism.

The American leadership of the Western world (and thus the imposition of its values) is the greatest influence on the sympathetic perception of Jews and Israel. An important corollary is that sympathy for Israel is, generally, directly proportionate to the support which national government, a party or a movement gives to the United States and its foreign policy goals. Almost invariably – as the EEC declaration on the Middle East illustrated in June 1980 – a Western nation's responsiveness to Arab demands and its insensitivity to the Israeli position or to expressed Jewish opinion is linked with its independence from American policy on other matters. Those Western nations – France being the most obvious example – most independent of the United States on a variety of foreign policy and military issues are also most likely to be antagonistic to American aims in the Middle East.

Implied in this is the fact that the United States is consistently Israel's most reliable supporter in its struggle for survival, as well as the nation most sympathetic to Jewish interests. Although the large size of America's Jewish voting bloc and the penetration of Jews into the American elite are, of course, important factors in this, neither is sufficiently important to explain the widespread degree of American sympathy for Israel or its sensitivity to the Jewish experience. Since President Eisenhower, who effectively stopped the Israelis during the 1956 Suez campaign, through Richard Nixon, up to Ronald Reagan, who has been termed 'more Israeli than the Israelis', a transformation has occurred in the attitude of the Republican party, a change reflected in the increased percentage of Jewish appointees in Republican administrations. Today's right-wing Republicans place great emphasis on Israel's importance to Western security interests in the Middle East. 'Israel represents the one stable democracy sharing values with us in that part of the world, and [has] a proven military capability that stands as a deterrent to further disruption and chaos', as Ronald Reagan has said.[45] The historical irony of Western conservatives now praising the Jewish state – the homeland of those who would formerly have been described as the leaders of the 'sinister Bolshevik cosmopolitan conspiracy' – because of its importance to the security of the Western world should be savoured in full.

In other Western nations the attitude of the conservative right toward the Jews and Israel has altered accordingly. In 1977 in Britain, for example, nearly two-thirds (65.8 per cent) of the sitting Conservative members of parliament were rated as pro-Israeli by one Jewish group – a complete reversal of the traditional patterns of prejudice. Of Britain's Conservative Prime Minister one well-placed Jewish source said that 'no Conservative leader since the days of Winston Churchill has been so personally committed to the ideals of the State of Israel as Mrs Thatcher'.[46] According to this report she 'sees Israel as the embodiment of many of her own values – self-help, hard work and a combination of stubborness and enterprise', and notes further that 'her fears about Russian ambition have confirmed her strong belief in the vital importance of the Jewish State'.[47] Mrs Thatcher was for many years President of the Finchley Anglo-Israel League and one of the earliest members of the Conservative Friends of Israel group.[48]

In the British media and among British intellectuals much the same reversal of attitudes towards the Jews and Israel is also evident. In general, the more right-wing the newspaper (with the exception, naturally, of the Fascist ultra-right), the more favourable it is to Israel and more sensitive to Jewish interests. While, conversely, the more left-wing, the more hostile to Israel and to Jewish interests; Conservative newspapers such as the *Daily Telegraph* and journals like *Encounter* are pro-Israeli and philo-semitic. The contrast between today's Conservative press and the often audacious and generally chronic anti-semitism of pre-war right-wing press – Leo Maxse's old *National Review*, the *Morning Post* or the Harmsworth tabloids which supported Oswald Mosley – cannot be greater. *The Times* is essentially friendly but critical, especially over the West Bank issue.[49] It employed Britain's most celebrated Jewish columnist, Bernard Levin (who frequently addresses himself to Jewish issues like the plight of Soviet dissidents, but almost never to the Middle East). On the left, papers like the *Guardian* and journals like the *New Statesman* are critical of Israel. The *Guardian's* chief Middle Eastern correspondent, David Hirst, is the author of a work on the Middle East,[50] which is ferociously anti-Israeli. The *New Statesman's* anti-Zionism has increased. The hostility of much of today's socialist left towards Israel has been a factor in the shift of many former left-wing intellectuals to the right.[51] Among Britain's Jewish intelligentsia (as among Jews everywhere else) this hostility has naturally produced a more marked shift to the right.

Whatever falling away of support for Israel has taken place since 1973, the astonishing thing is not that it should have happened but that any Western country dependent upon oil for its economic survival should persist in supporting Israel at all when it is so plainly in its direct and immediate interests to side with the Arabs. Support for Israel is gratuitous, if not irrational, and must be evidence of a deep commitment, sufficient to counteract the most pressing economic motives for supporting the Arabs.

This commitment to Jews and Israel must also be evidence of a recognition by conservatives of the legitimacy of the Jewish tradition within Western culture. In America, 'our Judaeo-Christian heritage' and 'all three faiths' – Protestants, Catholics and Jews – are, of course, much over-used stock phrases implying both a legitimacy and an approximate equality for Judaism *vis-à-vis* Christianity, whose adherents outnumber Jews by at least twenty times. The Jewish tradition has, indeed, been grafted onto the American tradition, and this often shows itself in unexpected ways. The American Jewish writer Milton Himmelfarb has cited one remarkable example of this. In the early 1970s Lewis F. Powell, a Southern Conservative lawyer and judge with no Jewish attachments, delivered a speech to the American Bar Association which included the following:

> Today, we are being cut adrift from the type of humanizing authority which in the past shaped the character of our people . . . This [old] sense of belonging was portrayed nostalgically in the film 'Fiddler on the Roof'. Those who saw it will remember the village of Anatoepka in the last faint traces of sunset on Sabbath eve. There was the picture of Tevye, the father, blessing his family, close together around their wooden dining room

table. They sang what must have been ancient Hebrew Hymns, transmitted from family to family through untold generations. The feeling of individual serenity in the common bond of family life was complete.

Sadly, this is not the portrait of contemporary American life.[52]

Since 1973 the West has, of course, been under immense pressure to compel Israel to compromise with the Arabs and, ultimately, to permit the establishment of an independent Palestinian state on the West Bank. This process necessarily would entail recognition of and negotiation with the Palestine Liberation Organisation, steps to which Israel is opposed. Some of this pressure has been economic,[53] aimed at boycotting Israeli products and Western companies which incidentally conduct business with Israeli firms. From the Western viewpoint, the aim of any Middle Eastern settlement must be to ensure the reliable and cheap supply of crude oil. But if a Palestinian state were created tomorrow, would OPEC lower the price of oil? Would it be any less scarce or irreplaceable? Would the attitude towards the West of radical Arab states like Libya and Iraq suddenly change? These doubts may be the reason why the West has not turned decisively against Israel.

In 1979–80 the Western powers appeared to become less friendly towards Israel. This hostility has taken two forms – growing exasperation with the Begin government's policy of building Jewish settlements on the West Bank and a general recognition that the PLO must be brought into direct negotiations. The latter of these demands, voiced most loudly by the EEC Declaration on the Middle East of June 1980, is unacceptable to virtually all Israelis. Israel regards the PLO as a terrorist body committed to the destruction of Israel. Whatever impression the Israelis or others might have had that the PLO was softening its policies was seemingly negated by the official declaration of Al-Fatah (the PLO's largest member), made after a ten-day Congress in Damascus at the same time as the EEC initiative, that its aim was to 'liberate Palestine completely, and to liquidate the Zionist entity [i.e. Israel] politically, economically, militarily, culturally, and ideologically',[54] virtually an announcement of the intent to commit genocide. It should be noted that Yasser Arafat subsequently denied that this statement was ever made 'officially', claiming it was only a 'draft'.

The moderate attempt by the EEC to bring the PLO into direct negotiations arose after seven years of ever-increasing oil prices (and more blatant use of the economic weapon by the Arabs), and in the midst of an American election year, against the background of an American administration generally perceived as weak. The lead for this initiative in the Middle East came from France, and appears to have been moderated by the remaining Western powers, including Britain. The provocative settlement-building policies of the Begin government have dismayed many who are normally strong supporters of Israel. Even so, there appear to be limits to the willingness of the West European powers to turn against Israel, despite the provocation of its government and the economic pressures applied by the Arabs.

In the United States some of the same factors have been at work, but here both the influence of American Jews, and the even greater reluctance of non-Jewish American policy-makers to injure Israel, appears to have stopped any alteration in American policy. Indeed, one can read the presidency of Jimmy Carter – a pro-Zionist Protestant fundamentalist – as a series of emotional accessions to Israeli pressure against the desires of the State Department and other official makers of American foreign policy, who would unquestionably prefer to bring the PLO into the Middle Eastern peace-making process in a direct way. During its first three years of office the Carter administration might well have been far more anti-Israeli than it proved to be. Carter's first Secretary of State, Cyrus Vance, was perceived by many Jews as essentially hostile to Israel, a product of the old-fashioned WASP elite and its attitudes towards the Jews and their interests. Thus Mayor Ed Koch of New York (who is Jewish) in early 1980 termed Secretary Vance the leader of an anti-Israeli 'gang of five' in the Carter Administration.[55] After Vance's resignation in May 1980 he was replaced by Edmund Muskie, a more traditional liberal Democratic politician who is perceived as friendly to Israel in the manner of Hubert Humphrey and Vice-President Walter Mondale. At the other extreme, UN Ambassador Andrew Young, the controversial and outspoken black leader, was widely perceived by many Jews as essentially hostile to Israel and friendly to the radical Arabs in the manner of most pro-Third World radicals. Young resigned his UN post in August 1979 as a result of an unauthorised meeting with a PLO representative.

The year 1979–80 could be regarded as one when the Carter

administration rid itself of foreign policy officials who were hostile, or potentially hostile to Israel: in the case of Andrew Young, the administration seemed to have to choose between upsetting Israel's Jewish supporters and offending the increasingly important and numerous radical black (and other) supporters of the Palestinians, and they unequivocally chose the latter. In the wake of the Iranian revolution, the seizure of the American embassy hostages and the Soviet invasion of Afghanistan, the Carter administration also became much more defence-minded and responsive to those who see America as dangerously weak and hesitant. In objective neopolitical terms, this will benefit the security of Israel and the other anti-Communist states of the Middle East. America's attitude towards Israel then, can reasonably be read as one of a deliberate refusal to work against her, despite the provocation offered by the Begin government and despite, perhaps, her own better judgement. Whatever happens in the 1980s, the same philo-semitic, pro-Zionist emotional framework will exist, although Israel's supporters will have to work much harder to mobilise it, while demands for a 'just and comprehensive' Middle Eastern settlement will also continue to grow.

The Left and the Jews

The animosity of much of the political left towards the Jews is complicated by two factors: the historical development of the attitude of the extreme left towards the Jews and the very great differences which exist between the Marxist and revolutionary left and the moderate social democratic left in their perceptions of the Jews and Israel. The attitude of the Marxist left towards the Jews has been consistent since Karl Marx first discussed the Jewish question in 1844. This attitude has been one of hostility to the Jews *as an ethnic and religious group*. Jews were significant both in the Marxist tradition itself and in forming its attitudes towards the Jewish people. The longstanding attitude of the Marxist left towards the Jews has been summarised very neatly by Arthur Hertzburg as that of 'a marked and lasting tradition of imagining a new heaven on earth without Jews',[56] and by Robert S. Wistrich as Marxism's 'rejection of any special pleading or moral obligation to further a distinctively Jewish existence in group form'.[57] This is firmly based in Marxism's commitment to secularism.

Some of Marxism's anti-Jewishness derives from Marx himself and stems from the self-hatred of the many Jewish founders and contributors to the Marxist tradition, who were often demonstrably more antipathetic to the Jews than non-Jewish Marxists. Marx's writings contain anti-semitic remarks, sometimes of an extreme nature.[58] In 1853 Marx wrote of Lionel Rothschild: 'It may be questioned whether the English people will be contented with this extension of the suffrage to a Jewish usurer.'[59] In 1856 he observed

> The loanmongering Jews of Europe do only on a larger and more obnoxious scale what many others do on one smaller and less significant. But it is only because the Jews are so strong that it is timely and expedient to expose and stigmatize their organization.[60]

Marx's writings contain many other examples of anti-semitism.[61] On a more basic level, Marx's system of historical materiaism elevated the industrial bourgeoisie and proletariat to a position of key historical significance in the dialectical process in place of the disproportionately Jewish commerical and financial spheres of the capitalist economy. The second persistent element in the Marxist perception is its view that the Jews are a medieval survival who owe their existence in the modern world to their financial links with feudalism's kings and princes. Karl Kautsky, the (non-Jewish) Marxist who wrote one of the important early socialist works on the Jews, *Rasse und Judentum*, 'dismissed Judaism as a relic of the medieval past and a parasitic ghetto phenomenon in the pores of feudal society'.[62] The notion that modern Jews are a relic or curiosity, and not really a 'people' in the same sense as other peoples leads to the third strand in Marxism's treatment of the Jewish question, its refusal to recognise any special claims which the Jews may have on the moral conscience of mankind, including, naturally, a claim to a nation-state or homeland. Rosa Luxemburg – who was, of course, a Jewess – complained to a friend in 1917, 'Why do you come with your special Jewish sorrow? I feel just as sorry for the wretched Indian victim in Putamayo, the Negroes in Africa . . . I cannot find a special corner in my heart for the ghetto'.[63] Karl Kautsky, uniting Marxism's belief in the atavistic nature of Jewish survival with its refusal to recognise their special claims, believed that the Jews would eventually disappear. But – as Walter Laqueur paraphrases him – 'The disappearance of the Jews would not be a tragedy, like the disappearance of the American Indians or the Tasmanians. For it would not be a decline into degradation but an ascent to an immense field of activity, making possible the creation of a new and higher type of man'. Kautsky concluded his book with the oft-quoted remark that under socialism, 'The wandering Jew will thus at last find a haven of rest. He will continue to live in the memory of man as man's greatest sufferer, as he who has been dealt with most severely by mankind, to whom he has given most'.[64]

This view of the Jewish question was chiefly expressed by Jewish Marxists, and almost invariably represented the opinion of the best-known Jewish Marxists towards Jewish affairs, especially towards Zionism. In Wistrich's words

> If there was one fact that united such well-known Marxist Jews as Leon Trotsky, Paul Axelrod, Julius Martov, Rosa Luxemburg, Leon Jogiches, Victor Adler, and Otto Bauer, it was their complete rejection of the very principle of Jewish national self-determination. There can be little doubt that this hostility of Marxist Jews to the Jewish national movement greatly influenced the attitude of other revolutionaries to the problem.[65]

Concerning the hostility of Jewish Marxists to Jewish nationalism, Wistrich cites the remark of the historian Simon Dubnow, 'How much a Jew must hate himself who recognizes the right to every nationality and every language to self-determination but doubts it or restricts it for his own people whose "self-determination" began 3,000 years ago'.[66]

Crucial to the Marxist view of the Jewish question is its further belief that anti-semitism is a product of capitalism and will disappear under socialism. Because Marxism is a system which believes in the ultimate importance of economic determinism in history it is unable to allot an independent role to other, non-economic historical factors. It is unable to grasp the discrete nature of most forms of modern anti-semitism, whose origins lie in the realm of psychology, nationalism or theology rather than in the economic bases of society. It cannot understand, for instance, the irrational, non-economic basis of Hitler's anti-semitism seeking to reduce Nazism to a form of 'finance capital' and thereby failing to explain the virulence of its hatred for Jews. This economic determinism also has the effect of reinforcing Marxism's hostility to

Zionism as a 'solution' to the Jewish problem. In the words of George Novack, a contemporary Trotskyite,

> The salvation of the Jewish people cannot come from reliance upon Zionist chauvinism, American imperialism, or Stalinist bureaucratism. Every expedient short of the struggle for socialism, any substitute for that, will end in calamity for the Jews. They cannot achieve security for themselves or anyone else so long as the root causes of discrimination, racism, and reactionary nationalism continue to exist.
>
> The Jews have to link themselves with those forces in their own country and on a world scale that are fighting to overthrow imperialism and striving to build the new society. The solution of the Jewish question is indissolubly bound up with the complete emancipation of humanity that can be brought about only along the road of international socialism.[67]

Marxism would, then, fundamentally reject either Zionism or the general movement of Jews into the capitalist large elite as fantasy. Anti-semitism will disappear only under universal socialism.

The fifth theme is Marxism's failure to recognise the peculiar situation of the Jews as a tiny minority, uniquely subjected to persecution yet uniquely achieving. For not only is Marxism generally hostile to Zionism as a solution to the problem of the Jews but it would make extremely difficult, if not impossible, any veto on anti-semitism deriving from the over-representation of Jews in the large and small elites. Although it is possible under a Marxist government for Jews as individuals to be over-represented at the elite level (as they certainly have been in the Soviet Union and probably are even now), it has proved impossible in any Communist country for them to function, as a coherent religious, national or cultural group, to support Zionism or, by the nature of all Communist regimes, to amass personal wealth and economic influence.

Soviet Communism has been hostile to Jewish national culture throughout its history. The current position of Soviet Jewry is a result of the history of Jews in the Soviet Union. In Wistrich's words

> Lenin . . . was quite unequivocal in his condemnation of Jewish national culture, even when proclaimed in its most moderate

form by the Jewish Bund, as 'a slogan of the rabbis and the bourgeoisie' . . . Any manifestation of Jewish nationalism could not be progressive but was, by definition, motivated by a desire to perpetuate [the] 'caste position of Jews' in Eastern Europe . . . [A]lthough Lenin (like Marx) supported the national liberation movements of oppressed nationalities when it suited his revolutionary strategy, that support categorically did not apply to Jewish nationalism.[68]

The many fringe Marxist groupings which regard the Soviet Union as little better than 'Western imperialism' share a common antipathy for the Jews. The most consistently abusive and extreme anti-Zionist and anti-Israeli propaganda in the Western world today emanates from Trotskyite, Maoist and 'revolutionary' Marxist sources; the Soviet Union's *official* policies on the Middle East, which have never *officially* gone beyond demanding the creation of a Palestinian state on the West Bank, appear models of moderation and compromise by comparison.[69]

The left contains other groupings than Marxism, and in attitudes towards the Jews the difference between Marxism and social democracy show most clearly. For there is a fundamental difference which must be drawn between the attitudes of the moderate, social democratic wings of the mainstream left parties throughout the Western world and either the Marxist left within these parties or the Communist and other Marxist parties outside of them. In general, social democrats remain committed to Israel's existence in security, and are sensitive to Jewish history. Social democracy contains few traces of the hostility to the Jews inherent in Marxism. Social democrats continue to perceive Israel as a model of a social democratic society, established and maintained against the most overwhelming odds. Western social democrats still remember the Nazi period and its horrors. Social democrats like Harold Wilson in Britain, Willy Brandt in West Germany and Bob Hawke[70] in Australia were among Israel's most valuable supporters in the Western world.

Social democrats have so sided with the Jews and Israel for three reasons. First, social democracy is the heir to nineteenth-century liberalism. Historically, liberalism has opposed religious persecution, and has acted as the principal agent for the removal of legal barriers to the full participation of Jews in Western society. Until recently, most Jews have situated themselves within the ambit of social democratic left-liberalism. Second, social democracy is reformist rather than revolutionary, and rejects crude Marxism. It also shares the view that the existence of Israel is historically justified. This view is one which is naturally associated with social democracy (or with American left-liberalism), rather than with Marxism or (until recently) with conservatism.

Third, Jews have hitherto associated disproportionately with social democratic parties, which has proved beneficial to both. Harold Wilson's 'court' consisted largely of Jews and in Australia Bob Hawke has close associations with the Jewish community.

Self-made East European Jewish entrepreneurs feel much more at ease within a social democratic party than a conservative party, even after amassing great wealth, because they fear rejection by the wealthy gentile establishment. Such men also retain a self-perception of their working-class origins (and even, in some cases, continuing membership), while their 'Jewish social conscience' works to maintain left-wing ties long after this would have vanished in most gentile businessmen of similar class origins. Successful (gentile) socialist politicians, who have often travelled a similar route by different means, are naturally highly sympathetic to such men, especially if these politicians have no real ideological commitment to socialism. In such an environment, both the influence and the visibility of wealthy Jews is increased simply by the fact that so few gentile businessmen of similar origins would normally maintain even residual ties with a socialist party.

The Left and the Jews in Today's World

Marxism came to power in Europe in countries which had long possessed a native tradition of anti-semitism. As the Communist elite in the Soviet Union and the other European states was cut off from outside influences and without a substantial minority component, its hostility to Jews increased accordingly. Because of the nature of the Soviet Communist system Jews were and are unable to fight back.[71]

The 'cold war' coincided with the increasing embourgoisement of Western Jewry and with the creation of Israel. Because of their affluence and their commitment to the state of Israel any political links which might have been forged between the Soviet Union and Western Jewry have progressively become impossible. A generation ago many Jews had some admiration for the Soviet experiment, with its promise of a utopian society freed from prejudice, unemployment and exploitation. This god failed many people in the West, but none more thoroughly than the Jews. To most Western Jews the Soviet Union is today perceived as the world's most anti-semitic, anti-Zionist state, a society as far removed from the Jewish utopia as any in the world.

Marxism in its various forms now controls more than one-third of the world's population and the Marxist left is the most important and dangerous source of anti-semitism in today's world. We should here briefly examine four key manifestations of the Marxist left's hostility to Jews and to Israel. One is the treatment of Jews in the Soviet Union, the only Communist country with a very sizeable Jewish population.[72] The second is the abusive anti-Zionism often found in the Marxist press. The third is the complete opposition to Israel and Zionism voiced by even those Marxist intellectuals who are in no sense fringe political extremists. The fourth is the Marxist left's abuse and violation of the Holocaust in a way which is deliberately offensive to all Jews.

Organised Jewish life in the Soviet Union is all but impossible under today's conditions. The Jewish religion and Jewish culture are persecuted, while Zionism

> which has not been considered significant enough to warrant a single article by Lenin or the early Bolshevik revolutionaries has today been elevated to a central role in Soviet demonology. Not even Stalin's paranoid, anti-semitic delusions of 1952–53 can compare in their scope and range with the thousands of articles, lectures, broadcasts and films which daily vilify Judaism, Zionism and Israel in the USSR. The only comparable analogy would be the monstrous and terrifying spectre of *Das Weltjudentum* in Nazi propaganda of the 1930s and the '40s – this time with the roles reversed. In place of the Nazi myth about 'Jewish Bolshevism', the Russians have fabricated the even more mendacious thesis of 'Jewish Nazism'.[73]

At the same time, the officially propagated Soviet view of the 'international Jewish conspiracy' closely resembles (if it is not actually identical to) that of traditional right-wing anti-semitism, including Nazism. Again, in Robert Wistrich's words

According to Yevgeny Yevseyev, author or *Fascism Under the Blue Star*, one of the leading examples of this licensed state pornography, the octopus-like tentacles of world Zionism are more far-reaching and dangerous than those of all other varieties of fascism put together. The villany of the Jewish bourgeoisie is in fact unequalled anywhere in the world.[74]

The situation in several of the eastern European satellites like Czechoslavakia and East Germany is, if anything, even worse.[75] Nevertheless, despite Soviet anti-semitism it is not completely fair to compare the Soviet Union's treatment of its Jews with the policies of the Nazis. For a variety of reasons, Jews have been over-represented at the elite level throughout Soviet history, and, up to a certain point, the Soviet government is willing to use the talents of its Jews for its own ends.

Throughout the Western world a glance at most Marxist newspapers or journals will reveal a hostility to Israel and Zionism out of all proportion to the intrinsic interest or importance of the future of Israel and the Palestinians for the Western 'working class'. As in the case of the Soviet Union's domestic propaganda, much of this borders on open anti-semitism, and often depicts the Jews, Israel and Zionism in the same imagery as the stereotypes of yesterday's right-wing anti-semitism. For example, the Socialist Labour Party, a Trotskyite fringe group, currently publishes a large number of books and pamphlets on Israel and Zionism. One of these, already mentioned, is George Novack's pamphlet *How Can the Jews Survive? A Socialist Answer to Zionism*. This contains the following:

> [T]he upper and middle ranges of American Jewry, comfortably ensconced in bourgeois America, some of them bankers, landlords, big and little businessmen, participate in the system of oppressing and exploiting the black masses, just as the Zionists have become oppressors of the Palestinian Arabs. Jewish teachers in New York, reluctant to give up their small priveleges, resist the Afro-American demand for control of the schools in their own communities.[76]

We have here in a few sentences three images which might well have come from the czar's Black Hundreds: the Jew as international oppressor, the Jew as oppressor of the 'working masses' and the linking of 'Zionist oppression' of the Palestinians with the 'exploitation' of American blacks by rich American Jews, a bracketing conceptually irrelevant unless *Jews* as such rather than 'Zionists' are the intended target.

The fringe ultra-left is in itself electorally insignificant and politically unimportant, although it does have disproportionate influence among many student groups, some trade unions and even a section of the intelligentsia. But there are others in the Western intelligentsia, those Marxist academics and people in the media, whose views must be taken more seriously. Such intellectuals have absorbed the theoretical bases of Marxism and are fully aware of its application to today's events. Consider, for example, the following passage by V.G. Kiernan, formerly Professor of History at Edinburgh University and author of the well-known work on nineteenth-century imperialism, *The Lords of Human Kind*, who has described himself as 'a socialist all his life' and 'an adherent of the Marxist method in history':

> There is, unquestionably, an Israeli expansionism; and while the original mischief was done as usual by Europe, American Zionism has added its contribution. It led the way by demanding all Palestine . . . there is an observable association between American Zionism and 'right-wing chauvinistic tendencies within Israel' . . . These [excesses] have been accompanied by a steady erosion of the socialist ideal with which many of the pioneers set out, but which had to be abandoned if a flow of American arms on the necessary scale was to be maintained. Non-Jewish American capital has been invested in Israel in large quantities and South Africa . . . Meanwhile there has been a parallel drift of American Jewry away from progressive ideals towards support of, for instance, the Vietnam War, another required sacrifice on the Zionist altar.[77]

Nigel Maslin, one of the producers of *Palestine*, a series of television documentaries on the pre-1948 history of that region shown on British television in 1978, writes:

> We discovered a great truth: the more rational and fair-minded we were, the more violence we did to the Palestinian case. The British Mandate was a fair and rational instrument so long as one accepted the legal and ethical system which produced it . . . We

had to revise our ideas of balance. We had to admit that our knowledge of the Holocaust, our sympathy for the Jewish catastrophe, and our unconscious liberalism had produced an anti-Arab bias. So we tried, again to be impartial, but from a revised stand point.[78]

Even a perspicacious libertarian socialist intellectual like Noam Chomsky, the celebrated linguisticist, a Jew who 'grew up with a deep interest in the revival of Hebrew culture',[79] and who is sufficiently sensitive to Jewish aspirations to write that the 'Zionist case relies on the aspirations of a people who suffered two millennia of exile and savage persecution culminating in the most fantastic outburst of collective insanity in human existence',[80] can, in the same work, call for the dismantling of Israel and its transformation into a utopian and obviously politically impossible 'socialist binational' state, a proposal voiced amidst severe criticism of Israeli socielty.[81]

The extreme left turns the Holocaust against the Jews in ways which, while they differ from the extreme right in content, have the same intention.[82] The Soviet Union has long ignored the Holocaust in its history books, and one can search in vain in any recent Soviet work for any mention of an event in which two million Soviet Jews were deliberately murdered. The Soviet 'final solution' to the Holocaust question does not entail, as on the extreme right, any elaborate rewriting of history but simply the cold death of silence always handed out to Soviet unpersons and movements. Since the Soviet Union has no wish to whitewash the Nazis, under whom 20 million of their citizens perished, Jews are merely subsumed under the losses suffered by other nationalities. Thus three million dead Poles and three million dead Polish Jews become 6 million dead Poles, and so on, country by country. What might be termed the 'radical' or 'ultra-leftist' solution to the Holocaust question consists of comparing Israel with the Nazis and the Palestinians with the Jews of occupied Europe. The extreme left's most recent method of employing the Holocaust against the Jews is the claim that 'Zionists' collaborated with the Nazis throughout their rule, including the Holocaust. This remarkable argument, which has quickly become a stock-in-trade of left-wing anti-Zionists around the world, is more truly analogous to the claims of the ultra-right 'no-Holocaust' theorists than anything else the left has propounded. In Britain, this view of history has been propagated mainly by the British Anti-

Zionist Organisation (BAZO), an umbrella group with considerable influence on the radical student left, and is typically voiced in the most abusive language.[83] Speaking of the Union of Jewish Students, the mainstream Jewish student society in Britain, a typical article from *Against Zionism!*, BAZO's journal, noted

> There is little doubt that these poor brainwashed kids have picked up a lot in the way of learning Zionist techniques of slander from their summer sojourn to the Zionist state. But what can one expect from an outfit which is financed by the World Zionist Organisation to the tune of at least £22,000 [a year] as a propaganda and publicity outfit for the new Zionist Nazis in occupied Palestine.[84]

On Radio 3CR, Melbourne's ultra-left-dominated fringe radio station, 'Palestine Speaks', one of three anti-Zionist programmes broadcast weekly, stated in June 1977

> Few aspects of Zionism are as treacherous and inexcusable as the role they played during the Second World War . . . Clearly World Zionism was saying: we are interested in Zionism, not in saving Jews. They will come to Palestine or as far as we are concerned they can rot in concentration camps.[85]

Of what do these claims of Nazi-Zionist collaboration consist? It consists in moving from the earliest years of the Nazi regime – In August 1933 the first official agreement between Zionism and Nazism was signed [the Ha'avara agreement][86] – to 1938, when

> the Zionists sent Pino Ginsberg to Berlin and Moshe Bar-Giland to Vienna, to sign further agreements. Cooperation between Zionists and Nazis on the basis of the secret accords signed by Ginsberg and Bar-Giland operated smoothly until 1941.[87]

Then came the Holocaust: a somewhat inexplicable event, one might have thought, given the close friendship between Nazism and Zionism:

> Not only did the international Zionist movement fail to send arms or ammunition to help the ghetto [resistance] fighters, but also many European Zionists helped to sabotage Jewish

resistance. Revisionist Zionist Jacob Gens betrayed Vilno resistance leader Itzit Witenberg to the Nazis . . . Hashomer Hatzair leader Abraham Gancwajch gave weekly intelligence reports to the Gestapo and headed a 300 man pro-Nazi 'police force' in the Warsaw Ghetto, while liberal Zionist Ephraim Barasz tried to prevent resistance in Bialystok by withholding information on Nazi plans from the ghetto inhabitants.[88]

'The last known Zionist-Nazi agreement',[89] and the one which the 'collaborationist' left makes the most of was the Kastner Affair, a squalid by-product of Eichmann's infamous attempt to barter the lives of a million Hungarian Jews for 10,000 trucks in 1944, which emerged in the 1950s when Rudolph Kastner, a mediator in this attempted deal, was involved in a bitter lawsuit in Israel.

The extreme left makes a second charge against 'Zionism' which is, if anything, more remarkable. The Zionists, it is alleged, deliberately and cold-bloodedly murdered large numbers of other Jews to further their ends. It was the Haganah, according to this perspective on history, which blew up two hundred would-be immigrants aboard the *Patria* in November 1940 to prevent its departure from Palestine; similarly

Two hundred victims did not suffice the Zionist propaganda purposes. On 24 February 1942, the ship 'Struma' which was loaded with 769 illegal Jewish immigrants exploded in the Black Sea . . . By a strange coincidence, the Haganah officer, David Stoliar, was the sole survivor of the explosion.[90]

There are, it seems, two reasons why the Zionists were so ready to collaborate with the Nazis and murder other Jews. First, Zionism is simply a form of Nazism. This notion is frequently found in Soviet anti-semitic propaganda; we find there such claims as the Nazi leaders 'sought to create a pro-fascist Jewish state in the Middle East',[91] and is implicit in the 1975 United Nations resolution declaring Zionism to be a form of racism. Also implied in this argument, and a major key to understanding it, is the suggestion that Zionists regard non-Zionist Jews as sub-humans who could quite rightly perish if they persisted in their views. Second, Zionism is not interested in Jewish liberation as such, but exclusively in bringing Jews to Palestine: Jews who did not wish to go to Palestine were of no interest to Zionism. Zionism prescribed immigration to Palestine as the only answer to anti-Semitism, it criticised and rejected any struggle for emancipation, civil rights legislation, etc. . . . The fiercer the struggle [against Nazism] became, the further apart did the Zionist organisation stand from the rest of Jewry.[92]

What is one to make of all this? First, 'collaboration' with Nazism was the one option never open to Jews. Zionist or non-Zionist, Jews were regarded as *a priori* sub-human, and went to their deaths indiscriminately, without regard to their views on the future government of Palestine. Second, 'Zionism' was a movement without a sovereign national base until 1948. Its leaders had little or no freedom of action, and were subject to restriction by the British in Palestine as well as to anti-semitism wherever they lived in Europe. Had Israel existed as a sovereign state during the 1930s millions of lives would have been saved; 'Zionists' who helped German and other Jews to escape from Nazi rule prior to the Second World War saved those lives. Third, proponents of the view of Zionist 'collaboration' with the Nazis often mean nothing more than that both had a common desire to see Europe's Jews moved elsewhere.

Although features of extreme right and extreme left can be found in anti-semitic writings of the 1950s and 1960s, both have fully emerged only recently. In the case of the 'collaborationist' line, the key articles appear to be 'Danger: Zionism', published in an Odessa periodical in 1975, and a semi-scholarly article by an East German journalist, Klaus Polkehn, 'The Secret Contacts: Zionism and Nazi Germany 1933–1941', published in Beirut's *Journal of Palestine Studies* in 1976.[93] This latter article claims *inter alia* that Eichmann visited Palestine in 1937 as a guest of the Hagana, despite his own admission at his trial that he came to make contact with the Palestinian leader Haj Amin el Husseini, Grand Mufti of Jerusalem, and asserts that the Irgun offered Hitler a pact under which Palestine would become a Fascist Jewish state allied to Nazi Germany.[94] When presented in this way, charges of Nazi-Zionist collaboration are plainly designed to mask the very real history of Nazi-Arab friendship and collaboration, especially in the case of the Grand Mufti of Jerusalem.

Most important of all the parallels between right and left, however, is the fact that both focus on the Holocaust in a particularly repellent way. For the 'collaborationist' line transforms the nature of the Holocaust in just the same way as the 'no-Holocaust' theory: the Holocaust now emerges as the Jews' (or Jewish nationalism's) greatest crime; not the 'hoax of the twentieth century' but the autogenocide of the twentieth century.

Social Democracy and the Jews Today

The consistent opposition of the extreme Marxist left to Jewish aspirations has not been of paramount concern in the Western world because Marxism has had little influence in post-war Western social democracy. But the continued support for Israel from social democrats cannot be taken for granted:

(1) As support for a West Bank Palestinian state has grown, so support for Israel has weakened.
(2) Two principal factors can be identified within the framework of present-day social democratic policies: (a) a perception of the Palestinians as victims of Israeli policy with a legitimate grievance requiring redress; and (b) the growing influence of Marxism within the mainstream social democratic parties of the West coupled with a decline of consensus welfare politics and the end of post-war economic growth.
(3) At present social democrats are less resistant to Palestinian claims than are establishment conservatives, and in the growing ranks of those who condemn Israel for its continuing occupation of the West Bank, social democrats have gone further than conservatives.
(4) However, it is unlikely that Western social democrats will move from criticism of Israel to open opposition to its existence in the same way as the extreme left, because of its legacy of sympathy for the historical oppression of the Jews and of the situation of Western social democracy well within the American-influenced Western system. A shift to outright hostility to Israel is likely only if the United States leads the way or if the extreme left captures control of a social democratic party. Nevertheless, uncritical support for Israel policy from social democrats is dwindling, a process assisted by the energy shortage of the 1980s.

Over the past thirty years Jews have benefited in the eyes of social democrats because they were perceived as a persecuted minority whose historical tragedy demanded redress. But the establishment of Israel at the expense of the Palestinians has tended to reverse this perception. Western social democratic parties have also increasingly accommodated a vocal and growing extreme socialist element. The growth of this radical sector is strongly associated both with the revival of Western Marxism in all of its manifestations and with the breakdown of economic consensus and continuing affluence in the 1970s.[95] It is neither the case that all such radicals are anti-Zionists[96] nor, obviously, that all anti-Zionists are radicals. Yet as the balance of power in the Western social democratic parties changes, it is likely that attitudes towards Israel will change accordingly.

As an example of this process, the mainstream Australian social democratic party, the Australian Labour Party (ALP) contains a socialist left-wing faction, especially in the state of Victoria, which is anti-Zionist and pro-Arab. In June 1980 the leader of the opposition ALP in Parliament, Bill Hayden, announced that he would meet Yasser Arafat, the PLO leader, on a forthcoming trip to the Middle East, despite the concerted protests of Australian Jewish leaders.[97] Most observers concluded that Hayden had decided on this course in part because of his need for left-wing support within the ALP in his fight for the leadership of the party with Bob Hawke, Australia's most important trade union leader, who was about to enter parliament. Hawke, a political moderate, has been described as 'probably Australia's most vehement champion of Israel's cause'.[98] The growing strength of the extreme left *within* the mainstream ALP and the surprising centrality its leaders give to anti-Zionism have assured that its attitude towards Israel has changed profoundly since 1948, when Dr H.V. Evatt, Australian Foreign Minister and ALP leader, had served as President of the United Nations General Assembly session which brought Israel into existence and had assisted materially in this decision.

A generation ago it was simply part of the natural order of things that social democrats were more sympathetic to Jewish aspirations than conservatives. Today, more often than not the reverse is true. In Australia, in the words of one observer, 'one of the never publicised but significant features of Australian foreign policy in recent years' has been the continuing and all-out support of Israel by the conservative government headed by Malcolm Fraser.'[99] It is to the world's conservative rather than social democratic parties and governments that many Western Jewish communities now look for support and, in return, give their allegiance and their votes.

Notes

1. See Leon Poliakov, *The History of Anti-semitism* (4 vols., London, 1973); Michael N. Dobkowski, *The Tarnished Dream: The Basis of American Anti-Semitism* (Westport, Conn., 1979) is an interesting study of American anti-semitism, especially during the nineteenth century.

2. The classical exposition of this aspect of anti-semitism is Arnold M. Rose, 'Anti-Semitism's Root in City-Hatred', *Commentary*, Oct. 1948.

3. Of course, many European peoples did not possess sovereign nation-states until 1918 or even later, for instance, the Poles or the Czechs. But they enjoyed territorial integrity within a contiguous area and were hence 'rooted' to a particular area in a way which Jews were not.

4. See the stimulating essay by Bela Vago, 'The Attitude Toward the Jews as a Criterion of the Left-Right Concept', in George Mosse and Bela Vargo, *Jews and Non-Jews in Eastern Europe* (Jerusalem, 1974).

5. See Meir Michaelis, *Mussolini and the Jews* (Oxford, 1978).

6. Edward Alexander, 'Stealing the Holocaust', *Midstream*, Nov. 1980., p. 13.

7. Lois Carol Dubin, 'Survival and Witness', *Jewish Frontiers*, Apr. 1974, p. 23.

8. See, e.g., Yaffa Eliach, 'Despair in Search of a Method', *The Jewish Spectator*, Spring 1977.

9. Michael Billig, *Fascists. A Social Psychological View of the National Front* (London, 1978), p. 305.

10. *Midstream*, March 1979, pp. 3–5.

11. Edward S. Shapiro, 'American Anti-Semitism Reconsidered', *Congress Monthly* (Jan. 1980), p. 16.

12. Henry Siegman, 'Liberalism and the Jews', *Congress Monthly* (Jan. 1980), pp. 3–4.

13. On the National Front, see, e.g., Billig, *Fascists*, who devotes considerable space to the Front's attitude towards Jews and Israel.

14. William Schneider, *Anti-Semitism and Israel: A Report on American Public Opinion* (American Jewish Committee, Dec. 1978), pp. 7–8.

15. Ibid., p. 118.

16. To cite one Australian example of this personally known to the author, the National and Victorian state branches of the Young Liberal Party (Australia's conservative party) unanimously passed resolutions condemning the ultra-left-wing anti-Zionist broadcasts of Melbourne radio station 3CR in 1978–9.

17. The reference here is to *The Protocols of the Learned Elders of Zion*, a notorious anti-semitic forgery produced in czarist Russia which is one of the classics of right-wing anti-semitism. It describes an alleged secret Jewish conspiracy to dominate the world.

18. Billig, *Fascists*, p. 167. The quotations here are from issues of *Spearhead*, the National Front's newspaper.

19. Ibid.

20. Rassinier published the curiously titled *Le Mensonge d'Ulysses*, *Ullysses Trahit les Siens* and *Le Drame des Juifs Européens* between 1951 and 1964.

21. All serious academic scholars who have studied the Nuremberg Trials have agreed on their extreme fairness, given the circumstances under which they were

held. See, e.g., Bradley F. Smith, *Reaching Judgement at Nuremberg* (New York, 1977).

22. A.R. Butz, *The Hoax of the Twentieth Century* (Southam, Warwickshire, 1977), p. 17. This incidentally raises the spectre of mass illegal Jewish migration.

23. Ibid., p. 14. This is surely one of the most blatant lies in the entire book.

24. Ibid., p. 249. Butz fails to explain why Britain, the rulers of Palestine in 1945–6, would be so obliging to Zionist interests at Nuremberg, even while they were engaged in suppressing the Zionist dream in Palestine.

25. Ibid., p. 250.

26. Ibid., p. 247.

27. There is a complete account of this conference in the right-wing American magazine *Spotlight*, 24 Sep. 1979. The best accounts of the claims of this 'school' is Gitta Sereny's 'The Men Who Whitewash Hitler', *New Statesman*, 2 Nov. 1979, and 'Holocaust "Revisionism": A Denial of History', *Facts*, June 1980. (*Facts* is published by the Anti-Defamation League, New York.)

28. Yehuda Svoray, 'A Letter to *The Age*', *Australia/Israel Review*, 28 Mar. 1979.

29. See, for instance, the references to Butz in Alfred Kazin's autobiography, *New York Jew* (New York, 1978), p. 285. See also, e.g., C.C. Aronsfeld, 'The Hoax of the Century', *Patterns of Prejudice*, Nov./Dec. 1976, and Yehuda Bauer, *The Holocaust in Historical Perspective* (Seattle, 1978), pp. 38–41.

30. About a dozen cases (in the United States, Britain and Australia) are known to the author of journals deliberately refusing to print letters in support of the 'no Holocaust' school or to accept advertisements for Butz's book and similar works. Most of these journals are establishment-right (or conservative) in their orientation.

31. Norman Podhoretz, *Making It* (New York, 1969).

32. I owe this suggestion to Professor S.N. Eisenstadt. On this matter see the perceptive article by B. Eugene Griessman, 'Philo-Semitism and Protestant Fundamentalism: The Unlikely Zionists', *Phylon*, Autumn 1976.

33. One would not, of course, wish to push this argument too far. The Ku Klux Klan emerged from just this Calvinist milieu. Conversely, the *absence* of an anti-semitic tradition has occurred in the most unlikely places, for example in Catholic Ireland.

34. *Midstream*, Feb. 1977, p. 40.

35. Ibid.

36. Ibid.

37. Cited in *Canadian Jewish Herald* (Nov. 1978), p. 67.

38. Hertzberg, 'Liberalism and the Jews', p. 5.

39. Marvin Maurer, 'Quakers in Politics: Israel, the PLO, and Social Revolution', *Midstream*, November 1977. See also Rael Jean Isaac, 'From Friendly Persuasion to PLO Support', and Marvin Maurer, 'Quakers and Communists – Vietnam and Israel', *Midstream*, Nov. 1979.

40. Ibid., pp. 37, 39.

41. Ibid., p. 44.

42. See Pichas E. Lapide, *The Last Three Popes and the Jews* (London, 1967), pp. 306ff.

43. See, e.g., *The National Outlook*, April 1980, a left-wing Catholic monthly published in Sydney which compared the Jewish claim to Israel with Catholic claims to the Papal States in the nineteenth century and noted (p. 5) that 'most Catholics would now admit the loss of the Papal States was a great blessing', implying that the loss of Israel would be an equally great blessing for Jews. This editorial also, most presumptuously, enjoins Israel to 'deal justly' with the Palestinians since 'this is not just political good sense, but urgent religious duty for the men of the Bible'.

44. By 'establishment right' we mean both those governments strongly

committed to defending the Western Alliance and those business, governmental, professional and media sectors of the elite normally regarded as most supportive of contemporary Western capitalist democracy. Extreme right neo-Fascist groupings are, of course, not a part of the establishment right. The position of the moderate left is more complex; in general its leaders and elite representatives (social democratic politicians, trade union leaders, intellectuals) are not included within our definition of the 'establishment right'.

45.   *The Times*, 30 June 1980, p. 19. Reagan also said: 'I do not see how it is illegal for Israel to move in settlements' on the occupied West Bank (ibid.).

46.   *Australian Jewish News*, 18 May 1979. This report was taken from reliable Jewish sources in Britain.

47.   Ibid.

48.   Ibid.

49.   *The Times* is widely regarded by many Jews as pro-Arab. A closer reading reveals a much more balanced picture.

50.   David Hirst, *The Gun and the Olive Branch* (London, 1977).

51.   See Paul Johnson, *Enemies of Society* (New York, 1977), especially Ch. 18.

52.   Milton Himmelfarb, 'Jews and Gentiles', *Forum on the Zionist People, Zionism, and Israel*, 23 (Spring 1975), p. 35.

53.   On this process see Terence Prittie and Walter Henry Nelson, *The Economic War Against the Jews* (London, 1978).

54.   *Time*, 16 June 1980, pp. 12–14.

55.   This is, needless to say, a distortion of Vance's attitudes and background. I am here merely stating a widespread feeling in the American Jewish community.

56.   Hertzberg, 'Liberalism and the Jews'.

57.   Robert S. Wistrich, 'Marxism and Jewish Nationalism. The Theoretical Roots of Confrontation', in Wistrich (ed.), *The Left Against Zion* (London, 1979), p. 1. This book and Wistrich's *Revolutionary Jews From Marx to Trotsky* (London, 1976) are excellent introductions to this subject.

58.   The best guide to this is Nathaniel Weyl's important *Karl Marx-Racist* (New Rochelle, New York, 1980). Weyl's interpretation of Marx's system as *inherently* racist is a major new perspective on Marx and Engels. See also Julius Carlebach, *Karl Marx and the Radical Critique of Judaism* (London, 1978).

59.   Cited in Saul K. Padover, *Karl Marx on Religion* (New York, 1974), p. 215.

60.   Cited in ibid., p. 235.

61.   See ibid., pp. 169–228, and Weyl, *Karl Marx–Racist, passim*.

62.   Wistrich, *The Left against Zion*, p. 70.

63.   Cited in Walter Laqueur, *A History of Zionism* (New York, 1972), p. 435.

64.   Ibid., p. 420.

65.   Wistrich, *The Left against Zionism*, pp. 2–3.

66.   Ibid., p. 3.

67.   George Novack, *How Can the Jews Survive? A Socialist Answer to Zionism* (New York, 1969), pp. 21–2.

68.   Wistrich, *The Left against Zionism*, pp. 12–13.

69.   Of course, the Soviet Union's treatment of its own Jews, and its substantial aid for the most radical Arab terrorists and governments, are another matter.

70.   Bob Hawke is President of the Australian Council of Trade Unions (ACTU), the equivalent of the TUC or AFL-C10. In contrast to the attitude of many important figures in the Australian Labour Party, he is fervently pro-Israel. In 1979, Hawke negotiated with Soviet trade union officials for the release of imprisoned Jewish dissidents in the USSR.

71.   This oversimplifies a complex historical evolution which will be discussed later. In particular, no mention is made here of either the Biro-Bidzhan project or of the considerable representation of Jews in the Soviet elite.

72. Hungary and Romania, however, each contain about 90,000 Jews, the largest communities remaining in eastern Europe, the old centre of European Jewry. For a variety of reasons, the condition of these Jews is considerably better than that of Jews in the Soviet Union, and Jewish communal life continues to exist. Both countries are, however, anti-Zionist in their foreign policy (although Romania maintains diplomatic relations with Israel). The other Soviet satellites in eastern Europe – which before the Second World War contained four million Jews – are virtually devoid of Jews and are bitterly anti-Israeli.

73. Robert S. Wistrich, 'Anti-Zionism in the USSR: From Lenin to the Soviet Black Hundreds', in Wistrich, *The Left against Zionism*, pp. 287–8.

74. Ibid., p. 288.

75. See, e.g., Adam Ciolkosz, '"Anti-Zionism" in Polish Communist Party Politics', and W. Oschlies, 'Neo-Stalinist Anti-semitism in Czechoslovakia', in ibid.

76. Novack, *How Can the Jews Survive?*, pp. 15–16.

77. V.G. Kiernan, *America: The New Imperialism* (London, 1978), pp. 240–1.

78. Nigel Maslin, 'Palestine', *History Workshop*, Spring 1980, p. 185.

79. Noam Chomsky, *Peace In the Middle East?* (New York, 1974), p. 49.

80. Ibid., pp. 57–8.

81. Ibid., *passim;* see also Chomsky's essay 'Israel and the Palestinians', in Uri Davis, Andrew Mack and Nira Yuval-Davis (eds.), *Israel and the Palestinians* (London, 1975).

82. See Edward Alexander, 'Stealing the Holocaust', *Midstream*, Nov. 1980, Yehuda Bauer, 'Whose Holocaust?', *Midstream*, Nov.1980, and Bauer, *Holocaust in Historical Perspective*.

83. See Dr Jacob Gerwitz, 'The Life of Zionist-Nazi Collaboration' (London), *Jewish Chronicle*, 25 Jan. 1980.

84. *Against Zionism!*, n.d. (*c* 1978–9).

85. Cited in Victorian Jewish Board of Deputies, *3CR: A Matter of Concern* (Melbourne, 1978).

86. 'Zionism and Nazism', *Farrago* (Melbourne University's student newspaper), 18 April 1980. Similar historical details are given by other anti-Zionist groups around the world.

87. Ibid.

88. Ibid.

89. Ibid.

90. 'Zionist Immigration Policy', BAZO pamphlet.

91. Gerwitz, 'The Lie of Zionist-Nazi Collaboration'.

92. *The Other Israel*, p. 9, cited in 'Zionism and Nazism'. *The Other Israel* is a pamphlet published in Tel Aviv by a Trotskyite fringe group.

93. Gerwitz, 'The Lie of Zionist-Nazi Collaboration'.

94. Ibid.

95. On these developments in the British Labour party see Michael Hatfield, *The House the Left Built. Inside Labor Policy-Making* (London, 1978), and the (admittedly partisan) *The Hidden Face of the Labour Party* (Richmond, Surrey, 1978).

96. For instance, Eric Heffer is one example of a left social democrat who continues to be strongly pro-Israel, and has written many times in support of Israel in the press.

97. See, e.g., Paul Kelly, 'Arafat Meets Australian Diplomats', *National Times*, 6–12 July 1980.

98. Ibid., and private information.

99. Ibid. Extreme hostility to Israeli policy has been voiced repeatedly since 1980 by Hayden and by Lionel Bowen, the ALP's Deputy Leader.

4 THE JEWISH REACTION

The Jewish Political Response

It would be unusual if the changes in the source of anti-semitism and the socio-economic status of Western Jewry that we have described failed to meet with an equally pronounced Jewish response. Thus Jews have reacted by moving to the political right throughout the Western world. The United States, where Jews continue to support the centre-left Democractic party, presents an apparently different picture, although American politics are so different from those of other Western societies that comparisons are difficult. Elsewhere, however, Jews are now generally conservatives *en bloc*. Considering the contribution of Jews to socialist thought and action from Marx onwards, and the equally lengthy history of right-wing anti-semitism, culminating in Hitler, this political shift is of profound significance; given the degree of Jewish participation in both the 'large' and 'small' elites of most Western countries, this shift has had a considerable impact upon Western perceptions of Jewish interests.[1]

Accurate Jewish voting statistics are difficult to obtain, except in the United States, because of the small size of most Jewish communities and the resultant difficulties in sampling – and, indeed, in defining – who is a Jew. Several recent studies, however, may provide at least a partial indication of the present state of affairs in Britain and Australia, two Western societies with a fairly typical ideological spectrum. In Geoffrey Alderman's survey of the party preferences of Jews in the marginal constituency of Hendon North in February 1974 the percentage of support for the three major parties among those declaring their intention to vote was Conservative, 59.1 per cent, Labour, 15.9 per cent, Liberal, 25.0 per cent.[2] Hendon North lies in the heart of today's London Jewish community. As Alderman remarks, 'Hendon North is Conservative because so many Jews (around five per cent of the total Jewish vote of Great Britain) live there'.[3] At the February 1974 General Election the division of the national vote among the three major parties was Conservative, 38 per cent; Labour, 37 per cent; Liberals, 19 per cent.

118

Alderman has recently reported on Jewish voting behaviour at the May 1979 General Election.[4] According to his research, British Jews voted overwhelmingly Conservative, even those Jews who continued to reside in predominantly working-class districts. The May 1979 general election saw a pronounced swing to the Tories in just those north London seats where most Jews reside; the Conservative majority in Hendon North, for example, rose from 1,754 to 6,392. It remains to be seen whether hyperinflation and the apparently pro-Arab bias of the EEC, with which the Thatcher government has concurred, will result in any perceptible return by Jews to Labour in the future.[5] The consensus view is that, for the indefinite future, British Jews will continue to vote Conservative in keeping with their socio-economic status.

In Australia, the strictures concerning the difficulties of sampling the Jewish vote apply with even greater force than in Britain, given the small size (about 70,000) of its Jewish community. Nevertheless, some valuable but as yet unpublished research on this subject has been undertaken by Professor Robert Taft and Mr Chanan Reich of Melbourne's Monash University; in addition, there is a considerable body of oral evidence and impressions provided by knowledgeable Jewish leaders in Australia. Both types of evidence point unmistakably to a decline in support for the Australian Labour Party (ALP) and to a growth in support for the conservative coalition, the Liberal and National Country Parties (L-NCP), since 1972. Electoral support for the ALP among Melbourne Jews totalled 75 per cent in the late 1940s, 62 per cent in 1961 and was probably as high as about 60 per cent even in 1972.[6] Thereafter the defection from left to right was comprehensive. In both the 1975 and 1977 Australian general elections the L-NCP received two-thirds of the Australian Jewish vote, with ALP support dwindling to one-third or less. To a large extent this change was a reaction to Labour Prime Minister Gough Whitlam's 'even-handed' Middle Eastern policies and to other more direct manifestations of hostility to Israel within the ALP; this change also reflects the objective socio-economic interests of the Australian Jewish community and their newly acquired high income and status attainments. After 1977 these trends developed, Bill Hayden, Whitlam's successor as leader of the Australian Labour Party, held a widely-publicised meeting with Yaser Arafat in July 1980. Meanwhile, the ruling L-NCP government continued to court the Australian Jewish community by voting very favourably for Israel in the UN and other international bodies. As in Britain, most observers regarded the shift of the Australian Jewish vote to the right as unlikely to alter in the foreseeable future, and possibly a decisive factor in those Sydney and Melbourne parliamentary seats where Jews were numerous.

In the United States support by the large Jewish community for the left-liberal Democratic Party since the 1930s has been overwhelming.[7] In the Johnson-Goldwater election of 1964, when the Republican candidate was perceived as a right-wing extremist, it was estimated that he received only 11 per cent of the Jewish vote, despite his own Jewish antecedents.[8] Shortly before, American Jews supported Adlai Stevenson even over Dwight Eisenhower – the man who liberated Germany's concentration camps – by majorities of three to one or more.[9] Although there has been a decrease in this Democratic trend during the 1970s, it had not really altered in a fundamental manner until the 1980 Presidential election.[10] Even Nixon failed to win more than about 35 per cent of the national Jewish vote in 1972, despite his large majority and George McGovern's pro-Palestinian statements.

The reasons for this apparent anomaly lie in the nature of the American political structure. The United States has no socialist party, and hence no *mainstream* source of left-wing anti-Zionism. Instead it has two parties explicitly committed to capitalism – one left of centre and, historically, the advocate of welfare state reforms within capitalism, the other right of centre. Jews can remain well within the Democratic Party despite their new affluence and high-status attainments. Many of the left would argue, of course, that the Democratic Party in the United States, despite the welfare state reforms it has introduced, is simply a party of multinational capitalism and is in no real sense on the political left. Certainly its recent national leaders, like the Kennedys and Lyndon Johnson, were men of great personal wealth; certainly its links with America's corporate structure and business world are manifold; certainly it has led anti-Communist military excursions and wars in Korea, Vietnam, the Dominican Republic and elsewhere. In many respects, indeed, from the left point of view its post-war record has been more aggressive than that of the Republicans.

There is evidence that American Jews do alter their voting behaviour whenever they perceive a *specific* threat to Jewish interests or to their way of life – which, in the post-war United States, has occurred rarely. Such shifts took place during the 1960s

and early 1970s, when extreme black demands were put to the
ballot. The most famous example of this was the New York City
referendum in 1966 over a proposed Civilian Review Board, a
suggestion perceived by many Jews as weakening 'law and order' in
a time of rising urban crime and violence. Sixty per cent of New
York's Jews voted against this proposal.[11] This particular vote was
also remarkable for revealing that working-class and lower-middle
class Jews were much *more* conservative than were wealthy Jews. In
this referendum, while only 20 per cent and 31 per cent of clerical
and blue-collar Brooklyn Jews favoured the Civilian Review
Board's proposal, 63 per cent of professional Jews did so.[12]

Many observers see in this and other recent trends a portent of a
flight of American Jewish voters to the Republican Party. William
Ray Heitzman from Villanova University asked in 1975 'Must we
then conclude that the Republican Party must "write off" the
Jewish vote?' and answered, 'No, I believe several factors will
return the Jewish electorate to the GOP'[13] – among them, 'removal
of the WASP stigma', suburbanisation and increasing political
conservatism among many Jews, especially younger Jews.[14]
Heitzman also cites disillusionment with 'the excesses of the civil
rights movement' and 'turmoil in foreign policy'.[15] Even since this
author wrote (1975) both these factors have become markedly more
important in the American Jewish consciousness – the movements
for 'reverse discrimination' in hiring and promotion and a
weakening of American resolve to support Israel in the wake of the
energy crisis and America's military deterioration. Should the left
wing of the Democratic Party ever succeed in adopting a
meaningful pro-Palestinian resolution, this may well cause many
American Jews to vote for the Republic Party; the situation now is
certainly more fluid than at any time since the New Deal.[16]

The Jewish Intelligentsia

Just as the ordinary Jewish voter has shifted to the right so, for
essentially the same reasons, has the Jewish intelligentsia. In some
respects this is even more novel. As a rule, Jewish intellectuals have
infrequently been found in the conservative camp. In the 1920s and
1930s, according to the well-known American Jewish literary critic
Alfred Kazin,

'Socialism' was a way of life, since everyone else I knew in New York was a socialist, more or less . . . My socialism, though I felt it deeply, did not require any conscious personal assent or decision on my part. I was a Socialist as so many Americans were 'Christians'; I had always lived in a socialist atmosphere.[17]

It is probably fair to state that most American Jewish intellectuals were left-liberal Democrats by the 1940s and 1950s, situated within the American political mainstream, though largely at the extreme left of that mainstream. American Jews rarely gave their support to any of the emergent right-wing movements of the period. On the contrary, most perceived them as a direct threat to American Jewish welfare, despite the fact that only rarely were such movements explicitly anti-semitic, while some of the key right-wing leaders of the time, like Senator Joseph McCarthy, had Jewish advisers and confidants. The Civil Rights movement and, most importantly of all, the anti-Vietnam demonstrations of the 1960s, possibly moved the American Jewish intelligentsia temporarily even further to the left. Lipset and Ladd's study of Jewish academics in the United States, undertaken in 1969, at the height of the Vietnam War, revealed that Jewish faculty members were much more inclined to the left than other academics, with more than 12 per cent describing themselves as 'leftists'. The relevant table (Table 4.1) is worth reproducing in full:[18]

This study also revealed that 79.1 per cent of all Jewish faculty members voted for Hubert Humphrey, the Democratic candidate.[19]

Table 4.1: Question: How Would You Characterise Yourself Politically at the Present Time (%)

	Left	Liberal	Middle of the road	Moderately conservative	Strongly conservative
Jewish faculty ($n = 5,907$)	12.4	62.1	18.2	6.6	0.7
Catholic faculty ($n = 9,096$)	4.4	40.3	30.0	23.2	2.1
Protestant faculty ($n = 37,804$)	3.8	36.9	28.0	28.4	3.0
All faculties ($n = 60,028$)	4.9	40.2	27.2	25.0	2.6

Although American Jewish faculty members are thus obviously far to the left of the American centre, this should perhaps not be overestimated. Only a small minority were so far to the left as to be entirely outside the normal range of American politics. This stance must also be seen in its international perspective. In every Western country, university academics form a major part of the political left; in many countries where Marxism is a part of the political system academics are disproportionately Marxist. Nevertheless, it is clear that the American Jewish academic intelligentsia of the late 1960s contained few conservatives in the American, let alone the European, sense. Jewish academics in America were profoundly alienated from the policies of the American government, and desired basic and far-reaching changes in the American political and economic structure. Moreover, a significant, although probably decreasing, segment of the Jewish intelligentsia continues to be Marxist. Among the Western world's leading Marxist theorists and writers at present, possibly one-quarter or more continue to be Jews; they have played a major role in the revival of Western Marxism at both an academic and a political level during the past two decades.

In recent years, however, there has emerged a genuinely conservative Jewish intellgentsia in the Western world. Its most significant American manifestation, the so-called 'neo-conservative' movement, has been described by the movement's historian, a man generally critical of this circle's aims, as 'the serious and intelligent conservatism American has lacked, and whose absence has been lamented by the American Left'.[20]

Because of its exclusively liberal origins, America has lacked a genuine conservatism; the 'conservatives' it produced, in Sheldon Wolin's phrase, were marked by a 'permanent identity crisis', for they necessarily defended the traditions of a country whose foundations were antagonistic to everything which European conservatism embodied; in particular, American conservatism could never easily come to terms with the significance of American capitalism.

American 'neo-conservatism', as the primary facet of this contemporary shift to the right is generally termed, took shape in the 1960s as a reaction to the excesses of the period.[21] At the height of the opposition to the Vietnam war in the middle and late 1960s, it is safe to say that 95 per cent of all reputable American academics and intellectuals opposed the war; the majority believed that it was symptomatic of a deep malignity within American society. Any serious voice raised in support of the Vietnam war – and, by implication, in support of American society – among the liberal academic intelligentsia was often greeted with disbelief. Norman Podhoretz, the editor of *Commentary*, and possibly the most important single voice in the movement, describes something of the atmosphere of this period in New York left-liberal circles:

At a ceremony of the National Book Awards being held in Lincoln Center [New York] . . . in 1967 when Vice-President Hubert Humphrey was scheduled to speak and a move got started to walk out on him in protest against the war . . . A group debated the wisdom and propriety of the demonstration . . . The argument grew heated until someone turned to the one stranger who happened to be standing there, the pianist Eugene Istomin, and asked him what he meant to do. 'Oh', he said calmly, 'I'm not going to walk out. I'm all in favour of American policy in Vietnam'. From the amazement which greeted this announcement I realized that not a single person of the ten or so in the group had ever actually met a supporter of the war; and from the way they all glared at him in horrified disbelief, I could see how this community of 'dissenters' felt about anyone who dissented from *them*.[22]

It was probably Podhoretz's conversion, around 1969 or 1970, to what Steinfels has termed a 'scorched-earth campaign against the New Left and counterculture'[23] which gave wide publicity and a centre of direction to a movement which had been gathering strength for a decade. This shift to the right was essentially a movement of the 1960s and 1970s,[24] and should be distinguished from another, earlier, similar trend: the 'God that failed' phenomenon of 1930s Communists who, in the 1950s, became cold-war Liberals.

Not all neo-conservatives are Jews but most of its leading members are Jewish, and its locus is very much the West Side New York-Harvard faculty. Jews are especially prominent among the neo-conservative movement for several reasons: the radical black demands for 'affirmative action' and 'reverse discrimination', moves which effectively discriminate against Jews; the decline of so many older eastern cities where Jews predominantly live;

perhaps, too, the new-found conservatism of any *arriviste* group.[25] For Milton Himmelfarb, among the most perceptive and incisive neo-conservatives, the Jewish outlook is essentially conservative. In the words of two commentators on his writings, Himmelfarb suggests that

> the notion that Jews are by centuries-long tradition a people of liberal inclinations, is a parochial error, the consequence of ignorance of Jewish history. Before the Enlightenment, Jewish attitudes toward politics were essentially static, detached, and conservative.[26]

But the most important motive is the threat posed to Israel by the Soviet bloc and revolutionary Marxism abroad, and the indirect threat posed to it by the American quasi-isolationist foreign policy in the post-Vietnam era. In Podhoretz's words,

> If the anti-intellectualism of the [New Left] Movement . . . gave plausibility in arguing with the intellectuals to the idea that radicalism was an enemy rather than a friend, so too did the hostility to Jews and Jewish interests within the Movement. By 1970 almost everyone knew that the radical Left was antagonistic to Israel; and even though opposition to the State of Israel was in theory not necessarily a form of anti-Semitism, the 'anti-Zionism' of the radical Left was becoming increasingly difficult to distinguish from anti-Semitism in the more familiar sense.[27]

Because neo-conservatism is so fundamentally identified with the north-eastern culture, as a movement it can account for only a small fraction of the American intelligentsia, and, indeed, has played only a relatively minor part in the American Jewish intelligentsia's movement to the right. Many key figures among today's American Jewish conservative intelligentsia have no real connection with the neo-conservative movement. They range from *laissez-faire* economists like Milton Friedman to public figures like Henry Kissinger. Of particular interest are the many Zionist writers who publish in American journals like *Midstream* and *Judaism*. Although generally more concerned with religious affairs, and writing from a less secular and openly political standpoint than the *Commentary* school, in their ideological stance today they reflect a virtually identical perception of the world and the dangers facing contemporary Jewry. The case of *Midstream* – after *Commentary* probably the most respected and widely read Jewish journal of opinion – is fairly typical. A publication of the Theodor Herzl Foundation of New York, it generally reflected the left-liberal values typical of most American Jews until the past decade. Under the editorship of Joel Carmichael, the historian and biographer of Trotsky, today it attacks Soviet aggression and anti-semitism, American military weakness and left-wing dangers to Jewry such as 'reverse discrimination' and liberal Christian supporters of the PLO; rarely does it attack right-wing threats to Jewry. Behind such a stance, of course, is its recognition that Israel's existence is threatened by forces on the left rather than on the right.

To claim that American Jewry intelligentsia is now wholly on the right would be unjustifiable. As recently as the late 1960s, as we have seen, the great majority of American Jewish academics were on the left, in some cases on the extreme left. The American Jewish intelligentsia straddles the entire political spectrum. Yet for the first time in American Jewish history, it can no longer be assumed that Jews will inevitably position themselves on the left, as had been the case throughout this century.

It is surprising that the most clear evidence for a widespread movement of the Jewish intelligentsia to the right should emerge in the United States, where the 'left' is less socialistic, and more committed to bourgeois values and the capitalist system, than elsewhere. It is, perhaps, the lack of a highly distinctive socialist ideology which best explains this apparent paradox: 'liberals' become 'neo-conservatives' so easily because there is so little difference between the two. Yet elsewhere in the Western world, where a Marxist left does exist, much the same movement of the Jewish intelligentsia to the right has occurred. In Britain, the closest equivalent to *Commentary* is *Encounter*, the monthly, founded in the 1950s as a deliberate response to the Soviet menace. *Encounter* does not occupy the place in English intellectual life which *Commentary* does for so much of the American intelligentsia, and its alleged associations with the CIA have probably harmed its reputation. Yet it retains its significance and following. A glance at its editorial board, its contributors or its subject-matter reveals a considerable and very disproportionate Jewish input; editorially and ideologically, it is largely a

Europeanised version of *Commentary*, with English or European anti-Communists like Orwell, von Hayek, Koestler and Mieses figuring prominently. Naturally, its specifically Jewish content is much less than is the case with *Commentary* (which is published by the American Jewish Committee), but the similarities are far more apparent than the difference. Again this must be seen in its proper historical context: would an intellectual journal of British conservatism have had the smallest Jewish input fifty or even thirty years ago?[28]

Because of the hostility of the political left to Israel and to Jewish aspirations, and the open anti-semitism of the Soviet Union and its allies, it has become increasingly difficult for sensitive Jewish left-wingers to continue on the political left unless they, too, are hostile to Israel. Even in the mainstream, many left-liberal American Jews effectively parted company with the American New Left 'Movement' when it became sharply critical of Israel in the late 1960s.[29] Professor Max Beloff, a long-standing Liberal Party activist, recounts that

> In retrospect my main reasons for leaving the Liberal party seven years ago [i.e., 1971] was my growing conviction that it was being increasingly influenced by ideas that owed more to socialism that to traditional liberalism . . . But the occasion of the break was in the field of foreign affairs. The Young Liberals had taken up positions on some questions which put them well to the left of the Labour party itself; in particular they insisted upon giving a platform to members of the PLO, a self-confessed terrorist organisation.[30]

On the extreme left, the 'shock of recognition' of the realities of the situation are felt even more. Peggy Dennis, who is a Jew and a member of the American Communist Party since the mid-1920s, and widow of Eugene Dennis, General Secretary of the party in the 1940s, dated her disillusionment with the Communist Party from a visit to the Soviet Union in 1972:

> In casual exchanges of non-political subjects among these circles of upward-moving Party activists, I heard strange phrases, all the more disturbing because they were said so nonchalantly. Referring to a mutual acquaintance of those present, one says and the others agree, 'For a Jew, he's quite a good fellow.'

At another time I am told, 'You can appreciate how capable
he is, he holds such a responsible position even though he is
a Jew.'

Among these bright, political career-minded persons, none
can give me an answer to the question why blatantly anti-semitic
articles appear in popular Soviet magazines, in the form of
book reviews, when a *glavlit* – an official government censor
– has to approve everything that appears in print.[31]

A young American socialist academic, Roger S. Gottlieb, finds
it necessary to argue that

'Zionism is a form of racism and racial discrimination.' So
declared the United Nations in 1975. So many socialists believe.
In this essay I hope to show that such a belief is mistaken;
and that, besides being many other things, Zionism is also a
legitimate expression of Jewish national self-determination.
Establishing this claim will require an examination of left-wing
antisemitism . . .[32]

Significantly, Gottlieb explicitly terms much left-wing hostility
to Israel *anti-semitism* – that is, hostility to Jews as such – rather
than *anti-Zionism*, hostility to Israel:

A significant portion of the left has treated the Jews with a
variety of double standards, condescension, and outright denial
of experienced oppression. This left-wing antisemitism has many
features in common with other forms of oppression: blaming
the victim, expecting the oppressed to be 'better' than the
oppressor, equating the validity of the leadership of a liberation
struggle with that of the struggle itself; failing to see the relation
between a group's past experience and present practice.[33]

In Australia, when in 1974–5 the Australian Union of Students'
executive committed itself to a series of anti-Israeli motions a
leading younger socialist and writer on politics, Dennis Altmann,
who has described himself as 'both Jewish and anti-Zionist', stated
that even radical Jews 'felt very uncomfortable in this situation
and often felt impelled to question just how far a Jew can refuse
to identify with Israel'.[34]

The automatic association of Jews with left-liberalism has

declined in the same way that the Jewish association with social democracy has declined, although many Jewish intellectuals still perceive themselves as on the left; some are socialists or Marxists; a small but appreciable element are anti-Zionists, rejecting Israel's right to exist or calling for basic changes in its constitution.[35] But for large numbers of Jewish intellectuals and academics the hostility of the left to Jewish interests and aspirations has meant that it is no longer rationally possible for Jews to situate themselves there, amongst an ideology opposed to Jewish claims and lacking sympathy for Jewish history. The existence of substantial numbers of well-placed conservative Jewish intellectuals and academics, emerging from diverse backgrounds but agreed on the dangers to Jewry presented in today's world by the extreme left, is a phenomenon which will obviously take on a life of its own; future generations of younger Jewish intellectuals will gravitate to the conservative pole in much the same way as previous generations of Jews naturally moved towards the left. The implications of this for the Western world's intelligentsia and its mainstream ideological stance will be profound.

The Zionist Reaction

Both the rightward political movement of Western Jewry and the emergence of a conservative Jewish intelligentsia are the reactions of the Jewish people to external events. But the growth of the Zionist movement has also profoundly influenced the ideological perspective of contemporary Jewry in much the same way as the pressure of world events.

It is first necessary to say something about the meaning of Israel for Western Jewry, otherwise the implications of Zionism for Jewish ideological perceptions may be lost. Nathan Glazer has put the situation concisely: Israel is now the religion of American Jews[36] – and, of course, of all other diaspora Jewish communities. Israel's emotional significance to Western Jewry has grown to the point where the destruction of Israel would probably destroy Jewish religious and communal practice in the Western world. To hundreds of thousands of Western Jews Israel is the living embodiment of the Jewish religion. This situation, which is certainly without precedent in modern Jewish history, is also unparalleled among the world's major religions.

Until the Holocaust, and even after, most of Reform Jewry and much of Orthodox and Conservative Jewry was opposed to the Zionist ideal, seeing in its claims a threat to their secure existence in the Western democratic world. Zionism was a minority faction within Jewry and one which was, up to 1933, arguably declining in influence and importance from the promise of Herzl and the achievement of the Balfour Declaration in 1917. In 1930 Rabbi Stephen Wise, in the words of one recent historian,

> summed up the position of American Zionism in 1930 in pessimistic terms: There is a complete lull in things Zionistic [*sic*] in America . . . The Zionist Organisation is gone . . . My pessimism is not of the moment . . . It [i.e., the Zionist hope] will come to pass, I have no doubt, but only despite us of the Diaspora who have miserably trifled with a great situation.[37]

Throughout the late 1940s *anti*-Zionist organisations flourished within mainstream Jewry. Many of these were associated with Reform Jewry which in the United States continued to oppose the establishment of Israel with considerable force.[38] Indeed, the very aims of the Zionist movement – the establishment of an independent, wholly Jewish state (as opposed to a binational or federative state) in Palestine – were not finally established among mainstream American Jews until the Biltmore Program of 1942, when the reality of the Holocaust was becoming clear.[39] Even in the 1950s, after Israel was established as a state and long after the Nazi war criminals had been hanged, there remained some notable anti-Zionist mainstream voices, especially in America, and a much wider and more general feeling of apathy towards Israel in some sections of the diaspora.[40] While nearly all Western Jews took pride in its re-establishment, it is probably incorrect to see Israel as *central* to diaspora Jewish existence until recently: specifically, until the 1967 and 1973 wars in the Middle East.

As a result of the military victories of 1967, and of the peril which faced Israel in 1973, many previously apathetic Western Jews discovered that their concern for Israel's well-being was considerably greater than they had recognised,[41] while mainstream anti-Zionism all but disappeared. The American Council for Judaism, the best-known mainstream anti-Zionist organisation in the United States, lost most of its remaining membership and, as a matter of policy, in 1967 ceased to criticise Israel's internal affairs.[42] In 1961 *Commentary* magazine had interviewed a group of distinguished American Jewish writers and academics to ascertain their attitudes to Israel and other aspects of Jewish life. The same group was re-interviewed thirteen years later, in 1974, by the American journal *Judaism* to discover how their views had changed. Perhaps the major change was a greater fervour for Israel.

The period between 1967 and 1974 witnessed the re-emergence of anti-Zionism as a central issue and rallying-point of the extreme left. It is important to keep in mind that the appearance of contemporary left-wing anti-Zionism coincided with a great increase in the support given by Western Jewry for the state of Israel. In part as a result of this, the post-war period has also seen a considerable revival of interest in traditional Jewish forms of worship. The ultra-Orthodox Chassidic sects of the Western world have become relatively more important and popular; at the other extreme of religious Jewry, Reform and Liberal Judaism have progressively added more elements of Hebrew and traditional practice to their services. In the wake of the Holocaust and the creation of Israel there is a newfound sense of awe, reverence and respect for the burden of Jewish history, for the responsibilities of Jewish religious life and for the cultural and historical traditions of the Jewish people.

There has been a widespread turning away from a 'universalistic' interpretation of the spiritual message of Judaism to one emphasising its uniqueness.[43] Equally, there is a widespread feeling among Jewish theologians that the Holocaust and the creation of Israel require a radical reinterpretation of the meaning of Jewish existence in the contemporary world. The implications of this re-evaluation of Jewish thought are profoundly 'conservative' in the accepted sense of Western intellectual conservatism. Naturally, given the course of diaspora Jewish history until the establishment of Israel, Zionism absorbed many things, and drew upon many people, who were 'conservative'. In particular, Zionism was founded by 'socialists'; Israel's best-known institutions – the Kibbutzim and the state welfare system – are 'socialist'; for the first twenty-nine years of its independent existence Israel was governed by a Labour rather than a Conservative government. Yet, *in essence*, Israel was founded and has been maintained in order to enact for Jews, in their sovereign state, values of traditional conservatism. Professor Harold Fisch, said of Moses Hess, one of the founders of the Zionist movement in the nineteenth century,

> The images used by the more visionary Zionist thinkers should
> therefore be taken seriously. Let us consider . . . one of Hess's
> typical images. Throughout *Rome and Jerusalem* he uses the
> imagery of *growth* or *organism*: 'Humanity', he declares, 'is
> a living organism of which races and peoples are the members'
> . . . The Jewish people is part of the larger organic unity of
> mankind, but it is also an organism in its own right with its
> own principle of growth and vitality. In fact if we view Israel
> in these terms, Israel's spiritual endowment, remarkable though
> it is, seems to be part of its natural condition, part, almost,
> of its biological character.[44]

Fisch goes on to note that

> The metaphors of organism which we noted as pervasive in
> Moses Hess also pervades the writings of many other Zionist
> thinkers down to the time of the creation of the Jewish state.
> It is, in fact, a fundamental metaphor . . . The image suggests
> vitality and also liberation: the Jewish people, long artificially
> uprooted from its natural environment, will now resume the
> life granted to all natural, healthy organisms.[45]

Even more explicitly, Fisch notes that the Zionist ideal 'implies
a reaction to a bourgeois, urban culture and an implicit affirmation
of the value of living by what Wordsworth called 'natural
sympathy': the life of the field and farm is held up in preference
to that of the market-place and the house of study'.[46] The idea
of society as an 'organism' is, of course, basic to the ideology
of European conservatism – perhaps the most basic of all its tenets.
The most important consequence of this interpretation is that
diaspora Zionists, whatever their own ideological positions believe
that the tenets of European conservatism are justified in the Jewish
case. Diaspora Zionists must surely believe this, even if they regard
somebody else's conservatism – French or German or American
conservatism – as dangerous and undesirable. This has several
important consequences. It helps to explain, for example, the
apparent contradiction frequently noted among American Jewish
left-liberals, who enthusiastically support American military
assistance for Israel but are bitterly hostile (or have been in the

past, as in the case of Vietnam) to American military expenditure elsewhere. In the words of Rosenberg and Howe:

> the paradox that must be recognised is that in so far as Israel functions – must function – as a state dealing with other States, its impact upon American Jews is – perhaps must be – conservative . . . Some American Jews now ask not, 'Is it good for the Jews?' but, 'Is it good for Israel?' Such people worried about Nixon's abandonment of Taiwan, not because they admired Chiang Kai-Shek but because they feared it might presage abandonment of Israel – perhaps as part of an overall retreat to 'isolationism' . . .
>
> It is betraying no secrets to report that in 1972 intimations came from at least some Israeli officials [to vote for Nixon]. How many Jews . . . responded to such intimations we cannot say; indeed, we have the impression that some Jews acted in accord with this position *without needing to be told* that it was held by influential Israelis.[47]

More importantly, it has the effect of justifying domestic conservatism in countries where diaspora Jews live in numbers. It does this both for utilitarian reasons – Israel's existence is dependent upon the political success of Western conservatives – and for ideological reasons: Jews can begin to symphathise with conservative thinking in countries where they live. Unless Western conservatives are hostile to Jews or to Israel such conservatives and Jews see themselves as allies rather than enemies.

Such a change in the ideological stance of Western Jewry is important and fundamental in its own right, but it is merely ancillary to, and perhaps less important than, another change. In the post-war world, Western Jews can (perhaps for the first time) genuinely advocate and play a role in political conservatism *within the countries* where they live, without disassociating themselves from Jewry and without seeming anomalous to these countries. The reason for this change is clear: the nature of political conservatism and of the establishment right has changed throughout the Western world (see Chapters 2 and 3). While emphasising most of the values of traditional European conservatism, contemporary Western conservatism has shed its pre-modern elements, and, in particular, its anti-semitism. It basis lies much more firmly than before 1945 in the rational values inherent in capitalism. Its view of the Western world and its history includes, rather than excludes, the Jews and Jewish history as a legitimate part of Western history.

Because of these *two* simultaneous changes in Western conservatism – the establishment of Zionism as the Jewish conservatism and the alteration in the nature of Western establishment conservatism – Jews can be 'at home' on the political right for the first time in modern history. There is no reason to believe that this situation, still relatively new, will not continue indefinitely.

Notes

1. This must be qualified in a number of ways. See especially below concerning the Jewish intelligentsia.
2. Geoffrey Alderman, 'Not Quite British: The Political Attitudes of Anglo-Jewry', *British Sociology Yearbook*, vol. 2 (London, 1975), p. 205.
3. Ibid.
4. *The Times*, 9 May 1980. See Geoffrey Alderman, *The Jewish Vote in Great Britain Since 1945* (University of Strathclyde, 1980).
5. But see, e.g., the letters of protest from prominent British Zionists to *The Times* in June-July 1980, shortly after the EEC's new policy on the Middle East was announced.
6. These figures are taken from an unpublished study by Chanan Reich of Monash University. On Australian Jewish voting behaviour, see also several of the essays in Peter Y. Medding, *Jews in Australian Society* (Melbourne, 1973).
7. On this subject, see William Ray Heitzmann, *American Jewish Voting Behaviour: A History and Analysis* (San Francisco, 1975).
8. Ibid., p. 79.
9. See Ibid., pp. 56–7 and 96. Stevenson is estimated to have received 74% of the national Jewish vote in 1952 (Ibid., p. 56). Other estimates are somewhat lower, in the range of 60% to 64%. See Mark R. Levy and Michael S. Kramer, *The Ethnic Factor* (New York, 1972), p. 103.
10. Most surveys of the 1980 election result put the Jewish vote as splitting about 42% for Carter, 37% for Reagan and 12% for Anderson. Some put Reagan's vote slightly higher. See *The New York Times*, 5–9 November 1980; *The Jewish Press*, 14–20 November 1980. This matter is discussed more fully in Chapter 5.
11. Levy and Kramer, *The Ethnic Factor*, p. 110.
12. Ibid., p. 110.
13. Heitzmann, *American Jewish Voting Behaviour*, p. 79. By 'return' to the GOP Heitzman has in mind the predominant Republican loyalties of American Jews prior to the New Deal.
14. Ibid., pp. 79–84.
15. Ibid., p. 84.
16. We shall discuss the American situation (as well as that in Britain and in Australia) in more detail in Chapter 5.
17. Alfred Kazin, *Starting Out in the Thirties* (Boston, 1965), p. 4.
18. Seymour Martin Lipset and Everett C. Ladd, Jr, 'Jewish Academics in the United States: Their Achievements, Culture and Politics', *American Jewish*

Yearbook 1971, table 21, p. 114.

19. Ibid., table 23, p. 115. Only 2.1% of Jewish faculty members voted for Barry Goldwater in 1964 (ibid., table 24).

20. Peter Steinfels, *The Neoconservatives* (New York, 1979), p. 15.

21. On this subject see also Jeffrey Hart, 'New Directions: Catholics and Jews', *National Review*, 28 Apr. 1978.

22. Norman Podhoretz, *Breaking ranks* (New York, 1979), p. 155.

23. Steinfels, *The Neoconservatives*, p. 21.

24. On the evolution of the movement, see ibid., Ch. 2.

25. For a frank discussion of this subject, see Podhoretz's earlier book, *Making It* (New York, 1969).

26. Bernard Rosenberg and Irving Howe, 'Are American Jews Turning Toward the Right?', in Lewis A. Coser and Irving Howe (eds.), *The New Conservatives: A Critique from the Left* (New York, 1977), p. 66.

27. Podhoretz, *Breaking Ranks*, p. 329.

28. In Australia, a very similar role is played by *Quadrant*, also a distinguished conservative (and right-wing social democratic) monthly specialising in culture, literature and politics. Published by the Australian Association for Culture Freedom, and with a member of the Packer publishing family as its chairman, it, too, has a very disproportionate Jewish input, especially given the small number of Jews in Australia.

29. Podhoretz, *Breaking Ranks*, pp. 329–32.

30. Max Beloff, 'Facing the World', in Patrick Cormack (ed.), *Right Turn* (London, 1978), p. 27.

31. Peggy Dennis, *The Autobiography of an American Communist. A Personal View of a Political Life 1925–1975* (Berkeley, California, 1977), p. 283. Mrs Dennis resigned from the Communist Party in June 1976.

32. Roger S. Gottlieb, 'The Dialectics of National Identity: Left-Wing Antisemitism and the Arab-Israeli Conflict', *Socialist Review*, vol. 47 (Sept.–Oct. 1979), p. 19.

33. Ibid., p. 21.

34. Dennis Altman, 'A Secular Democratic Palestine: A New Litmus Test for the Left', *Politics*, vol. x (1975), p. 174.

35. See, e.g., the essay in Uri Davis, Andrew Mack, Nira Yuval-Davis (eds.), *Israel and the Palestinians* (London, 1975).

36. Cited in Podhoretz, *Breaking Ranks*, p. 335.

37. Cited in Naomi W. Cohen, *American Jews and the Zionist Idea* (New York, 1975), p. 35.

38. There is a pressing need for a detailed history of Western (non-Marxist) Jewish anti-Zionism. On this subject, see Moishe Menuhin, *The Decadence of Judaism in our Time* (Beirut, 1969).

39. See Cohen, *American Jews*, pp. 51–69.

40. See Menuhin, *The Decadence of Judaism*. There was also a notable tradition of ultra-Orthodox opposition to Israel's existence. Some sects among Chassidic Jewry regarded the establishment of Israel as a sacrilegious attempt to usurp the work of the future Messiah.

41. Such a sentiment did *not* exist (or was not as widespread) during the 1956 war.

42. See Menuhin, *The Decadence of Judaism*.

43. See, e.g., Richard G. Hirsch, 'Jewish Peoplehood. Implications For Reform Judaism', *Forum*, vol. 37, Spring 1980.

44. Harold Fisch, *The Zionist Revolution. A New Perspective* (London, 1978), pp. 51–2.

45. Ibid., p. 55.

46. Ibid.

47. Rosenberg and Howe, 'Are American Jews Turning Towards the Right?', pp. 77–8 (their italics).

5 THE WESTERN DEMOCRACIES: THE UNITED STATES, BRITAIN AND AUSTRALIA

This chapter extends the discussion of previous chapters by a closer analysis of three Western democracies where the socio-economic and political evolution of the Jews has been fairly similar, as have been the forces antagonistic to them, and brings our analysis up to date.

The United States

The most striking feature of American Jewry is its comparatively large size: it is twice as large as the entire population of Israel, three times as large as the official Jewish population of the Soviet Union and more than eight times as large as France's Jewish community. The size of the American Jewish community – generally estimated at about six million[1] – endows it with some features unique to any diaspora community. Only in the United States is the 'Jewish vote' a significant electoral factor to which all presidential candidates routinely pay court; perhaps only in the United States does such a wealth of Jewish institutions, organisations and community leaders exist in large numbers. Nevertheless, the importance of the Jewish vote and even of Jewish numbers should not be exaggerated. Jews are a very small minority in the United States except in a handful of urban conurbations. Of the fifteen most popular American conurbations (as defined by the United States Census Bureau), only in four do Jews number as much as five per cent of the population – in Greater New York (21.0 per cent), Nassau-Suffolk, Long Island (22.6 per cent), Philadelphia (7.3 per cent) and Los Angeles (6.5 per cent). Jews are, moreover, relatively more numerous in the decaying and problem-ridden older cities of the north-east than in the newer and more dynamic 'Sunbelt' centres. In cities like Atlanta (where Jews number 21,000 out of 1.8 million), New Orleans (only 10,600 of 1.1 million) or San Diego (21,000 of 1.6 million), the Jewish presence is largely unfelt. Although Jews may be widely perceived as a key group at election time, their potential for influence by weight of numbers alone is very limited. What is true of America's largest urban areas, where Jews are more numerous than in non-metropolitan areas, is true of the whole United States. It is probably fair to say that most commentators on the extent of Jewish political influence in America have exaggerated its actual importance. American Jewish numbers, moreover, will not grow and in all likelihood will inevitably shrink – absolutely as well as relatively – without large-scale immigration or a substantial rise in the Jewish birth rate.[2]

Given these very real and increasing limitations on Jewish influence in the United States, how can one account for the undoubted success of American Jewry in securing America's deep and perhaps growing commitment to the continuing secure existence of the State of Israel, a commitment unbroken for nearly 35 years and unique in the world? There would seem to be several main reasons. American Jewish lobbying efforts – a clear example of the magnified power of the large elite – are unquestionably very good, extremely sophisticated and undertaken by men and women of undoubted dedication and considerable skill. More generally, the over-representation of Jews in the American large and small elites, so notable a feature of post-war society, has ensured a considerable Jewish over-representation at the elite level. Although these are important factors, they are insufficient to explain fully the degree of American commitment to Israel's existence.

This favourable attitude towards Israel is basically due to the general philo-semitism which is now so pervasive in the United States that, when it draws attention to itself, it often appears to be a kind of disguised anti-semitism. Richard Reeves, a non-Jewish journalist, recalled talking to 'an AFL–CIO official', an Alabama delegate at the 1974 'Midterm Convention' of the Democratic Party. Asked whether he believed his people would support American military action to save Israel,

'Hell no!' he answered. 'I guess we sympathise with Israel – *we kind of grew up that way*. But nobody talks about it down here'. [Author's italics.][3]

By far the most interesting part of this statement is that in italics. That working-class Alabamans have 'grown up' sympathising with Israel is certainly an attitude not generally associated with the

Deep South.

Important statistical evidence concerning the pervasiveness of philo-semitism in the United States has been documented by William Schneider in a recent report to the American Jewish Committe.[4] Schneider's research demonstrated that in contemporary America 'positive stereotypes expressing admiration for Jews are accepted by the public by a three-to-one margin', 'Jews tend to overestimate the amount of anti-Semitism in the non-Jewish population', that 'support for Israel increased substantially in the American public after the 1967 War' and that 'Americans strongly condemn the PLO'.[5] Schneider found that 'there is evidence of anti-Semitic backlash from an unanticipated direction, namely the extreme left', which included '(1) overt anti-Semitism and anti-Zionism among black militants; (2) criticism of Israel and of US military support for Israel from the radical left' and 'although both blacks and whites became more sympathic to Israel between 1964 and 1974, the difference between blacks and whites increased noticeably. The data also show southerners becoming increasingly more pro-Israel than northerners in 1974 . . .'[6] According to Schneider, 'the [American] public has shown no strong tendency to blame Jews, Israel, or Zionists for our economic difficulties or for the energy crisis, especially in comparison with business and government, which are widely blamed for these problems'.

Friendliness towards Israel showed little correlation with over-anti-semitism: surprisingly, according to a Harris Poll taken in 1974 and reported in Schneider's study, among those who scored 'very high' on a scale of anti-semitism, 39 per cent regarded themselves as sympathetic to Israel and only 18 per cent to the Arabs.[7]

To understand why Jewish influence in the United States is so strong and why Americans demonstrate so little anti-semitism and so great a commitment to Israel's welfare it is necessary to look further at the exceptional and unique features of the American political structures. As mentioned earlier, alone among the world's democratic nations, America has no socialist party. Although some commentators have seen an 'underground' tradition of tacitly socialist goals among the liberal wing of the Democratic Party,[8] the Democratic Party is not a socialist party and none of its prominent leaders, even its advocates of the advanced welfare state like Edward Kennedy and the late Hubert Humphrey, ever paid lip-service to the eventual goal of socialism. Instead, at least since the New Deal, American liberalism has had as its principal aims the overall growth of the American economy and the bringing into the prosperous mainstream of groups – generally ethnic groups rather than social classes – previously excluded from America's bounty. It has never, even theoretically, advocated socialism. From the New Deal until the 1970s American Jews perceived themselves as among the main beneficiaries of the Democratic Party's goals, and, at least until the 1976 presidential election, normally delivered Democratic majorities of four to one or more. Even Jews whose economic status should have made them support the Republican Party long continued to vote Democratic in percentages markedly higher than other white Americans of similar status.

Because the Democratic Party is not a socialist party – and, too, because of the substantial Jewish presence within the Democratic Party – it possesses no distinct anti-Zionist or pro-Palestinian sector. In perhaps no other left-of-centre party in the Western world is this true. American Jews have not perceived an anti-Zionist threat from within the Democratic Party because none has existed. Instead, Democratic politicians have continued to outbid one another, particularly during presidential campaigns, in promising military and economic aid for Israel, and declaring their deep concerns for Israel's secure existence. There is no evidence that this situation has changed in the recent past, despite the energy crisis and the unpopularity of some Israeli policies.

There is one notable exception to this generalisation. American blacks have demonstrated increasing anti-Israeli, pro-Arab and, occasionally, anti-semitic sentiments. These have, moreover, perceptibly increased in recent years while overt anti-semitism among American whites has continued to decline since 1945. A detailed Harris Survey of 'Attitudes Toward Racial and Religious Minorities and Toward Women', made in October 1978 showed a marked increase in black anti-semitism since the 1974 Schneider survey reported above, and had reached levels notably more anti-semitic than among white gentiles.[9] Negative stereotypes about the Jews were more pervasive still among a sample of fifty-three 'national black leaders' interviewed by Harris, and had reached what this memorandum described as 'shockingly high' levels. 'This is not the anti-Semitism of ignorance or religious bigotry; it is the anti-Semitism of political conflict and confrontation', the memorandum continued.[10] These results are given in Table 5.1.[11]

Table 5.1: Negative Stereotypes About Jews:'Agree' (%)

	Non-Jewish whites		Blacks		Black leaders
1974	1974	1978	1974	1978	1978
(1) When it comes to choosing between people and money, Jews will choose money	32	32	48	56	81
(2) Jews are more loyal to Israel than to America	33	28	34	37	50
(3) Jews are irritating because they are too aggressive	32	27	25	29	65
(4) Most of the slumland lords are Jewish	20	17	37	41	67

The growing degree of anti-semitism and anti-Zionism among blacks, especially among its vocal leadership, has been evident to American Jews for some time. A recent article in *Commentary* termed *The New Amsterdam News* – the 'voice of Harlem' and perhaps the leading black newspaper in America – anti-semitic in its reporting and editorials.[12] In mid-1979 came two extremely disturbing events: the resignation of America's UN Ambassador, Andrew Young, following his secret meeting with a PLO official, and the visit of the Reverend Jesse Jackson, the prominent black spokesman, to the Middle East, where he met and embraced Yassir Arafat. That American blacks, the most liberal and disadvantaged group in America, should apparently be the first major American group to turn against Israel should surprise no-one who properly understands today's sources of anti-semitism and philo-semitism.[13] The political significance of this flows from the black's potentially large voting block – 11 per cent of the American population – its usually near-solid Democratic majorities and the increasing presence of blacks in positions of power at the national and local levels, almost always as Democrats. It is far from easy to see why the hostility of blacks towards the Jews and their aspirations should be so discernible, or why this should have increased between 1974 and 1978. Urban blacks often come into direct personal contact with Jews as retailers and landlords, but this has long been true and should not be exaggerated. It is likely that many blacks – especially the young, better-educated black leadership element – perceive themselves as in some real sense allied to the

Third World anti-Western movement, of which militant Islam and the PLO are major parts.

Nevertheless, the position of the Democratic Party and its leaders towards the Middle East has not altered in a fundamental way; under Democratic administrations the United States has remained more committed to the survival of Israel than any other country. Perhaps the main reason for this is the continuing allegiance of the Democratic Party to capitalism and to the Western alliance, despite the problems of the 1960s and 1970s. This has meant that the 'left' party in America has viewed the Jews and Israel in the same philo-semitic light as the establishment right, and has contained virtually no voices inimical to Zionism and the State of Israel. For this reason, the American Senate, where Democrats were the majority party, can produce votes of 80–0 condemning the 1975 United Nations General Assembly vote equating Zionism with racism, or 79–11 (in May 1979), voting billions of dollars for Israel and Egypt in support of their recently-concluded peace treaty.

Because of the absence of a political anti-Zionism in America, American Jews have until recently continued to adhere to that variant of left–liberalism so typically American with its tradition of near-anarchism and its emphasis on moralism, individual rights, 'civil liberties' and self-realisation. There is little specifically Jewish, but much that is mainstream American, about this tradition, whose progenitors were America's political and cultural founding fathers: Jefferson and Thoreau, Jackson, Whitman and Mark Twain. The areas where Jews have most prominently come into conflict with the American 'mainstream' are the efficacy of violence, racism and anti-socialism.

It is, then, not surprising that Jews have been so prominently and disproportionately involved in American left–liberal movements. The very absence of an anti-Zionist left has allowed American Jews the self-indulgence of a continuing attack upon established authority, American 'militarism', *laissez-faire* capitalism and even the basic cultural assumptions of Western civilisations, of which the Jewish tradition was, ironically, the cornerstone. This might help to explain some of the basic paradoxes of the Jewish situation in post-war America: for example, the support given by the American Civil Liberties Union (whose membership is frequently stated to be two-thirds Jewish) to the proposed march by members of the American Nazi Party in Skokie,

Illinois – a town inhabited by large numbers of Jewish Holocaust survivors.[14] Another is the support given by left-wing Jews to 'reverse discrimination' measures which, however, admirable their goal of securing greater opportunities for minorities, entail deliberate discrimination against those classified as belonging to the majority. Despite the long history of anti-semitism, Jews have always been categorised by the American government as members of the majority, rather than as a minority group standing to benefit from these schemes.[15] Similarly, the left–liberalism of America's television writers and producers – about half of whom are Jewish – has been described by one writer who knows the industry well:[16]

> In Hollywood, almost nothing is explained except on the basis of conspiracies and cabals. It is here, for example, that serious intelligent people believe that the world is run by a consortium of former Nazis and executives of multinational corporations . . . All [television producers and writers interviewed by the author] thought themselves as politically 'progressive', a term that I rarely heard elsewhere but that was quite popular among those I interviewed and knew as colleagues.[17]

Despite their own wordly success, the attitude of such men towards capitalism, according to Stein, could hardly be more critical:

> one of the clearest messages of television is that businessmen are bad, evil people, and that big businessmen are the worst of all! This concept is shared by a distinct majority of the writers and producers I spoke with . . . In TV comedies, businessmen play several different roles, all highly unflattering. Often they are con men . . . Sometimes they simply appear as pompous fools.[18]

The customary depiction of the military – 'military men . . . are at best [portrayed] as part of a bureaucratic background noise that sets off the heroes' humanity. At worst, they are identical to Nazis . . .', small towns ('. . . wicked, dangerous places . . .'), the police and many other institutions are of a piece, according to Stein.[19]

There is considerable evidence that the familiar left-liberal stance of most American Jews is undergoing a significant shift, despite the absence of a mainstream left-wing anti-Zionism. It is noteworthy that this change has also occurred in the dangers perceived by America's best-informed Jewish defence organisations, which were formerly orientated to an almost automatic left–liberalism similar to that of the New Deal. In 1964 Arnold Forster and Benjamin R. Epstein of the Anti-Defamation League of the B'nai Brith, published a work entitled *Danger on the Right* which examined – exclusively – the dangers to democracy presented by such right-wing extremist groups as the John Birch Society and the Christian Anti-Communist Crusade. The extreme left was ignored.[20] It is likely that this was the last time that a mainstream Jewish defence organisation could attack the extreme right while ignoring the extreme left. Ten years later the same authors produced a second work, *The New Anti-Semitism*, which devoted far more space to attacking left-wing anti-Zionism, especially that found on the American left and among black extremists, than the remaining anti-semites of the far right.

There are several reasons why this perceptible shift should have taken place, even in a country without a significant element of left-wing anti-Zionism. First, the left–liberalism of most American Jews has long been highly anomalous in that their heavy Democratic majorities did not accord with their largely prosperous socio-economic circumstances. Even in the American economic context, the relatively heavier taxation and welfare state measures typically proferred by liberal Democrats no longer served the interests of a successful and affluent community. Second, the weakening of America's economic strength at home, and of its military prowess abroad since the mid-1960s – 'shown by its frustrated inability to release the embassy hostages held by Iran's student militants from 1979 to 1981 – have been perceived as intolerable by many American Jews, just as they have by many other American groups.[21] Jews thus shared in a very general shift to a more conservative stance throughout America. Two other elements, however, are much more specific to the Jewish situation. The special tensions which exist between urban Jews and blacks have already been mentioned. There seems little doubt that Jewish fears of black crime and rioting, of 'reverse discrimination' programmes designed to aid blacks at the expense of whites (including Jews) and of growing black political power, especially at the local level, lies at the root of much of American Jewry's disenchantment with left-liberalism. This first became evident during the 1960s, when working- and lower-middle class Jews voted against such measures as the proposed New York City Police Review Board (which was perceived as 'anti-police') and when Jews began to draw away from their previously close association with the movement for black civil rights; a Jewish constituency, conservative on 'social issues' like other white urban ethnic groups, became evident.[22] The growth of 'affirmative action' and 'reverse discrimination' programmes during the 1970s and the further deterioration of race relations in many American cities were widely seen by Jews as a deliberate attempt by black leaders to reduce Jewish power in urban America. According to Marvin Weitz,

> If we continue to support affirmative action programs, we only encourage self-destruction. A truly frightening possibility of this kind was raised not long ago in the meeting between the mayor of a large urban area and a group of black community leaders. The implications of this confrontation were so explosive that news of it was withheld from the media; few were made aware of what passed between the mayor and the black spokesmen. In his own home the mayor was told by the black group that they would not tolerate the positions of power held by Jews in the city government and community economy. They demanded that immediate steps be taken by the mayor to reshape in favour of blacks what they considered to be the disproportionate Jewish power structure. If the mayor would not voluntarily acquiesce in this, they said, the black community would force the situation with threats, coercion, and violence.[23]

By the late 1970s survey data had appeared which indicated that Jews were more anti-black than non-Jewish whites, certainly a significant reversal of attitudes from only ten years before. According to the 1978 Harris Survey discussed above, Jews were less likely to state that they wanted their children to go to school with blacks (21 per cent of Jews, 32 per cent of non-Jewish whites), and more likely to say that they did not want their children to go to school with blacks (21 per cent of Jews, 14 per cent of non-Jewish whites), less likely to favour residential integration than non-Jewish whites (46 per cent versus 39 per cent), less likely to favour 'full racial integration' than non-Jewish whites (25 per cent versus 35 per cent).[24] The Harris Survey blandly observed, 'It is fair to conclude that as a group, Jews are not today in the vanguard of non-black people pressing for integration and progress for blacks'.[25] Conversely, as we have seen, 'blacks tend to be more anti-Jewish than any other people'.[26]

The second of the specifically Jewish concerns which has moved American Jewry to the right is, of course, concern for Israel. To the American Jewish community, Israel is central. This is the case amongst all diaspora Jewish communities but is especially true of American Jewry as the Western world's largest, wealthiest and most important community, and that containing the greatest diversity of attitudes in other spheres. In the words of Edward S. Shapiro,

> For the American Jew the impact of Israel is all-pervasive, with Israel partially filling the vacuum created by the diminishing importance of traditional religions, practices and beliefs. Israel has become *the* focal point in the search for Jewish identity, in combatting anti-Semitism, and in asserting Jewish patriotism. Support for Israel brings together the religious and non-religious Jew, the former seeing Israel as a fulfilment of biblical prophecy, the latter finding Israel as a means of expressing Jewish identity or a possible paradigm for a contemporary state.[27]

During the past fifteen years not merely has American Jewry's depth of feeling for Israel markedly increased but its expectations for the normal degree of American governmental support for Israel have grown. American Jewry has become far more, rather than less successful, in winning presidential and Congressional approval for Israel's security; this reflects a greater general support for Israel throughout the American community, but it is also indicative of increasing success by the Jewish community. Because expectations have been so high, any disappointments, even minor ones, are viewed with great disquiet, especially at a time when much of the rest of the Western world seems to be adopting distinctly pro-Arab leanings. Despite his diplomatic *coup* at Camp David, President Carter alienated a large segment of American Jewry by a number of his actions, particularly at the United Nations. There were also widespread Jewish fears of what a second-term Carter administration, in no fear of Jewish wrath at election time, would do. Nevertheless, no observer can fairly claim that the Carter administration was anti-Israel or pro-Arab; it was certainly not seen in these terms in Israel itself. But Ronald Reagan's sweeping victory in the presidential election of November 1980 was accomplished with possibly the largest swing of Jewish electoral loyalties since Roosevelt's win in 1932.

Since 1932, Jewish support for the Republican Party has always been extremely slim; in most elections up to 1976 the Republican presidential candidate secured only 20–25 per cent of the Jewish vote. It is difficult to see any objective reason why this should have been so, apart from a very general mistrust of any conservative political movement which has so marked American Jewry in modern times. Dwight Eisenhower was certainly friendly towards Israel and its interests, while Richard Nixon and Gerald Ford were probably more supportive of Israel than any other American presidents. Republican congressmen support Israel as regularly as Democratic congressmen, and the Republican Party contains no anti-semitic or anti-Zionist voices. At the local level, some liberal Republicans, most notably Nelson Rockefeller and Jacob Javits (who is Jewish) in New York, enjoyed widespread Jewish support, but at most times in modern America Jews have been exceedingly unenthusiastic about Republican candidates. Despite his Jewish grandparents, Barry Goldwater secured only about ten per cent of the Jewish vote in 1964, a figure even lower than usual.

Although most initial surveys indicate that Carter won somewhat more Jewish support than Reagan (42 per cent compared with 37 per cent), Carter's percentage of the Jewish vote was the lowest and Reagan's the highest of any candidate of their respective parties since 1932.[28] Some surveys indeed believe that Reagan and Carter split the Jewish vote evenly, at 45 per cent. each.[29] Reagan did especially well in Orthodox Jewish areas. According to the Orthodox, pro-Zionist New York weekly *The Jewish News*, which enthusiastically endorsed Reagan and claimed credit for Reagan's majority in New York State,[30] 'every Orthodox Jewish community [in New York] gave Reagan over a two-to-one plurality. This also held true in other [Orthodox] areas . . . Such as [in] Miami, Chicago, and California'.[31] In the Borough Park and Flatbush, areas in Brooklyn containing perhaps the greatest concentration of Orthodox Jews in America and previously heavily Democratic, Reagan received 15,779 votes and Carter only 8,773. Reagan also scored well in such non-Orthorox, heavily Jewish and traditionally Democratic districts as Sheepshead Bay and Flatlands in Brooklyn, Stuyvesant Town–Murray Hill in Manhattan and Douglaston–Bayside in Queens. Throughout New York state,

Reagan polled 42 per cent to Carter's 37 per cent and Anderson's ten per cent. According to ABC–TV's survey of voters leaving voting booths, Reagan secured 70 per cent of the Jewish vote in California, 56 per cent in Michigan and 60 per cent in the Miami area.[32] The shift of over one-third of the votes of Jewish Democrats to the Republican candidate in only four years represented the greatest erosion of support for Carter among any identifiable American group.

Although Carter was widely perceived by Jews as anti-Israel, there was much in Reagan's entourage to give cause for disquiet to supporters of Israel, most notably the Christian Fundamentalism of many of his prominent supporters and the Arab business and oil connections of John Connolly and George Schultze. Yet Reagan's own personal commitment to Israel was unquestioned. Reagan saw Israel, as many conservatives do, as a pro-American security asset for the West in the troubled Middle East. Beyond this, there was a widely held belief among Jews that in toughening America's military capability and more actively combatting Soviet aggression, Reagan would automatically help Israel. 'A strong defense posture for the United States also is important for Israel', noted George Klein, a leading Jewish campaigner for Reagan.[33] There was an expectation that the growth of the American government bureaucracy would be halted and reverse discrimination measures eliminated.[34] There was, in other words, much tacit belief that the policies of increased American military strength and defence of the Western world abroad, and a decrease in federal government influence and power at home, would be in the interests of American and world Jewry in their present circumstances, even if Jews had relatively less direct impact or influence with the Republican administration than with the previous Democratic one, and even, indeed, if the new administration contained its share of right-wing figures who appeared at best remote from Jewish concerns and at worst at least superficially antagonistic to them. This perception evidently influenced large numbers of Jewish voters in 1980.

It is far too early to speculate whether a large portion of American Jewry would continue to identify with the Republican rather than the Democratic Party, although, according to a post-election press release of Jewish Reagan activists, 'Many political experts have determined that the Jewish voter now represents a swing constituency . . . [the] Jewish community is now available to Republican candidates who make a determined effort to address the issues of concern to them'.[35] The behaviour of the Republican-dominated Senate, where several enthusiastically pro-Israeli Democrats were replaced by untested Republicans, is a particular matter of concern.[36] While voting for Reagan in record numbers, New York Jewish voters also gave a large majority of their votes to the liberal Democratic senatorial candidate, Elizabeth Holtzman, and probably favoured other Democrats at the state level.[37]

Nevertheless, it may well be that American Jews are at last moving – as elsewhere in the West – to their 'natural' political home. This may help to end the political paradox of American Jewry – unexampled wealth, influence, freedom and mobility productive not of conservatism but (within the American context) of disproportionate left–liberalism. At its base, the lingering hatred for any right-wing movements occasioned by memories of czardom and Nazism may go far to understanding this. Most sociologists have interpreted the behaviour as the perceptible inconsistency between their wealth and their status: what Nathanial Weyl has termed the phenomenon of the 'despised elite'.[38] Such an inconsistency has often been productive of a radical political outlook: a similar historical example may be found in the American progressive movement of 1890–1917, whose 'status anxieties' have been identified by the historian Richard Hofstadter as engendering their ideology.[39]

In the case of American Jews this inconsistency has created a profound, deep-seated and long-standing sense of alienation from the traditional 'American way of life' which has led American Jews to place themselves largely on the extreme left of the American mainstream, often in a way which would seem to work directly against their interests. In Weyl's words,

> A powerful force driving Jews toward radicalism is a sense of alienation from American society. This is not specifically a Jewish problem, but . . . American Jews seem to be more susceptible to the disease of alienation than American Gentiles . . . One . . . factor would seem to be self-imposed Jewish apartheid after the religious reason for it has disappeared. The disintegration of religious faith often causes a frantic search for substitute religious faiths. To the extent that the latter expresses alienation and the desire to huddle in a psychic ghetto,

they often espouse values at variance with those of the majority and coalesce in a congregation or political party with the characteristics of a *despised elite*.[40]

There is, of course, sufficient truth in the dichotomy between American Jewish wealth and status to make it a dismaying reality for many Jews. There remains a continuing perception, among both Jews and gentiles, that Jews are not yet fully at ease in America. One recent textbook, for instance, presented a detailed examination of several 'representative American minorities' – blacks, Mexican–Americans and Jews – although the socio-economic statistics of American Jewry presented by the author clearly point to the elite status of Jews.[41] The author notes that

Popular stereotypes to the contrary, American Jews are not concentrated in positions of control in the American economy . . . According to Carey McWilliams, 'Generally speaking, the businesses in which Jews are concentrated are those in which a large risk-factor is involved; businesses peripheral to the economy; business originally regarded as unimportant; new industries and businesses; and businesses which have traditionally carried a certain element of social stigma . . .' In sum, American Jews have enjoyed considerable class success without accruing comparable economic power.[42]

We have previously argued that the relative lack of Jewish success in American corporate capitalism is more than compensated, given the nature of power in capitalist societies, by their over-representation in other ways in the large and small American elites. Yet in all likelihood this lack of corporate success is seen by many American Jews as indicating their virtual exclusion from the real American power structure, and thus as an indictment of American society. Whatever the reasons for the deep sense of alienation, it must finally be said that it has long existed and is a major feature of Jewish life in the United States.

It is possible, however, to begin, at least in a tentative way, to chart those groups within American Jewry who are most likely to adopt an increasingly right-wing stance in the American sense of 'right-wing'. The small though influential group of Jewish conservative intellectuals will certainly continue to grow. The increasing support given by Jewish (and other) academics and

authors to American conservatism is indicated by the petition by
'members of the intellectual, academic and professional
communities of the United States' in support of Reagan's candidacy
which appeared in the *New York Times* on 2 November 1980.
Claiming that 'it was not until the Soviet invasion of Afghanistan
that Carter, in his own words, began to understand the nature
and objectives of Soviet policy. The same misjudgment is reflected
in his astounding comparison of the American civil rights
movement to Palestinian Arab terrorism. A Reagan administration
would . . . build a foreign policy on close relationships with
dependable allies such as Israel, Japan, and the NATO countries',
it was signed by such well-known Jews as the pianist David Bar-
Illan, authors Midge Decter, Lucy Davidowicz and Dorothy
Rabinowitz, and academics Michael Katz and Eugene Rostow.[43]
Much more numerous are three groups within American Jewry
who have been increasingly resistant to left–liberalism and
conservative in their political outlook: Jewish businessmen,
especially those running small businesses, Orthodox Jews,
especially those ultra-Orthodox Jews living in self-contained
Orthodox communities, and working- and lower-middle-class Jews
resident at the edge of the black ghettoes and other decaying
neighbourhoods. The case of America's Orthodox Jews is
particularly interesting. Ultra-Orthodox Jews marry young, do not
practise birth control and take seriously the biblical admonition
to 'be fruitful and multiply'. They seldom intermarry, and observe
Jewry's biblical code to the letter. Given the very low Jewish
birth rate in America, the high rate of intermarriage and the decline
of religious observance in many quarters they will certainly become
an ever-increasing percentage of American Jewry as a whole.
Within the New York area, many are employed in the diamond
trade and the garment industry. Like the Mormons and Amish
peoples in the United States they decline, as a matter of conscience,
to accept government aid or relief, and both their religious
fundamentalism and 'self-help' principles have doubtless
influenced their shift to the right.

Not every group within American Jewry is likely to shift towards
the right. Jewish community leaders are unlikely to move from
a dispassionate political neutrality.[44] More significantly, many
wealthy, well-educated Jewish professionals and managers are
likely, paradoxically, to remain within the left-liberal camp. It
has frequently been argued since this trend first became apparent

in the mid-1960s that left–liberalism among American Jews is inversely proportional to wealth and socio-economic standing: the higher up the income and social ladder, the more liberal Jews tend to be.[45] Thus, the wealthy Upper East Side and the traditionally left-liberal Jewish Upper West Side of Manhattan returned large majorities for Carter and Holtzman. (Many of these wealthy Jews are unaffiliated with Jewish congregations.) Finally, many Jewish teachers, social workers, civil servants and 'technostructure' employees will continue to retain a vested interest in high government expenditure and a large public service, and are unlikely to desert the higher-spending Democrats.[46]

It might finally be asked whether such a movement of American Jewry to the right serves the interests of American Jews. Two points should be made here: this shift is in part a response to a perceived weakening of Jewish influence in the United States in terms of both domestic and foreign policy; and from the viewpoint of commonsense it would seem to be profitable to maintain strong channels of influence in both major parties. It is a tribute to the philo-semitism of virtually all Americans that post-war Republican administrations have been as satisfactory to Jewish interests as Democratic administrations (perhaps more so). despite the smallness of the Republican Jewish vote.

Many observers would point to two pitfalls inherent in such a shift. Many American Jews believe that left–liberalism is somehow implicit in Jewish theology or the Jewish tradition. Such a perception seems to be both a misinterpretation of Jewish history and chimerical. More significantly, perhaps, it might be urged that a severance of the strong Jewish nexus with the Democratic Party and left–liberal interests in the United States will hasten the very prospects which are most to be feared: the growth of a significant anti-Zionist left within the Democratic Party, probably linked to black and white radical caucuses sympathetic to Third World revolutionary movements like the PLO. This may happen and a move to the right by American Jews may hasten its occurrence. But in strengthening American defence and the American economy, and restoring American values, a triumphant American conservatism would surely strengthen those very forces which have given American Jewry – and world Jewry – the singular success they have enjoyed since 1945.[47]

Britain

The Jews of Britain live in a society markedly different from that of the American Jews. Although it is the third largest European Jewish community, Britain's Jewish population is much smaller than America's – most estimates put its number at between 400,000 and 450,000.[48] British Jewry is much more (and increasingly) centred upon London – especially north and north-west London – to an even greater extent than American Jewry is centred around New York. Britain's three major political parties, while each is a coalition of groups and interests and all operate within the framework of the British constitution and its traditions, are ideologically motivated and principled in a way which America's two major parties are not. British Jews live in a society which is poorer, weaker, less self-confident and less resistant to foreign economic pressures than is the United States. As the most sizeable European Jewish community to survive the Holocaust intact,[49] and as citizens of the mandate power in Palestine, British Jews are placed at a central vantage point of modern Jewish history.

The British Jewish community is an exceedingly interesting one. As elsewhere in the West, British Jewry has moved largely into the upper middle class, and occupies an increasing place in Britain's elites. They are a respected and influential community, nearly as prominent in some elite spheres – the arts, academic life and publishing, for instance – as their American counterparts, and have made a contribution to contemporary British culture out of all proportion to their numbers. But a number of factors threaten their secure existence. From the extreme left, the gains made by the socialist left within the Labour Party brings the threat of left-wing anti-Zionism. Because of the ideological and class dimensions of the British political system, as well as the nature of power within the Labour Party, British Jews are potentially far less able to negate the gains of left anti-Zionists than are American Jews. From the right, since 1979 Britain has increasingly adopted the Middle Eastern policies of the EEC, perceived by most British Jews as distinctly pro-Arab and anti-Israeli. From the extreme right is the danger of a revitalised neo-Nazism via the National Front, the British Movement and similar bodies. This section will examine both the nature and strength of these forces in contemporary Britain and the response of British Jewry to them.

During the past ten years most of the pro-Arab and anti-Israeli feeling in Britain, especially among the political elite, emanates from the Labour Party, especially (though not entirely) from its socialist left wing. Conversely, to a disproportionate extent it has been the British Conservative Party – particularly when in opposition – which has been pro-Israeli and anti-Palestinian. This alignment has been disguised by several important factors, including the friendliness of Harold Wilson towards Israel and British Jewry and the pro-Arab oil business and defence links of several leading Conservative politicians. Nevertheless, since the early 1970s a small but growing body of Labour politicans have been actively anti-Zionist and pro-Palestinian; they far outnumber the pro-Arab and anti-Zionist Conservatives. In contrast, a substantial majority of Conservatives were actively pro-Israel during their recent period of opposition in 1974–9, and they outnumber the pro-Israeli Labour members. Totalling the number of members of parliament belonging to the three (Tory, Labour and Liberal) 'Friends of Israel' groups, as well as the signatories of pro-Israeli Early Day motions,[50] and, conversely, membership of one of the pro-Arab parliamentary groups or signatories of pro-Arab Early Day motions, the final Report of this investigation disclosed an analysis of attitudes towards the Middle East among British members of parliament in the period 1974–8 (Table 5.2).

Table 5.2: Attitudes Towards the Middle East Among British Members of Parliament

Total		Total pro-Arab	Strongly[a] pro-Arab	Total pro-Israel	Strongly[a] pro-Israel
Labour	307	51 (16.6%)[b]	24	153 (49.8%)	41
Conservative	280	16 (5.7%)	4	184 (65.7%)	53
Liberal	13	1	0	10	4
Ulster Unionists	10	0	0	4	0
Scottish Nationalists	11	0	0	2	0
Others	11	0	0	1	0

Notes: a. Two points were awarded to all members of a pro-Israeli or pro-Arab group, one extra point to each officer in these groups and one point for every Early Day motion signed. 'Strongly' pro-Arab or pro-Israeli members scored four or more points.
   b. Percentage of that party's total of members.

The degree of pro-Israeli sentiment on the Tory side is magnified still further if Jewish members of parliament – sixteen among the forty-one strongly pro-Israeli Labour total, compared with only six of fifty-three such Tories – are subtracted from the totals for the two major parties. Among these strongly pro-Israeli members there remain only twenty-five gentile Labour members, compared with forty-seven gentile Tories. These Conservative pro-Israeli members included some of the most right-wing members in the House, among them Rhodes Boyson, Julian Amery, Winston Churchill, Sir John Eden, John Biggs-Davidson (Chairman of the right-wing Monday Club) and Ian Paisley.[51] Paisley – whose support for Israel probably flows from his Protestant fundamentalism – is said to have made a special flying visit from Ulster to Westminster in October 1973 to vote for Israel in the important division over the government's arms embargo during the Yom Kippur War.[52] A number of observers of the British political scene have attributed much of this variety of Conservative philo-Zionism to the considerable Jewish presence in north-west London marginal seats. According to Dr Geoffrey Alderman of the Royal Holloway College, who has investigated the Jewish political presence in contemporary Britain in great detail, 'in the mid-1970s . . . several MPs, mostly Conservatives, became prisoners of their Jewish voters'.[53] Alderman cites John Gorst, Geoffrey Finsburg, Tom Iremonger, Milly Miller, Tim Sainsbury, James Callaghan (of Middleton and Prestwich[54]) and, 'most intriguing of all', Margaret Thatcher as specific examples of this. However, still less than in the similar circumstances of the 'Jewish vote' in America can this motive be attributed to such demonstrably pro-Israeli Conservatives as Sir Stephen McAdden, Anthony Berry, Nicholas Winterton or Teddy Taylor. Among such Conservatives, support for Israel is entirely consistent with their right-wing ideology, and results from a mixture of religious philo-semitism, respect for the long historical tradition of the Jews and for the success achieved by them in spite of extreme adversity, as well as admiration for Israel as a fighting pro-Western bastion. The strange alchemy of time has transformed the values exemplified and upheld by the Jews and Israel into the locus for philo-semitism rather than anti-semitism.

Such sentiments are, of course, not always widely held in the Conservative Party. Economic necessity, geopolitical considerations and the peculiar variety of philo-Arabism long a notable feature of much of the British right have meant that Conservative governments have proved no more pro-Israeli than

Labour governments. Given her own commitment to Israel, Mrs Thatcher's government in particular has proved a disappointment,[55] especially as it has moved closer to the position adopted by Europe and away from that of the United States. A number of Conservatives with prominent Arab links, like Sir Ian Sinclair, were given high office in her administration, while Lord Carrington has edged closer to associating the PLO with any Middle Eastern peace process. Yet support for Israel appears genuinely well based and deeply felt among many Conservatives while ideological sympathy for the radical Arab cause is slight; Britain has, in general, acted as a moderating influence upon the more openly pro-Palestinian and anti-Israeli position of other EEC members such as France; and Britain's need for Arab oil and for good business connections with the Arab world are economic considerations which do not represent a genuine commitment to the Arab perspective.

At the other end of the political spectrum much has changed within the Labour Party since the late 1940s, when support for Israel found a place in the left-wing critique of Britain's colonial and imperial policies. Pro-Arab and pro-Palestinian groups on the Labour side existed as long ago at 1969,[56] while by 1978 the number of identifiably pro-Arab Labour politicians totalled fifty-one, one-sixth of Labour's parliamentary contingent. The majority of these men – e.g. Sidney Bidwell, Stan Newens and William Molloy – stand on the socialist left of the party on all significant issues, although Labour's Arab supporters span the whole ideological spectrum from far left to the right. Yet so long as the Palestinians are perceived as victims and the Israelis as agents of Western imperialism the importance of pro-Palestinian sentiment within the Labour Party is bound to grow. In March 1978, for instance, the Labour Party's student organisation voted to join the pro-Arab Labour Council for the Middle East rather than the Labour Friends of Israel group.[57] Many British Jews who have traditionally been supporters of the Labour Party are bewildered by this novel situation. A thoughtful article by Paul Rose, the former Labour member for Manchester Blackley, which appeared in the *Jewish Chronicle* immediately following the 1979 General Election, offers an excellent summary of this new mood:[58]

> Since I entered Parliament in 1964 until my recent decision to leave, there has been a slow but discernible erosion of

sympathy with Israel in the Labour Party. By the same token, there has been a movement away from the traditional affinity between the Anglo-Jewish community and the Labour Party in Britain.

The legacy of Nazism and the traditional hostility by the left to fascist movements associated with anti-semitism naturally drew the Jewish community towards the Labour Party and left-wing groups in Britain and abroad. Initially, the economic position of the wave of immigrants from Eastern Europe was at the bottom of the social scale . . .

Today, the descendants of those impoverished immigrants frequently play an active part at all levels of the Conservative Party, a role formerly reserved for those of long-standing and impeccable lineage. Middle-class Jews with a liberal tradition are more likely to see the Conservative Party as representative of their social and economic position . . .

When I entered Parliament, the Jews on the Tory benches were typified by the [aristocratic] d'Avigdor Goldsmids and Sir Keith Joseph. Today, the small crop of descendants of those impoverished immigrants no longer look out of place on the Tory benches and . . . more have joined them.

By the same token, the disproportionately high number of Labour MPs with Jewish connections has been sharply reduced. Four deaths during the last Parliament and eight retirements compounded by the loss of such members as Eric Moonman (a pro-Israel stalwart), Arnold Shaw, Helene Hayman . . . [and] Harold Lever. Thus, there is a gradual adjustment as the Jewish community begins to vote and act more closely in line with its socio-economic position, rather than the traditional allegiances of an ethnic or religious minority . . .

[T]he strident anti-Zionist rhetoric hardly distinguished from plain antisemitism in some university campuses, has alienated a traditionally non-conformist group. Left-wing sympathisers with Israel can feel deeply confused and isolated . . .

As the new MPs settle down in the House and the long-standing close relationship with the Israeli Labour Party recedes, there is a gradual diminution of the strong ties that once made the Labour Friends of Israel the strongest single Labour grouping in the House of Commons. It would be wrong to exaggerate the movement of opinion, and most of Labour's leading figures still display this traditional sentiment. But the longer Israel is regarded as an occupying power, and the further we get from the memories of 1948 and the preceding horrors, the more tenuous are those ties likely to become.

This growing movement towards a pro-Palestinian and anti-Zionist perspective must also be seen as part of a growing drift to the left by the Labour Party as a whole, a movement which resulted in Michael Foot's election to party leader in November 1980. Until it lost office in May 1979, the politically moderate pro-Israeli leadership of the party, though increasingly challenged by the left, remained in control of the party. Yet the generational passage from power of moderate social democrats first elected in the relatively affluent 1950s and 1960s, and their replacement by younger men and women far more ideologically orientated, has continued unabated. Membership of the Tribune Group, the best-known left-wing organisation within the parliamentary party, has grown with each new intake of members of parliament from ten per cent of those first elected before 1950 to 50 per cent of those who entered parliament in February 1974 and to 60 per cent first elected in October 1974.[59] While there is no necessary correlation between leftism within the Labour Party and support for Israel – a number of important party left-wingers, like Eric Heffer, remain outspoken supporters of Israel – it must be said that if the British pattern is anything like that found elsewhere in the Western world, support for Israel declines and support for the PLO increases as one moves further to the left. The foreign policy of a left-dominated Labour government would certainly be less friendly towards Israel than that of the moderate Labour governments of Harold Wilson and James Callaghan. *Labour's Programme 1976*, a policy statement produced by the left-dominated National Executive Committee, for instance, stated that the aim of a socialist Britain could only be achieved 'in alliance with socialist and liberation movements abroad', a description that the PLO would surely accept of itself. In Paul Rose's words, 'Labour's identification with the Third World includes the rise of Arab nationalism and a by-product has therefore been to cast Israel in a quasi-imperialist role'.[60]

Apart from Jews and a handful of other politicians with a specific and declared interest in the Middle East there are few members of parliament to whom the future of Israel is a matter of pressing importance. Yet to the extent that the ideological pursuit of socialism replaces moderate politics as the concern of many Labour members, and to the extent that support for the PLO replaces support for Israel as the commonplace attitude of the Western left, the balance within the Labour Party will surely continue to tilt against Israel until the party's declared policies are altered. The fact that the number of Jewish Labour members is now declining sharply – from thirty-five elected in October 1979 to only twenty-one elected in 1979[61] – will accelerate this trend, making it much more difficult for Jewish Labour members to counter the party's ideological trend and placing ever-growing reliance on the diminishing goodwill of the non-Jewish majority.

The other sphere which has caused British Jews to turn away from socialism is the economic one. The inegalitarian distribution of Britain's income structure, despite the welfare state, has in recent years emerged as a matter of central concern to British socialism, and it is likely that any future Labour government will enact a stringent tax upon wealth and private capital. As a disproportionately wealthy minority, British Jews would pay taxes upon wealth to a disproportionate extent. It is the argument of this book that British Jews, like other Western Jewish communities, rely upon the gap created at their over-representation at the elite level to compensate for anti-semitism. Wealth taxes would diminish the type of influence which flows from wealth-holding and economic success, and would make it extremely difficult for British Jews to compensate for their small numbers in this way. They would weaken the well-organised network of Jewish educational, charitable and religious institutions which are supported by the voluntary contributions of their members.

That British Jews now widely and increasingly perceive the long-term consequences of British socialism as injurious to their interests is evident from the research which has been done on Jewish voting behaviour over the past decade by Alderman. According to him, the 'drift to the right' among Jewish voters in the London parliamentary constituencies he has examines is 'dramatically reflected' in his survey data.[62] Alderman has analysed recent Jewish voting behaviour in two London seats – Hendon North and Ilford North – at the residential heart of London Jewish life, as well as the third London seat of Hackney North and Stoke Newington, which contains a declining population of older working-class Jews. His sample may be compared with the overall results of the poll in each constituency (Table 5.3).[63]

Table 5.3: Analysis of Recent Jewish Voting Behaviour in Three London Seats

Election		Hendon North Con. (%)	Hendon North Lab. (%)	Ilford North Con. (%)	Ilford North Lab. (%)	Hackney North and Stoke Newington Con. (%)	Hackney North and Stoke Newington Lab. (%)
1970[a]	Jewish sample	55.1	26.5	–	–	–	–
	Overall result	49.3	40.7	–	–	–	–
1974 (Feb)	Jewish sample	59.1	15.9	46.6	44.8	–	–
	Overall result	42.6	36.2	40.9	42.5	–	–
1974 (Oct)	Jewish sample	68.3	21.9	59.3	35.2	–	–
	Overall result	44.4	39.7	50.4	38.0	–	–
1978[b]	Jewish sample	–	–			36.4	49.1
	Overall result	–	–			33.2	51.7
1979	Jewish sample	(no data)		61.2	34.7		
	Overall result			51.3	37.3		

Notes: a. Voters were asked in 1974 about their votes in the general election of 1970.

b. By-election of March 1978.

Alderman notes that not merely was the proportion of Jews supporting the Conservative Party larger than the general support for the Tories in each constituency – and the support for Labour consistently lower – but the difference between the actual result and Jewish support for the Conservative candidate grew during this period. Studying this change in Hendon North, he concludes, 'it is almost as if the Jewish voters in Hendon North consciously compensated for the fall in popularity of the Conservative party over the five years in question [1970–4], in order to help Conservative M.P. John Gorst retain the seat'.[64]

In considering these findings it is important to keep in mind that neither Hendon North nor Ilford North contain many wealthy Jews, who are more likely to live in St John's Wood, Hampstead or Marylebone. Both seats are middle-class London districts whose Jewish residents reflect their overall character. Nor is this move to the right confined to the Jewish middle class: 'even in such a working-class area as Hackney', to quote Alderman, 'Jewish support for Labour was lower among all voters, and Jewish support for the Conservative and Liberal candidates was a few percent higher'.[65] Looking to the future, Alderman concludes that 'all the available evidence, qualitative as well as quantitative, suggests that Jewish Labour voters are becoming fewer in relation to Jewish Conservatives' as Jews mount the socio-economic ladder and the political realignments described above take place.

What most British Jews fear from a shift to open anti-Zionism by the British left may be seen in the frequent attempts made by the extreme left at various British universities and other academic institutions since 1974 to ban Zionist speakers and even Jewish religious meetings from these campuses.[66] This campaign began in April 1974, when the left-dominated National Union of Students voted by 205,000 to 183,000 to 'recognise the need to refuse any assistance (financial or otherwise) to openly racist and fascist organisations' and stated that it was 'necessary to prevent any member of these organisations from speaking in colleges by whatever means are necessary (including disruption of the meeting)'. Originally directed against the neo-fascist National Front, it soon came to be interpreted by the radical student left to encompass all those professing right-wing views of any kind. After the 1975 UN resolution equating Zionism with racism, it came increasingly to be applied by the left towards Zionist groups and against Jewish Student Unions whose members, as Jews, merely support Israel's right to exist.[68] Anti-Zionist and pro-PLO support have come chiefly from Arab students (of whom there are 15,000 in Britain) and other Third World students, as well as from the British extreme left, especially Trotskyites. Support for Israel has come from most Jewish students (who number 9,000–12,000 at the universities),[69] Tories, moderate Labour and – surprisingly – pro-Moscow orthodox Communists, who are opposed to the destruction of Israel. Since 1975, anti-Zionist resolutions calling for the destruction of Israel, labelling Zionism as racism, and proferring complete support for the PLO have been put to the vote at over twenty British universities and colleges and have been approved at eleven.[70] One such successful motion at the University College of Wales, Swansea, was followed by the appearance of an anti-semitic article in the student newspaper which warned of the 'Zionists' plot to conquer the world'.[71] The 'no platform to racists' resolution prompted York University's Student Union in June 1977 to strike the University Jewish Society from its register, and hence effectively banned it from that University.[72] At Salford University, whose enrolment included 700 Arab students but only thirty-five Jews, an intensely anti-Zionist resolution was passed by the University's Student Union in 1976. In the words of the Institute of Jewish Affair's research report on this matter,

> To give the flavour of the kind of reslutions being put forward, here are a few sample clauses from the 43-point 'indictment' [of Zionism]:
> 'This Union believes that Zionism is a discriminatory, racist, and unjust ideology which from the start to the present day discriminates between Jews and non-Jew.
> That Israel is committed to defending the interests of Imperialism.
> That Zionism, like apartheid, is and always will be a racist ideology.
> That the essence of racism is the mythical belief in race superiority. The South African racists, the Zionists, and fascists share this belief in common. Each professes to be the 'chosen people'. This action too, was justified by the 'no platform' policy.[73]

Another incident which occurred at Salford University is indicative of the mood of the student left:

> In March 1977, a Palestine Week was held at Salford . . . The Jewish Society then applied for permission to hold an Israel week but was told that no political activities would be allowed. The question was raised of a Rabbi, who was due to speak on the relationship between Zionism and Judaism. The Student Union president . . . was quoted as saying: 'It would be all right to speak about the differences between the two but not about the links'.[74]

Such incidents have continued to multiply since 1977.[75]

New and disturbing manifestations of right-wing anti-semitism also appeared during the late 1970s and early 1980s, lending credence to the notion, increasingly popular, that the period of tranquillity, enjoyed by British Jewry since about 1950, was now passing.[76] The British Movement, an extreme breakaway faction of the National Front which appeared in 1979, openly idolised Hitler, sold anti-semitic tracts and records and recruited unemployed teenagers in the manner of the early Nazi movement.

A report in the *Sunday Times* noted that 'Anti-semitic records [are] being openly sold outside and inside Arsenal [Football] stadium . . . [by] the hard-core Nazi British Movement . . . Yesterday's *Daily Mirror* repeated that the hate records by a group calling themselves the Sex Bristols, are directed against Tottenham's fans, especially the allegedly large Jewish segment'.[77] This is only one of many such incidents known to London Jewish sources of increasing extreme right-wing anti-semitism at a time of economic difficulty.

However offensive and dangerous these new manifestations of right-wing anti-semitism may be to British Jews, there remains a qualitative difference between the anti-semitic far right and the anti-Zionist far left. While ideas and people float, seemingly irresistibly, from Marxist fringe groups to the mainstream Labour Party, the National Front and similar fringe groups have no influence at all within the Conservative Party. Ideologically, the National Front advocates a policy of national socialist autarky; it is anti-semitic because Jews are 'cosmopolitan international financiers'.[78] The National Front desires an economy and social order centrally directed and run exclusively in the interests of the 'indigenous' people of Britain; it has little or nothing in common with the *laissez-faire* policies of Margaret Thatcher and Sir Geoffrey Howe. Similarly, it would oppose the system of structured inequality supported by conservatism and advocated in this book as the best antidote to endemic anti-semitism. Socially and sociologically, too, the National Front and similar groups are largely working-class and lower middle-class movements far removed from the British Conservative Party.

It remains to be said that the British people remain disproportionately pro-Israeli and anti-Arab, if the survey evidence which exists is accurate. Public opinion surveys taken since the 1967 war have repeatedly confirmed that 35–40 per cent of those sampled basically support Israel's stand, only 5–10 per cent favour the Arabs, with the percentage of 'don't knows' very high.[79]

There seems to have been little alteration in overall attitudes during this period, though some erosion of popular support was noted between 1969 and 1973. The 1973 war, however, saw public support for Israel rise from 30–40 per cent recorded in the two polls taken in May of that year to 36–47 per cent during the war itself.[80] This would suggest that the British public became more sympathetic towards Israel's plight when it is perceived as endangered.[81] Public support for Israel is, however, evidently less fervent and widespread in Britain than in the United States. While elite support and media support for Israel has also been strong, there is growing reason to believe that anti-Zionism is increasing at all levels and has a much stronger place in the mainstream than in the United States, fed as it is by left-wing extremism and right-wing anti-semitism. British Jewry is smaller than American Jewry and cannot work to negate these forces with the same likelihood of success as in the United States. As always, there. can be no substitute for a strong, disproportionate and direct Jewish presence at the elite level, in the context of a social and political structure which values upward mobility, capitalism and pluralism.

Australia

In Australia left-wing anti-Zionism of surprising depth and growing influence is to be found, coincident with increasing philo-semitism on the establishment right. This has occurred in a nation whose Jewish community is very small and which maintains a reasonably low profile, but which has undergone the same political and socio-economic shifts as those larger Jewries elsewhere in the Western world.

There are about 70,000 Jews in Australia today, just over 30,000 of whom live in Melbourne, and just under 30,000 in Sydney. Much smaller communities exist in the other large Australian cities, but only in Melbourne and Sydney do the Jews number as much as one per cent of the population of any Australian town. This percentage has remained broadly constant throughout most of Austrlian history. Jewish life began in Australia at the same time as European settlement in 1788; there were Jews among the convict transportees of the First Fleet which initiated British control of the continent. Jews have thus never been considered to be aliens to quite the same extent as elsewhere, although full religious toleration for Australia's Jews came only with the liberalising reforms of the mid-nineteenth century.[82] Until at least the end of the ninteenth century, most of Australia's Jews were English-speaking migrants from Britain and their descendants, rather than Continental Jews, which added to their acceptability. The nineteenth-century community produced its full share of wealthy and prominent men. As elsewhere, they were mainly businessmen in the largest cities, but Jews were also frequently traders and shopkeepers in the smaller towns and even, occasionally, successful pastoralists.[83] Intermarriage was frequent, and many of their descendants today retain no Jewish connections or links.

Because of their relatively favourable position, Australian Jewry produced, simultaneously, two commanding figures in Australian life – Sir John Monash and Sir Isaac Isaacs. Monash (1865–1931), a civil engineer prior to 1914, emerged during the First World War as lieutenant-general commanding the Australian Army Corps in Europe, and is regarded by military historians as among the ablest Allied generals.[84] Monash was possibly the first Jew to hold so high a military rank in any army since Roman times; in Australia, he was universally respected and admired, and his high repute probably diminished the volume of open anti-semitism in inter-war Australia. Isaacs (1855–1948) remained a vigorous and controversial figure for an exceptionally long period. A successful lawyer, he played a leading role in drafting the Australian Federal Constitution, held many high cabinet and judicial posts and eventually served as Australia's first native-born Governor-General in 1931–5. In 1898, Beatrice Webb described him in her diary as the 'only . . . man of talent in the [Victorian] Ministry . . . the only man we have met in the colonies who has an international mind determined to make use of international experience'.[85] Nearly fifty years later, during and after the Second World War, he proved a considerable embarrassment to most of Australia's Jews by his outspoken anti-Zionism and his vocal defence of British policy in Palestine.[86]

Conversely, there was little active anti-semitism in late nineteenth-century Australia once the battle for full religious toleration had been won. The only significant exception to this was cultural in nature, and emanated from the radical nationalist school of Henry Lawson and the *Bulletin* magazine; this school is regarded by most historians as important to Australia's national coming of age in the 1890s. Anti-British, anti-'finance capital' and militantly anti-Oriental, the *Bulletin* commonly depicted the Jew in its cartoons and sketches as the vulgar, fat, cigar-smoking figure common to all *fin-de-siècle* caricatures.[87] However, in contrast to Edwardian Britain, Jews formed only a small fraction of the wealth elite – certainly fewer than five per cent (and more probably only 1–2 per cent) – predominated in or 'controlled' no significant sector of the economy and remained peripheral to the growth of Australian society.[88] The *Bulletin* school made little permanent impact upon Australian political attitudes: it is interesting to note, for instance, that Australia's most important extreme right-wing movement of the 1930s, the New Guard, was not actively anti-semitic.[89]

Australian Jewish life was transformed in the 1930s and 1940s by the arrival of relatively large numbers of refugees from Hitler. In contrast to most previous Jewish migrants to Australia, few were English-speaking. Few would have settled in Australia had Hitler not existed. They were numerous enough and sufficiently alien to attract the prejudice attending all sizable and sudden migrations, which grew especially during the period of austerity following the war. By weight of numbers, they altered the demographic profile of Australian Jewry in a fundamental way: even in 1967, it was estimated that 11,000 of 30,000 Jews in Melbourne were post-war refugees who survived the Holocaust, a total which excludes either pre-war refugees or the children of either group.[90] These refugees typically arrived penniless, without a single relative in Australia and knowing virtually nothing about Australia or its way of life. Their success – which will be examined below – must be accounted one of the most singular achievements of any group of migrants to Australia, a nation of immigrants.

At the time, most opposition to this wave of Jewish migrants originated from the political right, while most support for them came from the social democratic left, especially from the post-war Australian Labour Party (ALP) government which had permitted them to come.[91] The most vociferously anti-semitic opposition to these migrants came from right-wing groups and politicians, most well within the political mainstream. For instance, in May 1947 a Liberal[92] member of the House of Representatives published in the Melbourne *Argus* a letter which Medding has described as 'the most vicious anti-semitic attack ever made in Australia by a person in public life',[93] and is typical of the mood aroused by this wave of Jewish settlement:

> The arrival of additional Jews is nothing less than the beginning of a national tragedy ... We should remember that they are European neither by race, standards, or culture . . . These are the people who, at the direction of international Jewish organisations, are being foisted upon us who are to become

the dumping ground for the world's unabsorbable.[94]

In contrast, the ALP was viewed by the bulk of Australian Jews as friendly to their interests. Dr H.V. Evatt, the then Foreign Minister and later (1951–60) leader of the ALP, was always held in particular esteem by Australian Jews. Evatt served as President of the United Nations General Assembly during the momentous year 1948–9 when Israeli independence was secured, and was instrumental in assisting its birth.[95] Australian Jews returned the friendliness of the ALP with their loyal support. Three-quarters of Australia's Jews voted for the ALP in the late 1940s when it fell from power and was replaced by the conservative coalition led by Robert Menzies.[96] As late as 1971 Medding found that Jewish voting samples demonstrated 'the continued predominance of the traditional left-of-centre Jewish voting pattern' in Australia.[97]

Over the next two decades, in common with nearly all Australian Jews, these migrants prospered exceedingly during the long post-war boom. An occupational survey of Melbourne Jewish males published in 1967 found that only 14.49 per cent of 146 non-British-born in the total of 200 sampled were employed in a skilled manual occupation, and only 8.28 per cent in an unskilled or semi-skilled one.[98] At the time, 15.87 per cent were to be found in the lower managerial and 29.98 per cent in the skilled/supervisory classes. Melbourne Jewry was already predominantly domiciled in the upper middle-class eastern and south-eastern suburbs, with few Jews resident in working-class areas.[99] In Sydney, the main areas of Jewish residence were the prosperous eastern beach suburbs of Bondi and Coogee and in middle-class areas north of the harbour. The other aspect was the remarkable degree of freedom from poverty which was enjoyed by Jews. Only twenty-three 'multiple-problem families' were known to the main Jewish welfare organisation in 1969.[100] This organisation dealt with only 300 cases of all kinds – including those of the elderly, family breakdowns and newly arrived migrants – in the first six months of 1969.[101] Most knowledgeable Australian sources who have commented on the subject agree that there has been a steady upward rise since the late 1960s in the incomes and status of Australian Jews, both as individuals and *en bloc*.

These changes in the socio-economic position of Australian Jews, together with the altering perceptions of the Middle Eastern conflict, have altered the sources of friendliness and hostility to Australian Jewry in a fundamental way. As elsewhere in the Western world, since the early 1970s left-wing anti-Zionism has emerged as a significant force in Australian political life, despite the remoteness of the Middle East and Zionism to the Australian people. As Dennis Altman noted in 1975, 'In the past couple of years support for the position of the Palestine Liberation Organisation has become a central tenet for those in Australia who wish to be identified as being on the left . . . This is most marked among the young left, for whom Palestine seems to have become an issue of prime symbolic importance and one by which leftish credentials can be measured.'[102] Most Australian Jews now clearly perceive the main danger to their untroubled future as the far left rather than the right, and most have moved – consistent with their socio-economic status – away from the ALP to vote for the governing conservative coalition, which has given Israel a remarkable degree of support at the United Nations and other international forums.

As elsewhere in the Western world, both the fringe left and the mainstream social democratic ALP have become increasingly hostile to Israel and Jewish interests. As in Britain, control of Australia's national student body, the Australian Union of Students (AUS) has long been in the hands of the fringe left and its various groupings. Anti-Zionism first surfaced as a major issue in AUS politics in 1973–4. In 1974–5 the AUS Annual Convention passed a series of extreme anti-Zionist and pro-Palestinian resolutions, among them one which explicitly committed the AUS to supporting 'armed struggle' against Israel in the Middle East. Another demanded the 'rejection of racist legislation such as the present Zionist "Law of Return"'. The most basic stated that 'AUS supports the establishment of a democratic secular state of Palestine (encompassing the area of mandate territory), wherein all people presently residing in Israel and all people forcibly exiled from their homeland will have the right to Palestinian citizenship . . . To counter the present media bias, AUS should continue to use its resources to publicise to both students and the general community the plight and continuing oppression of the Palestinian people . . .'[103] In early 1974, a number of such resolutions were put to the vote of affiliated campuses and, to the surprise of the AUS leadership, were rejected by large majorities.[104] But anti-Israeli and pro-PLO motions continued to emerge from left-wing sources in numbers. In 1975, for instance, the Australian Young Labour Conference, the official youth group of the ALP, adopted a resolution calling for a 'democratic secular state of Palestine'. Tensions between radical student leaders and young Jews heightened considerably.[105] As Altman – who describes himself as 'both Jewish and non-Zionist' – has noted, even radical Jews 'felt uncomfortable in this situation and often felt impelled to question just how far a Jew can refuse to identify with Israel'. What might be described as a hostile truce between Jewish students and the radical AUS has prevailed since about 1976, as the focus of student attention has shifted to other issues. The AUS leadership has, however, maintained a number of links with the PLO, despite the unpopularity of its Middle Eastern leanings with the majority of students.

Perhaps the most unusual source of left-wing anti-Zionism in Australia is Melbourne's radio station 3CR. In 1975 a number of new non-profit community-oriented stations were licensed by the Australian broadcasting authorities. Most of these are objective but among them is Melbourne radio station 3CR. Control of this station passed into the hands of a number of extreme left-wing groups whose stance was generally described as 'Maoist'.[106] Under 3CR's charter the station was to have a 'pro working-class bias' and was in its political content to broadcast only extreme left-wing material which, it was claimed, could not appear in the other media. Nearly every current revolutionary fringe movement was allotted its airtime; unsurprisingly extreme and uncompromising supporters of the PLO have obtained several hours of broadcast time per week. Most of the PLO broadcasts are made by radical Anglo-Saxon Australians rather than Arabs. The chief broadcaster on one of these programmes, 'Palestine Speaks', is a former President of the AUS. In Lipski's words,

> The broadcasts are unrelieved propaganda. The language is Orwellian and often vicious. The hatred of Israel and any of its supporters . . . is blatant . . . [E]very news and public affairs program on the station carried declarations of support for the war against 'Zionism, imperialism, fascism, and racism'.[107]

The Victorian Jewish Board of Deputies prepared a long list of such carefully monitored statements which it regarded as particularly abusive and anti-semitic.[108] Samples of the 3CR style included attacks upon '. . . the International Zionist movement with its world-wide political influence, its financial intelligence and arms-smuggling resources'; it promised 'to have a look historically at the close collaboration of the Zionist organisations with the Nazis during the Second World War and the assistance given by the top Zionist leadership to the Nazis in their murderous extermination of hundreds of thousands of Jewish people'. Not surprisingly, 'Zionism are [sic] like Hitler's Germany', and therefore, in the words of one speaker, 'I think the Zionists should be driven out of Australia'. 'The Palestine – Australia Solidarity Committee,' another speaker declared, 'believes in the absolute right of the Arab Palestinian Revolution to establish its own secular, independent, democratic state in the whole of Palestine as it existed under .the British Mandate . . . To achieve this it is necessary to use armed struggle because of the brutal nature of the Zionist occupation forces and also against whatever power stands in the way of the final armed liberation and independence of Palestine.'[109] Such quotations as these are not taken out of context or exaggerated; they were, moreover – in Lipski's words – 'accompanied by poetry and songs in Arabic and English which called for revenge, "eating the flesh of the marauder", and glorified every PLO raid'.[110] It should be noted that – citing the United Nations resolution equating Zionism with racism – supporters of the State of Israel have been denied any right of reply to these broadcasts, and any Jewish programmes even remotely advocating 'Zionism' have been consistently banned from the station. A lengthy and indecisive appeal by the Victorian Jewish Board of Deputies on the matter before the Australian Broadcasting Tribunal in 1978–9 led to a compromise of sorts; there is some evidence that 3CR has toned down its more virulent Palestinian broadcasts.[111] Meanwhile, however, as the *Weekend Australian* newspaper noted,

> Australians can listen to a steady stream of anti-semitic propaganda which is being broadcast regularly under the simple device of labelling all Jewish and Israeli activities as 'Zionist' – and then hiding under the United Nations resolution that 'Zionism is a form of racism' . . . 3CR's anti-semitism is conducted by playing the pea and thimble trick of equating Zionism with racism despite the fact that the overwhelming majority of Jews regard Zionism as the basis of [their] national

philosophy in the sense of agreement to Israel's right to exist.[112]

Although they would still be significant as indicating the current tenor of the extreme left's attitudes towards the Jews, neither the AUS nor 3CR would be particularly important if they merely represented a few small groups of isolated fringe extremists. However, such radical groups have many links with, and receive considerable support from, the socialist left wing of the ALP. Although the national ALP is largely led by moderate social democrats, at the state level, particularly in the state of Victoria, the extreme left is extremely influential. Bill Hartley, the recognised leader of this group, and probably the radical Arab cause's main spokesman in Australia, stated in June 1979, 'the Socialist Left virtually controls the Australian ALP'. Hartley had for many years served as a member of the Federal Executive of the ALP and of the Victorian State ALP Conference, both important party offices. He was an ALP candidate for the Australian Federal Senate in 1975, when he was narrowly defeated. Although certainly the best known and most vocal anti-Zionist on the ALP's socialist left, he is by no means the only one.[113] Within the Victorian ALP, anti-Zionism often functions as among its main driving forces in a way which is, by any standards, well in excess of its political importance. For example, in June 1979 the Australian government abandoned plans to hold its United Nations-sponsored International Crime Prevention Conference because the PLO was permitted to send delegates. This characteristic move was applauded by Australian Jewish groups; however, the Victorian ALP's newly-formed Administrative Committee, which is controlled by the socialist left, unanimously condemned the Australian government for cancelling the Conference. This virtually inexplicable attraction of anti-Zionism for much of the Australian left within the mainstream ALP has unquestionably hastened the movement of Australian Jewry to conservatism.

The hostility of the Australian left towards Israel has not been confined to socialists, even within the ALP. Gough Whitlam, ALP Prime Minister from 1972 to 1975, and his successor as leader of the ALP, Bill Hayden, although social democrats of the left-centre, have proved to be bitter disappointments to the Australian Jewish community. The Whitlam era, in particular, was widely viewed by Australian Jews as a period of betrayal which began with a calculated shift in Australian voting at the United Nations to a more 'even-handed' direction and which ended with what has become known as the 'Iraqi Election Funds Affair' – an attempt by ALP officials, including Whitlam and Hartley, to secure $500,000 from the Iraqi government to contest the 1975 general election.[114]

Whitlam's continuing hostility to Israel is something of a mystery. Some observers have viewed this as consistent with his attempts to orientate Australia much more towards the Third World countries and away from her traditional allies in the Western world, while others have quoted him as saying that contemporary Australia had more Muslim and Arab voters than Jewish voters, and that this new reality had to be taken into account.[115] When the Iraqi Election Funds Affair became public knowledge in early 1976 (shortly after the Whitlam government was removed from office by Governor-General Sir John Kerr), former ALP minister, Kim Beazley, remarked that 'it would be inevitable for the Australian Jewish community to regard any such [Iraqi] money as being in effect blood money that might be paid for ultimately, in Israeli blood'.[116] Whitlam's own views on the Middle East since leaving office apparently remain unchanged. In May 1979 he told a lecture audience at Harvard University – where he was Visiting Professor of Australian Studies – that the United States was being 'dragged through the nose' by Israel, and unambiguously supported the case for a Palestinian homeland in the Middle East.[117] Later, he accused the Australian Jewish community of engaging in 'crude political blackmail' in its efforts to influence Malcolm Fraser's conservative government over Israel's future,[118] a remark which caused widespread outrage in Australian Jewish circles. Whitlam's successor, Bill Hayden, who had been seen by Australian Jews as considerably closer to their interests than Whitlam, dissipated much of the goodwill he had built up by meeting Yasser Arafat in July 1980.[119]

Pro-Israeli sentiment within the ALP still exists, and is represented most importantly by Bob Hawke, formerly head of the Australian Council of Trade Unions and since October 1980 an ALP Federal Representative. Hawke has been described as Israel's greatest Australian supporter, and has built up close links with local Jewish leaders.[120] Yet Hawke's voice is one, increasingly, of a minority. As elsewhere in the Western world, Australian Jews have largely deserted the ALP, pushed by the growing volume of left-wing anti-Zionism and pulled by the natural attractions of conservatism to any prosperous groups.

The establishment right in Australia should be briefly considered by way of contrast. No part of the establishment right in Australia is anti-Zionist. On the contrary, the Liberal government of Malcolm Fraser, which took over from Whitlam in 1975, has reinstituted a policy of continuing support for Israel in its voting patterns at the UN and other bodies, despite the greatly increased threat of an oil boycott. Australia frequently votes in a minority of three or four of the most committed supporters of Israel. For instance, Australia was one of a handful of countries to vote against the final declaration of the 1980 International Women's Conference at Copenhagen because of its gratuitous insertion of an attack on 'Zionism' by Arab and Communist delegates; most other Western nations, including most West European countries, abstained on this vote.[121] Fraser and his ministers have made frequent references to their record on the Middle East and have enjoyed very close relationships with Australian Jewry. In the spheres of culture and media, there is a similarly sympathetic portrayal of Jews and Israel by conservative journals and newspapers. The *Bulletin*, for example, formerly connected with an anti-semitic journal, is now a right-wing news magazine owned by the Packer syndicate. It frequently contains pro-Israeli stories, as well as a continuous attack upon terrorists and left-wingers generally; in 1978 it published the most widely-read exposé of Radio 3CR and its practices. Since the Camp David agreement of 1978, as elsewhere in the Western world, there has been much evidence of erosion in support for Israel's current policies towards the West Bank, and much hostility towards the Begin government. In Australia, this erosion has come almost entirely from the left–liberal media – from newspapers like the *Melbourne Age* and radio stations like the non-commercial ABC – with little erosion among conservative sources like the *Australian* newspaper and the *Bulletin* magazine, sources which remain constant to the American-centred view of world affairs discussed in Chapters 2 and 3.

Australian Jews perceive these trends clearly enough, and have reacted, as have Jews elsewhere, with a move to the political right. From three-quarters support for the ALP in the late 1940s, the Australian Jewish vote, it is generally agreed by informed observers, has gone to the conservative coalition parties by majorities of between two and three to one at each of the three most recent general elections (1975, 1977, 1980), when the hostile attitudes of Whitlam and Hayden – and those much further to the left – stood in contrast to the friendliness of the conservative government. The Jewish vote, it is agreed, was instrumental in keeping a number of marginal seats in conservative hands.[122] As elsewhere, the social democratic nexus which long bound Jewish activists and leaders to the left has begun to unravel, and a new set of connections with Australia's conservative leadership has grown up.[123] Australian Jews plainly perceive the chief sources of hostility to its interests as situated on the far left and (increasingly) the centre-left, and largely discount the residual anti-semitic extreme right – Christian Fundamentalist groups like the League of Rights – as being significant in the same sense.[124] Though very small, the Australian Jewish community is considerably over-represented in the Australian small elite; this plainly benefits all Australian Jews and their interests.[125] Of at least equal importance is the ordering of world power which has existed since the Second World War. This factor has made for a reorientation of the perception of Jews and Israel by both the right and the left, and is likely to continue so long as this orientation remains.

Notes

1. Some estimates put this figure slightly lower; for instance, the recent study by Samuel S. Lieberman and Morton Weinfeld, 'Demographic Trends and Jewish Survival', *Midstream*, Nov. 1978 arrived at a total of 5.37 million Jews in the United States in 1970. There has been a fairly substantial Jewish migration to the United States in the decade 1970–80 – about 400,000 people, mainly from Israel and Russia.

2. Lieberman and Weinfeld conclude that the American Jewish population will decline to 3.9 million in 2070. This projection is relatively *optimistic*: for a still lower estimate, see Elihu Bergman, 'The American Jewish Population Erosion', *Midstream*, Oct. 1977.

3. Richard Reeves, 'If Jews Will Not Be For Themselves, Who Will Be For Them?' *New York*, 23 Dec. 1974, p. 46.

4. William Schneider, 'Anti-Semitism and Israel: A Report on American Public Opinion', American Jewish Committee, Dec. 1978 (unpublished).

5. Schneider, pp. 3–4.

6. Ibid., pp. 7–8. Schneider has more recently found 'increasing *absolute* levels of anti-Semitism among blacks since 1974'. ('Summary of Remarks of William Schneider to the American Jewish Committee', 11 May 1979, unpublished.)

7. Schneider, 'Anti-Semitism and Israel', p. 37. Among all those polled, 52% were sympathetic to Israel, 7% to the Arabs, while 41% were in a 'Neither, both or don't know' category. In 1964, the respective percentages in a similar poll were 25–7–68 (ibid.). Of 3,207 respondents in the 1974 poll, 280 scored 'very high' on a scale of anti-semitism.

8. E.g., Michael Harrison, *Socialism* (New York, 1972), pp. 109–33.

9. 'Memorandum. Update Data on Anti-Semitism and Jewish Attitudes' (unpublished mimeograph, American Jewish Committee, 6 March 1979), especially pp. 5–6. The Harris Survey was Study No. S2829-B in the Harris series.

10. Ibid., p. 6.

11. Ibid., p. 5.

12. Dorothy Rabinowitz, 'Blacks, Jews and New York Politics', *Commentary*, Nov. 1978.

13. Obviously, there are many American blacks who are still strongly supportive of Israel. Bayard Rustin is perhaps the best-known among vocal black leaders.

14. On this affair, see David M. Hamlin, 'Swastikas and Survivors: Inside the Skokie–Nazi Free Speech Case', *The Civil Liberties Review* 4 (March/Apr. 1978); and J. Anthony Lukas, 'The ACLU Against Itself', *New York Times Magazine*, 9 June 1978.

15. On 'reverse discrimination' see Nathan Glazer, *Affirmative Discrimination: Ethnic Inequality and Public Policy* (New York, 1978); McGeorge Bundy, 'Beyond Bakke: What Future for Affirmative Action?', *The Atlantic*, Nov. 1978; Thomas Sowell, 'Are Quotas Good for Blacks?', *Commentary*; Marvin Weitz, 'Affirmative Action: A Jewish Death Wish?', *Midstream*, Jan. 1979.

16. Ben Stein, *The View From Sunset Boulevard* (New York, 1979). Stein (who is Jewish) is a lawyer and newspaper columnist who interviewed many of America's leading television writers and columnists.

17. Ibid., pp. 26, 13.

18. Ibid., pp. 15–16.

19. This left–liberalism should be kept in proper perspective. BBC Television, with a far smaller Jewish input, is much more radical in many of its plays and current affairs programmes. American television shows almost never stray beyond left–liberalism. Thus their programmes are probably perceived abroad as largely conservative rather than radical.

20. It is noteworthy that several of these right-wing groups are certainly not anti-semitic in any explicit way, yet two Anti-Defamation League officials believed it proper to attack them. Conversely, the pervasiveness of Soviet anti-semitism was surely evident in 1964, yet its existence was ignored.

21. It is thus probable that the shift to the right among Jews which marked the 1980 presidential election would have occurred earlier but for two causes of short-term radicalisation: Vietnam and Watergate.

22. On this see, e.g., Mark R. Levy and Michael S. Kramer, *The Ethnic Factor* (New York, 1972), especially pp. 109–14, and Richard M. Scammon and Ben J. Wattenberg, *The Real Majority* (New York, 1970). This period also saw the emergence of radical black nationalist groups where whites (including Jews) were unwelcome.

23. Weitz, 'Affirmative Action', pp. 16–17. The 'large urban area' is not specified.

24. 'Memorandum Update . . .' pp. 11–12, citing the Harris Survey, pp. 42, 87. The author of the 'Memorandum' believes that in their attempt to find a polling sample of Jews of a size sufficient to draw valid inferences (who totalled 281 in this survey) it necessarily concentrated on older, heavily-Jewish neighbourhoods which, according to the author, are more likely to represent 'conservative' attitudes on social issues than amongst all Jews (ibid., pp. 17–18).

25. Ibid., p. 13, citing Harris, p. 87.

26. Ibid., citing Harris, p. xvii.

27. Edward S. Shapiro, 'American Jewry and the State of Israel', *Journal of Ecumenical Studies*, Winter 1977.

28. *New York Times*, 5–11 Nov. 1980; (Brooklyn) *The Jewish News*, 14–20 Nov.

1980; (London) *Jewish Chronicle*, 7 Nov. 1980.

29. *Jewish Press*, 14–20 Nov. 1980, p. 44.

30. 'The *Jewish Press* endorsed Reagan and gave out hundreds of thousands of papers in New York. This turned the tide and clinched the state for Reagan . . .'. In 'New York State Jewish Vote Elects Reagan', *The Jewish Press*, 14–20 Nov. 1980, p. 1.

31. Ibid.

32. Ibid., p. 44.

33. Ibid., p. 2, 'Politicos Assess Jewish Vote in Sweep by Reagan'.

34. See the remarks on this by Senator Orrin Hatch, the conservative Republican, in *The New York Times*, 6–10 Nov.1980.

35. Ibid., p. 44.

36. See, e.g., 'Israels's Critics Gain', *Jewish Chronicle*, 14 Nov. 1980, p. 1.

37. It is perhaps worth noting, however, that the right-wing pro-Zionist New York weekly *The Jewish Press* endorsed the Republican senatorial candidate, Alfonse D'Amato, instead of either Ms Holtzman or Senator Jacob Javits, who stood as a Liberal.

38. Nathaniel Weyl, *The Jew in American Politics* (New Rochelle, New York, 1968), p. 332.

39. Richard Hofstadter, *The Age of Reform: From Bryan to F.D.R.* (New York, 1955).

40. Weyl, *The Jew*, pp. 331–2 (his italics).

41. Daniel W. Rossides, *The American Class System* (Boston, 1976), pp. 144–71.

42. Ibid., pp. 169–71. Rossides does not note, unfortunately, that the McWilliams quote dates from *1948* and is derived from research conducted in *1936*.

43. It was also signed by numerous non-Jewish conservative academics like Edward Banfield, Robert Bork, Willard Quine, George Stigler and Ernest Van Den Haag.

44. An exception to this is probably to be found among the leaders of America's Zionist organisations. A very well-placed source told the author that 75% of these leaders supported Reagan over Carter.

45. See Levy and Kramer, *The Ethnic Factor*.

46. It is interesting to note that one of the few states which Carter carried in 1980 was Maryland, with its large number of federal employees in suburban Washington. Government employees were regarded as a major Carter voting bloc during the 1980 campaign.

47. It is worth making the point that most Arab leaders polled by the influential *Middle East* magazine preferred Carter to Reagan as 'the lesser of three evils' (the third being John Anderson).

48. *The World Almanac, 1979* (p. 218) puts the number of British Jews at 410,000, while the *Jewish Year Book 1975* (London, 1975) opts for 450,000 (p. 188).

49. As noted in Chapter 1, a large percentage of British Jewry are pre- or post-war refugees from Nazi Germany or Holocaust survivors. The only other major European Jewish community to survive the Holocaust completely intact, and the only nation occupied by the Nazis where no 'deportations' occurred, is Bulgaria.

50. These are motions on some public event or issue. For example, a pro-Israel Early Day Motion of May 1977 congratulated the new (Begin's) government of Israel and 'recognised the achievements of all previous ones'. It was signed by four members of parliament. One put forward in January 1976 condemned the United Nations for its 'Zionism equals racism' vote. It was signed by 122 members. Such Early Day motions on the Middle East are generally signed across party lines.

51. Paisley is, of course, a member of the Ulster Unionist Party, not a Conservative.

52. *Jewish Chronicle*, 26 Oct. 1973.

53. Dr Geoffrey Alderman, *The Jewish Vote in Great Britain Since 1945* (Centre for the Study of Public Policy, University of Strathclyde, Studies in Public Policy, no. 72, 1980), p. 18. Dr Alderman's work is the most important study of this topic to appear. On this topic see also Barry A. Kosmin, 'Jewish Voters in the United Kingdom. The Question of a Jewish Vote', Institute of Jewish Affairs Research Report (Aug. 1980), which disputes the concept of a 'Jewish vote' in Britain but relates Jewish voting patterns to their class situation.

54. Ibid. This James Callaghan is not to be confused with James Callaghan, member for Cardiff and Prime Minister in 1976–9.

55. For specific evidence, see Alderman, 'Jewish Vote', pp. 29–30.

56. See, e.g., *Jewish Chronicle*, 24 and 31 Jan. 1969.

57. *Jewish Chronicle*, 17 March 1978.

58. *Jewish Chronicle*, 29 June 1979; see also Alderman, 'Jewish Vote', p. 24.

59. *The Hidden Face of the Labour Party* (Richmond, Surrey, 1978), p. 16. The author has not seen statistics on the 1979 recruits.

60. *Jewish Chronicle*, 29 June 1979.

61. Alderman, 'Jewish Vote', Appendix, p. 31.

62. Alderman, 'Jewish Vote', p. 21.

63. Taken from ibid., pp. 21–3. The remaining electors voted for the Liberal or minor candidates.

64. Ibid., pp. 21–2.

65. Ibid., p. 23.

66. On campus anti-Zionism see 'Anti-Zionism at British Campuses', Institute of Jewish Affairs Report, London, July 1977; 'Anti-Zionism at British Universities', *Patterns of Prejudice*, July–Aug. 1977; Eric M. Breindel, 'The End of the Affair? Campus Anti-Semitism in Britain', *The New Leader*, 16 Jan. 1978; Ann Hulbert and Peter Galison, 'Zionism, Racism and Free Speech', *Commentary*, Oct. 1978.

67. 'Anti-Zionism on British Campuses', p. 2.

68. Ibid. It is worth noting that these resolutions do not apply to the banning of extreme left-wing speakers. The 'vote' of 205,000–183,000 was largely fictitious. No students voted directly for or against these resolutions; rather their NUS delegates, often drawn from the most vocal and militant left-wing faction, block-voted for them.

69. Only about 3,000 of whom are members of the Union of Jewish Students. Ibid., p. 1.

70. Ibid., p. 2.

71. Ibid.

72. Ibid., p. 3. This motion was later overturned by a close vote.

73. Ibid., pp. 3–4, citing Alan Elsner, 'Race, Tolerance and the NUS', *New Statesman*, 13 May 1977.

74. Ibid., p. 4, citing *The Times Higher Education Supplement*, 29 Apr. 1977.

75. See the weekly 'University News' column of the *Jewish Chronicle*, *passim*.

76. On this subject, see E.J. Hobsbawm, 'A New Anti-Semitism?', *The Listener*, 15 Dec. 1980.

77. 30 Nov. 1980.

78. See, e.g., 'The Nation Wreckers', *Britain First*, May 1975; 'Zionism is the Issue', *Spearhead*, Apr. 1976; Martin Webster, 'N.F. Stampedes the Zionist Racialists', *Spearhead*, Aug. 1977.

79. For figures up to 1976 see 'British Public Opinion Polls on the Arab–Israel Conflict Since the Six-Day War', Institute of Jewish Affairs Research Report, July 1976.

80. Ibid., p. 3.

81. On the other hand, according to a poll taken in December 1975, 27% of

those surveyed agreed that Zionism is a form of racism (while 42% did not), while a poll taken in January 1976 found that 17% of those polled believed that Israel should be excluded from the United Nations (compared with 53% who opposed this proposition). (Ibid., pp. 5–6.)

82. See Israel Getzler, *Neither Toleration Nor Favour. The Australian Chapter of Jewish Emancipation* (Melbourne, 1970). On the history of Australian Jewry see Peter Y. Medding, 'The Star of David Under the Southern Cross: Australian Jewry 1788–1976', in Daniel J. Elazer (ed.), *New Jewries in Four New Societies* (forthcoming), and J.S. Levi and G.F.J. Bergman, *Australian Genesis. Jewish Convicts and Settlers in 1788–1850* (Sydney, 1974).

83. See Medding, 'The Star of David', and Levi and Bergman, *Australian Genesis*, especially pp. 71–92, 236–54.

84. Lloyd George wrote that '. . . according to the testimony of those who knew well his genius for war and what he accomplished by it [he was] the most resourceful general in the whole British (*sic*) Army'.

85. A.G. Austin (ed.), *The Webb's Australian Diary 1898* (Melbourne, 1965), p. 68.

86. See Max Freilich, *Zion in Our Time. Memoirs of an Australian Zionist* (Sydney, 1967), pp. 91–110, and Alan D. Crown, 'The Initiatives and Influences in the Development of Australian Zionism, 1850–1948', *Jewish Social Studies* (Autumn 1977).

87. See Humphrey McQueen, *A New Britannia* (Melbourne, 1975), pp. 31–2, 104ff., 197.

88. On this subject see W.R. Rubinstein, 'Top Wealth-holders of New South Wales, 1817–1939', *Australian Economic History Review* (1980), and his 'The Wealthy in Australia', *Quadrant*, August 1980.

89. See Keith W. Amos, *The New Guard Movement, 1931–35* (Melbourne, 1976).

90. Peter Y. Medding, *From Assimilation to Group Survival* (Melbourne, 1968), Ch. 7, and Peter Y. Medding (ed.), *Jews in Australian Society* (Melbourne, 1973), Ch. 2.

91. The ALP was in power between 1941 and 1949.

92. The Liberal Party has been the main conservative party in contemporary Australia. Founded by Robert Menzies during the Second World War, it has held federal government between 1949 and 1972 and since 1975, at all times in coalition with the National Country Party (NCP), a rural-based conservative party.

93. Medding, *From Assimilation*, p. 154.

94. Cited in ibid. The writer added that 'I refer only to Jews from the Continent of Europe, not British Jews or Jews already in Australia'.

95. At the time Australia was viewed as a major spokesman for the world's middle-rank powers and was probably more influential internationally than today.

96. This figure is taken from an unpublished study made by Chanan Reich of the Department of Politics, Monash University, Melbourne, and is based upon a study undertaken at the time by Professor Robert Taft at Monash University. On Australian Jewish voting preferences, see also Peter Y. Medding, 'The Persistence of Ethnic Political Preferences: Factors Influencing the Voting Behaviour of Jews in Australia', *Jewish Journal of Sociology*, 13 (1971).

97. Ibid., p. 37.

98. Walter Lippmann, 'Melbourne Jewry: A Profile', in Medding (ed.), *Jews in Australian Society*, p. 20.

99. Ibid., p. 19.

100. Lionel S. Sharpe, 'A Study of Poverty Among Jews in Melbourne' in Medding (ed.), *Jews in Australian Society*, p. 33.

101. Ibid.

102. Dennis Altman, 'A Secular Democratic Palestine: A New Litmus Test for the Left', *Politics*, x (1975), p. 69.

103. Cited in Altman, 'A Secular Democratic Palestine', p. 176.

104. Ibid.

105. For an account of this mood in the mid-1970s, see Ibid., p. 174.

106. They also include Trotskyites, extreme left-wing ALP supporters and 'revolutionary' Communists. See Sam Lipski, 'The Voice of Terrorism', *Quadrant*, June 1978, and Lipski's article in the (Sydney) *Bulletin* of the same month.

107. Lipski, 'The Voice of Terrorism', p. 48.

108. Victorian Jewish Board of Deputies, *3CR, A Matter of Public Concern*, (Melbourne, 1978). See also Tim Hewat and David Wilson, 'The Voices of Hate', *Weekend Australia*, 13–14 Jan. 1979.

109. Cited in *3CR: A Matter of Concern*. These quotations are taken from verbatim transcripts of 3CR's Palestine programmes.

110. Lipski, 'The Voice of Terrorism', p. 48.

111. (Melbourne) *Age* 'Green Guide', 8 Aug. 1979.

112. Hewat and Wilson, 'Voices of Hate'.

113. A large number of other examples might be cited. The head of the Victorian Food Preservers Union and an important left-wing figure in the Victorian ALP, Tom Ryan, was visiting a PLO base in Southern Lebanon when he narrowly escaped death from an Israeli air attack in June 1979. Ryan said that though he found the attack very frightening, he 'was determined to continue to support the struggle of the Palestinian people to liberate their homeland from the Zionist entity' (Melbourne) *Herald*, 26 June 1979; *Free Palestine*, August 1979. In November 1978, a vote of the Victorian ALP executive *defeated* a motion deploring the treatment of Soviet Jews and dissidents. The reason given by socialist left spokesmen was that the Soviet Union was a 'working class state' and demands for better treatment of Soviet Jews was led by 'Zionists'. Moves by the Victorian Jewish Board of Deputies to modify 3CR's extreme anti-Zionism were denounced by the Victorian ALP State President, Kevin Hardiman, as emanating from 'the class interests which however sincere are trying to take away the worker's voice', and by a prominent left-wing member of the Victorian Parliament, Joan Coxsedge, as 'moves to stifle free speech . . . and introduce backdoor censorship'. (All quotations supplied by Australia–Israel Publications, Melbourne.) For further examples, see W.D. Rubinstein, 'The Left, the Right, and the Jews', *Quadrant*, Aug.-Sep. 1979.

114. On Whitlam's Middle Eastern policies, see Alan Reid, *The Whitlam Venture* (Melbourne, 1976) especially pp. 443–56; Paul Kelly, *The Unmaking of Gough* (Sydney, 1976), pp. 326–45 and Medding, 'Star of David'.

115. Reid, *Whitlam Venture*, p. 454; Don Chipp and John Larkin, *Don Chipp. The Third Man* (Melbourne, 1978), p. 158.

116. *Sydney Morning Herald*, 4 May 1979.

117. *Sydney Morning Herald*, 14 July 1979.

118. See *Jewish Herald* (Melbourne), July 1980.

119. See ibid; July-Aug. 1980. Following the October 1980 General Election, the Parliamentary ALP contained '9–10 members . . . committed to support of the PLO'. (AIP Background Memo, 13 October 1980.)

120. On Hawke's many pro-Israeli connections, see Robert Pullan, *Bob Hawke: A Portrait* (Sydney, 1980), pp. 141–62.

121. See *Jewish Herald* (Melbourne), June-July 1980, for an account of this vote. Similarly, in February 1981 Australia voted in a minority of three at the UN General Assembly against condemning Israel for its annexation of Jerusalem.

122. These electoral figures are taken from the unpublished findings of Chanan Reich of Monash University (Australia–Israel Publications (Melbourne)).

123. For instance, following the 1980 general election, the Parliamentary

Labour Party dropped the three long-serving Jewish Labour members of parliament from its Shadow Cabinet; at the same time Prime Minister Fraser added the first Jew to his government. These examples are, no doubt, coincidental in that Jewishness played little or no part in these events: but the trends are clear.

124. The League of Rights has existed since the 1930s and combines Christian fundamentalism, Empire Loyalism and social credit anti-banking economics. It is openly anti-semitic and anti-Zionist and distributes a wide range of anti-semitic tracts. On it, see K.D. Gott, *Voices of Hate; A Study of the Australian League of Rights and Its Director, Eric D. Butler* (Melbourne, n.d. (1965)).

Apart from residual anti-semitic social discrimination in clubs, the only other significant source of Australian anti-semitism stems from a group of right-wing Baltic migrants in Australia who publish a far-right anti-Communist journal, *News Digest-International*. This frequently publishes articles such as 'Judaism equals Bolshevism'. Australia also possesses at least one vocal advocate of the 'Holocaust was a Zionist hoax' theory, who has, because of his unusual background, caused great anguish to Australian Jewry. He is, however, unconnected with any known right-wing group.

125. For example, the present Governor-General of Australia, Sir Zelman Cowen, is a distinguished Jewish lawyer and academic; he was appointed by Fraser in 1976. Recent Lord Mayors of Melbourne and Sydney were Jews; there are two Jews in the Victorian Cabinet. For a description of Jewish businss success in today's Australia see *Financial Review*, 14 Oct. 1980.

6   THE SOVIET UNION

Our discussion of the Jewish situation in three Western democracies showed certain common patterns. In all three countries, the establishment right has become increasingly philo-semitic and pro-Israel; in the two countries where a socialist party is the party of the mainstream left, anti-Zionism has become a staple of the extreme left. In each country, the Jews as a whole have risen to upper middle-class status and are disproportionately influential because of their greatly disproportionate numbers at the elite level. To the degree that the culture and media of each reflect the values of capitalism and Western democracy, Jews and Israel are largely perceived as 'good', terrorists and Palestinians as 'bad'. In all three the extreme neo-Fascist right which continues to promulgate racist anti-semitism is unimportant and unconnected with the philo-semitic, pro-capitalist establishment right.

It would be very easy to present the Soviet Union in its values and policies as the obverse of the philo-semitic, pro-Israel capitalist West, and leave the story there. If a short answer were required as to why the situation of Soviet Jews is so lamentable, one could indeed do worse than ascribe it quite simply to socialism. This would, however, be an oversimplified explanation for Soviet anti-semitism.

Soviet Jewish life is an extension of Jewish life under the czars, and when examining the circumstances of Russian Jewry in the contemporary period one is often drawn into a comparison with Jewish life before 1917. Before the First World War, the Russian Jews numbered five million or more; because most of Poland was included within the Russian Empire, Russia was the centre of Europe's Jewish population. Russian Jews, even in the late czarist period, were subject to a large number of legal restrictions of all kinds; one annotated collection of these restrictions, *Gimpelson's Statutes Concerning the Jews* (1914–15), ran to nearly 1,000 pages.[1] The most important of these restrictions, and that with the most far-reaching consequences for both Russian and Jewish life, concerned the rights of residence and freedom of movement. From 1791 until 1915, Jews were legally restricted to living in the fifteen south-west Russian provinces and the ten provinces of Russian Poland, known

180

as the Pale of Settlement. About 95 per cent of Russia's Jewish population lived within the Pale.[2] The obvious result of the confinement of millions of Jews to one corner of the vast Russian Empire was chronic and dire poverty, which led in turn to mass migration to the United States and elsewhere, and to a well-justified and widespread hatred of czarism among nearly all Russian Jews. For its part, the Russian Empire lost the economic and intellectual contribution which these Jews might otherwise have made. Jews were also subject to restrictions and discrimination in many other spheres of Russian life – in trade and industry, in government employment, in military service and in education.[3] The last of these, perhaps the most irksome of all of to many Jews, was guaranteed by the quota system established for Jews in schools and universities throughout Russia. Within the Pale, only ten per cent of all school enrolment could be Jewish; outside the Pale the quota was five per cent, except in Moscow and St Petersburg, where it was three per cent.[4] Similar quotas existed at the universities. This led to the widespread employment of home study and university study abroad among young Jews desperate for an education.[5] One unintended result of the quota system was that the small Jewish portion of students, selected by competitive examinations, were, in Goldenweiser's words 'inevitably . . . the best students at the university',[6] and often the most revolutionary as well.

Anti-semitism in czarist Russia was officially sanctioned and state policy from the eighteenth century until the overthrow of the czarist regime in 1917.[7] Czarist hatred of the Jews added the word 'pogrom' to the language, and *The Protocols of the Elders of Zion* to the corpus of anti-semitism. The last period of czarism in Russia, the reign of Nicholas II (1894–1917), was, if anything, even worse for the Jews than the mid-nineteenth century had been.[8] There were violent and bloody pogroms against Russian Jewry in 1881–4 and again in 1903–6. These were tacitly or even officially sanctioned by the czarist authorities.

Every moderate commentator within czarist Russia regarded the situation of the Jews as both disgraceful and grossly counterproductive. Numerous Russian statesmen and legal and constitutional commissions recommended the liberalisation of anti-semitic legislation. Yet – chiefly because of the obstinacy of the czar – nothing was ever done to help the Jews until the First World War, when at last certain reforms were made.[9] Naturally by then it was too late. Freedom and equality came to Russia's Jews only in March

1917 when the Kerensky regime abolished all hitherto-existing legal restrictions based on religion.[10] This period of constitutional equality in the Western sense lasted for just seven months, until Lenin and the Bolsheviks came to power.

Although no one would wish to revise our estimation of the czarist regime or find mitigating circumstances for its systematic policy of anti-semitism, there are several factors of considerable importance concerning the welfare and status of Jews under czarism which must be taken into account in assessing their condition. First, czarist anti-semitism was purely religious in nature. Jews were defined as a religious rather than a racial group, and, once baptised, faced no *legal* restrictions of any kind. According to Goldenweiser, 'talented Jewish students were frequently offered access to university professorships if they consented to be baptized',[11] and this must have occurred throughout the range of activities closed by statute to Russian Jews. The careers of men like the composer and conductor Anton Rubinstein (1835–81) and his brother Nikolay (1829–94) illustrate the possiblities of professional success open to the assimilated, baptised Russian Jew. Their parents were baptised soon after Anton's birth. Anton founded and led the St Petersburg Conservatory and became a notable leader of Russia's musical establishment during the age of Tchaikovsky, Rimsky-Korsakov and Moussorgsky. His brother founded and led the Moscow Conservatory.[12]

A similar distinction had been drawn throughout Europe between baptised Jews, to whom no doors were officially closed, and practising Jews, to whom anti-semitic restrictions had recently exclusively applied, even in countries with an infinitely greater tradition of toleration than Russia. In Britain, for instance, no practising Jew could take his seat in the House of Commons until 1858, no Jew could graduate from Oxford or Cambridge until the 1860s and no practising Jew was given a peerage, or could take his seat in the House of Lords, until 1885. On the other hand, as early as the eighteenth century, baptised Jews had sat in the House of Commons and had even received peerages. It is thus a tribute to the religious fervour of Russian Jewry that so few of them abandoned their ancestral faith. Heavily Jewish areas within the Russian Empire like Poland and Lithuania were, on the contrary, centres of Jewish religious life and practice.

Second, as in all hereditary despotisms, there were numerous traditional anomalies. Some Jews *were* permitted to reside outside the Pale, own land or were granted other privileges. The Polish community of Jews to whom the family of Sir Lewis Namier belonged, for example, was singled out by special decree after 1815 for full rights of landownership, despite their Judaism. They were notable and virtually assimilated landowners near Warsaw.[13] Similarly, Jews were permitted to participate in national elections for the Dumas, first established in 1905, on an equal basis with the rest of the population, despite the fact that they lacked the right to take part in the less important city and rural elections.[14] Twelve deputies elected to the first Duma in 1905 were Jews.[15] Three of these were socialists, the others members of the moderate-liberal Constitutional Democrat party.[16] Only four Jews were elected to the second Duma of 1907, chiefly as a result of a change in the electoral law designed specifically to reduce Jewish success.[17] In the Third Duma, there were only two Jewish deputies, and in the fourth and final Duma elected before the Revolution, there were three.[18] Several of these delegates were men of some influence in pre–1917 Russian politics.[19] Had no specifically anti-semitic legislation existed in czarist Russia the bulk of Russian Jewry would probably have been relatively moderate in their politics and basically loyal to the regime. Third, wealthy Jews, as well as Jews who had succeeded in gaining admission to universities and graduating from them, were also specifically exempted from the worst of czarist oppression. Privileged 'First Guild' merchants, who paid an annual tax of 1,000 roubles, were permitted to reside throughout Russia, as were Jews with university degrees and those in certain other highly-skilled occupations, like dentists and pharmacists.[20] Since the best-educated and wealthiest Jews formed, by and large, the elite of Russian Jewry, to some extent these privileges, limited as they were, must have served both to diminish organised discontent and to increase, at least marginally, the influence and bargaining power of Jews in czarist Russia.

Finally, and perhaps most important of all, despite these formidable obstacles, pre-1917 Russian Jewry had already begun its economic ascent and was an important and powerful element in Russia's industrial and commercial elite.[21] According to a Russian economist, Professor M. Bernatsky, writing in 1916:

> The Jews constitute more than one third (35 per cent) of the Russian mercantile class . . . The role of the Jews in the commercial life of Russia is enormous, and they contribute

greatly to its progress and efficient functioning. Every obstacle to the manifestation of the commercial energies of the Jews hurts the national economic body of Russia.[22]

Industries named by Dijur as having a disproportionate and powerful Jewish contingent include textiles, sugar-refining, brewing, tobacco, leather-making, woodworking, bristle-making, grain and timber-merchandising, banking, railway finance and construction, shipping, oil and mining – virtually the whole range of non-agricultural economic life in czarist Russia.[23] According to the Russian census of 1897, 886 out of every 1,000 people engaged in commerce in the northwest provinces were Jews.[24] The proportion of Jewish grain merchants in this area was even higher[25] – 930 out of every 1,000. In 1912 the Moscow Manufacturers' Association submitted to the Council of Ministers the following memorandum concerning the economic role of the Jews:

> The Jews perform in the economic organism of the country the functions of an intermediary link between the consumers and the producers of goods. In the northwestern, southern and southwestern provinces, these functions are carried out almost exclusively by Jews. Under these conditions, the separation of the commercial and industrial population of a large part of the country from the centres of factory production is enormously damaging not only directly to Jewish merchants, but also to the many millions of non-Jews. Dividing the village from the city, the cities of the west and the south from the cities and villages of central and eastern Russia means a virtually deliberate disruption of the economic life of the country, the undermining of credit and the devaluation of the people's labor.[26]

The czarist regime refused to heed such pleas; as a result, the Jews of the Pale remained predominantly working-class and petty-bourgeois in character,[27] and proved a rich source of discontent for revolutionary leaders.

This over-representation of Jews even in the czarist period in areas which were open to them is also evident in the field of higher education, despite the stringent quotas applied by the regime. In 1886 Jews attending Russian higher education institutions numbered 1,856 and constituted *14.5* per cent of the total number of all students. In 1902 these declined, respectively, to 1,250 and seven per cent, but rose in 1907 to 4,266 (12.1 per cent) and then in 1911 declined again to 3,602 (9.4 per cent).[28] Large numbers of Jewish students also attended private institutions of higher learning which were not subject to the quota system, for instance the 1,875 Jewish students who were in 1912 attending the Kiev Commerical Institute, according to Ilya Trotsky.[29]

In looking at the tragic history of the Jews under czarism, one can only feel regret for the lost contributions which the Jews might have made to the building of a liberalised, economically progressive, cosmopolitan Russia. This hope is not far-fetched: time and again the Duma, or responsible and moderate groups of government officials, businessmen or legal professionals, would recommend the lifting of artificial restrictions on Jewish participation in Russian life.[30] Such recommendations often reached the point of acceptance when they would be vetoed by the czar and his reactionary officials. Nevertheless, it is fair to say that another fifteen or twenty years of peace would have made such changes inevitable.

There are several areas of life in czarist Russia in which the Jews *were* permitted their freedom. Jewish religious life flourished, and was, of course, not subject to discrimination by the czarist regime.[31] 'The study of the Torah attained its highest development in eastern Europe. In the cities and small towns of Lithuania, Russia, and Poland there were vast numbers of people studying the Torah, as well as groups dedicated to such study.'[32] The life of the religious Jew in eastern Europe up to 1914 – which chiefly meant czarist Russia – is well known to all Jews. Russian Jews developed a flourishing literature and popular culture in their own language, Yiddish, as well as in the newly revived Hebrew language. The 'golden age of Yiddish literature', which produced such writers as Sholem Aleichem, Mendele Sforim and Sholem Asch, occurred chiefly in czarist Russia in the latter part of the nineteenth century and up to 1917. Despite censorship and periodical government restrictions, there was a popular Yiddish-language press as well.[33]

Jewish life in czarist Russia, then, presents many paradoxical features. At its religious and cultural core there was much life which the oppression of the regime could not touch. What czarist anti-semitism could and did harm was the attempt of the Jews to normalise their life there, above all to be an accepted and acceptable part of Russian society without yielding their Jewishness. Even so, Jews made considerable economic and educational progress in the most unpromising of circumstances. But such Jewish penetration of the czarist 'small' and 'large' elite as there was, was irrelevant because wealth as such, particularly wealth based upon commerce and industry, was immaterial to Russia's neo-feudal power structure. This type of structure in czarist society automatically precluded significant political participation by Jews at a leadership level, while the purpose and intent of czarist anti-semitic legislation was precisely to limit the emergence of a powerful Jewish presence in its 'large' elite by restricting the Jews to peripheral geographical ghettos and in employment to artisan and petty-bourgeois trades. This policy was successful until the collapse of the regime.

When turning to the story of Soviet Jewry, especially in the contemporary period, we encounter once more a paradoxical and ambiguous situation. The Soviet Union contains the world's third largest Jewish population. According to official census figures, Jews numbered 2,151,000 in 1970 and 1,800,000 in 1979; it is known that there are substantial numbers of 'hidden' Jews who declare their nationality[34] to be something other than Jewish, presumably in order to escape from anti-semitism by assimilation. The usual estimate of the number of 'hidden' Jews is just over half-a-million; hence most informed sources place the total Soviet Jewish population at about 2.5–2.7 million at the present time.[35] Thus about 0.8 per cent of the Soviet population declares itself to be Jewish, while the 'real' percentage is probably just over 1.0 per cent of the total Soviet population of 260 milion. The Jewish population of the Soviet Union has been declining and will decrease still further. The number of Soviet Jews killed in the Holocaust or as a result of military actions in the Second World War is estimated at from 750,000 to two million or more, while the surviving community demonstates the same patterns of ageing, intermarriage and a very low birth rate evident among Western Jewry; in the Soviet case there is the additional factor of substantial emigration since 1970. Future Soviet censuses should reveal continuing declines in Jewish numbers.

It is clear to Western observers that the history of the Jews under Soviet rule presents a pattern of steady and continuous deterioriation in all spheres of life, relieved only by periods of relative liberalisation or – more usually – of decline at a more accelerated pace. At present, the Soviet Union has moved from encouraging and publicising 'merely' extreme anti-Zionist material to open anti-semitism, to which Soviet Jews have no right of reply. In the Soviet Union today there is a flourishing journalistic industry of anti-semitism at a level unknown in that country – with the possible exception of the 'black years' of 1948–53 – since the czarist period.

Beyond the explicit anti-semitism of today's Soviet propaganda is the unpleasant reality of Jewish life in the Soviet Union.[36] Virtually alone among Russian ethnic groups the Jews are denied adequate cultural facilities or institutions. Moscow, which contains an estimated 285,000 Jews, has only one functioning synagogue; in the entire Soviet Union there were only sixty-two synagogues in 1966 (compared with 1,103 in 1926), most of them in remote Asian areas containing few Jews.[37] No Jewish religious bulletin is published in the Soviet Union; no Jewish literature of a religious nature has been published there since 1928, with the exception of a prayer book in 1957 and several small Jewish calendars.[38] No Jewish religious education may be given to Jewish children, despite the expressed right granted to all Soviet citizens to teach their children religious doctrines 'in a private manner'.[39] Although the Soviet authorities have permitted over 200,000 Jews to emigrate from the Soviet Union since 1970, announcement to the authorities of the desire to leave is usually met with official harassment and loss of employment, occasionally with imprisonment. Those refused the right to leave – the 'refusniks' – have, of course, attracted worldwide publicity.[40]

Petty instances of open anti-semitism abound as well. Hedrick Smith, formerly the *New York Times* correspondent in Moscow, has described some of these:

I have heard Jews ruefully describe discrimination they have faced in education and at work. A Jewish graduate student once protested to a senior scientist whom I knew that he had been ordered by a Russian professor to give flunking grades to several Jewish applicants for Moscow State University despite their excellent examination results. A man who was formerly senior editor at a publishing house said that when the annual list of books for the coming year was sent to the Communist Party Central Committee for approval, it would invariably be returned with several titles by Jewish authors crossed off. No explanation was needed; a Jewish 'quota' had been imposed. The head of a laboratory, a Russian, told me that his superiors explicitly rejected some highly qualified Jewish scientists whom he had proposed hiring on grounds that 'we already have enough Jews'.[41]

But no account of the general position of Soviet Jewry can ignore the other side of the coin. Writing of the disproportionately *high* percentage of Soviet Communist party members who are Jews, Brown has shrewdly noted, 'the party membership figure does not signify the absence of anti-semitism in the Soviet Union; it is, however, a datum which should be taken into account by western commentators who have often presented an extreme and over-simplified account of the nature and extent of the anti-semitism which does exist.[42] Regardless of everything that has happened to Soviet Jewry since the 1930s, regardless of Stalin's anti-semitism, regardless of the racism and anti-semitism so evident during the past ten or fifteen years in the Soviet Union, Jews continue to be *over*-represented in the 'large' – and perhaps even in the 'small' Soviet elite – at all but the very highest levels. Trends in this area during the very recent past appear to be diverging: while the Jewish percentage among all Soviet university students is declining (although this may largely be the result of demographic trends rather than anti-semitic state policy), there is some evidence that the number of Jews at the highest levels of state and even party apparatus is increasing, albeit only marginally and doubtless as a cosmetic response to Western charges of Soviet anti-semitism.[43] According to Leon Shapiro,

> In the 1960s there were 20 Jewish members of the Academy of Medicine and 57 of the Academy of Sciences. Of a total of 664,584 academic workers[44] in 1965–6, 53,607, or 7.8 per cent, were Jews. Among the scholars who received the Lenin Prizes in 1965, 13 were Jews. Of the 19 scientists who received Lenin Prizes in 1966, 5 were Jews. The award was also given to 10 Jewish engineers out of a total of 102. In 1967, 29 Jews were among the 203 persons receiving the State Prize. In 1968, of the 192 who received the award, 30 were Jews, and in 1971, out of a total of 228 who received the award, 26 were Jews. In 1972, of 185 . . . 21 were Jews.[45]

Although there has been a steady decline in the relative number of Jews classified as 'scientific workers', they still numbered 6.94 per cent of the total in 1970, far outstripping their proportion in the Soviet population.[46] According to Altschuler's study of this situation, 8–9 per cent of the *total* number of Soviet Jews and one quarter of all Moscow Jews, 'were supported by individuals who were gainfully employed in scientific work'.[47] According to official statistics, Jews in 1966 accounted for 14.7 per cent of all Soviet doctors, 8.5 per cent of writers and journalists, 10.4 per cent of all judges and lawyers and 7.7 per cent of actors, musicians and artists.[48] Similarly, Jews are still prominent in many other spheres of cultural and even administrative life.[49]

During the 1970s the number of Jews elected to the highest bodies of the Soviet Communist Party actually rose. There were four Jews at the 24th Party Congress in 1971, and five at the 25th in 1976.[50] According to Hirszowicz, these totals 'compare not unfavourably with that of other ethnic minorities of similar size'.[51] The most important Jew in the Soviet hierarchy, Venyamin Emmannilovich Dymshits, is a Deputy Prime Minister of the Soviet Union, and a member of the Communist Party's Central Committee. He is the first Jewish full member of the Central Committee since 1961.[52] Hirszowicz also notes that 'for the first time since the 1940s, there are two Jewish candidate members of the . . . Central Committee', Alexander Chakovsky, editor of *Literaturnaya Gazeta*, and Lev M. Volodarsky, First Deputy Director of the Central Statistical Directorate.[53] Something of the price paid for success by these 'chosen Jews' is suggested by Hirszowicz's remark that all these Jewish officials 'played a conspicuous role in the anti-Zionist campaign of 1969–71. They made, or signed, statements and were presented by the media to the Soviet public – and to the world at large – as Jews who regarded the USSR as their only homeland and to whom their "Jewish nationality" constituted no obstacle to advancement to the highest positions in the country'.[54]

Jews are also still slightly over-represented in the Soviet Communist Party as a whole, though their percentage has been declining since the 1920s. However, even here, there is ambiguity and certainly little evidence of a pogrom-like purge of Jews from party echelons: while from 1961 to 1965 the percentage of Jews in the Soviet Communist Party declined from 2.8 to 1.5–1.7 per cent between 1961 and 1965, and stood at 1.5 per cent in 1969, the estimated Jewish percentage apparently *rose* to 1.8 per cent of the total in 1976, despite a declining Jewish population and increased anti-semitism.[55]

Therefore the Jewish situation under the Soviet regime remains as paradoxical as it did under the czars. Although the condition of the Soviet Union's remaining Jews appears to be becoming worse rather than better, it is still basically erroneous to liken the situation of Soviet Jews to that of the Jews under the Nazis.[56]

In order to understand the strengths and weaknesses of Soviet Jewry in the contemporary period it is first necessary to examine Soviet Communism. Is the Soviet Union a socialist society? Is it an egalitarian society? What are its leading ideals? Is the present position of Soviet Jewry a product of Marxism? Is it a product of the inbuilt features of Soviet society or of the peculiarities of its leaders? Or is it simply a reflection of the traditional and age-old Russian pattern?

The answers may be summarised as follows: the Soviet Union is a socialist society which is relatively egalitarian in terms of wealth and economic rewards, inegalitarian in terms of power and privilege. In its governing philosophy and structure, the Soviet Union continues to adopt the Leninist technocratic model of development entailing an elite, scientific leadership group. In general, the rational scientific and inegalitarian principles animating the Soviet state – its strong elitist features – largely account for the over-representation of Jews within the Soviet elite, while the present deterioration in the position of Soviet Jewry is ultimately the product of the Soviet Union's commitment to equality, as well as the atavistic persistence of traditional Russian[57] anti-semitism. The deteriorating condition of the Jews in the Soviet Union is exacerbated by two other central problems: the fact that Soviet socialism forbids private accumulation of great wealth or the ownership of the means of production, and hence the development of centres of economic power outside the government; and the atheism and secularism of the Soviet regime, which have all but destroyed Jewish religious (and cultural) life in the Soviet Union. In a sense, therefore, though the anti-semitic intent of the Soviet government increasingly resembles that of the Russian government during the late czarist period, the two strongest sources of Jewish strength in their efforts to overcome their disadvantages at that time – their economic rise and penetration into the industrial-commercial capitalist elite, and their continuing strength and cohesion as a distinctive religious-cultural community – now no longer exist. Instead, Jews have to rely upon the possibilities presented by the Leninist technocratic variety of socialism for elite-penetration and over-representation in a different way. The long agony of Jewish history under the Soviet regime would seem to demonstrate that this kind of elite offers them inherently fewer possibilities for successful elite-penetration, or the bending of official attitudes and ideologies in a direction favourable to themselves, than does Western capitalism.

It is impossible for Jews – or anyone else – to control sources of economic power independent of those existing in the Soviet Union's socialised economy and commanded by its Communist elite. This is one of the central differences between Soviet society and either the czarist or Western worlds, and an important key to understanding the tragic position of Soviet Jewry. For Jews cannot compensate for government-sanctioned anti-semitism by creating independent spheres of economic power and influence for themselves; they cannot use their entrepreneurial talents to compensate for their small numbers; they are, literally, at the mercy of the Soviet state and the whims of its ruling elite. By its very nature, the socialist society that is the Soviet Union eliminates one of the most important antidotes to anti-semitism.

But the worst effects of Soviet policy on Jewish life have occurred not at the elite, but at the mass level, in the spheres of Jewish religion and culture. Except as an underground movement and in a handful of 'showpiece' synagogues, Jewish religious life in the large Soviet cities has been virtually destroyed.[58] Stalin effectively nullified the still-flourishing secular Yiddish culture during the 'black years' of 1948–53.[59] Only a remnant of secular Jewish cultural life has been permitted to exist since his death. In a broad sense, the persecution of the Jewish religion since the Revolution must be attributed to the Soviet Union's secularism and its persistent refusal to tolerate religious practice on a free basis. This intolerance is especially severe towards non-Orthodox sects, but even here, the Jews suffer disproportionately even by the standards of other persecuted sects like the Baptists.[60] Similarly, the decline of Jewish cultural life must be attributed primarily to Russian anti-semitism, and its resolute unwillingness to permit any signs of Jewish nationalism, particularly if, directly or indirectly, this implies an admiration for the State of Israel.[61] While the persecution of Jewish religious and cultural life plainly has its roots in czarist policy, Soviet anti-semitism in an important sense goes far beyond that of the czars, who permitted – indeed, encouraged – a flourishing Jewish religious life and cultural activities.

Yet there are features of the technocratic model of development adopted by Lenin and adhered to by subsequent Soviet leaders which are elitist in nature and which both account for the Jewish over-representation in the Soviet elite and give grounds for hope that the overall situation of Soviet Jewry may not deteriorate to intolerable levels, at least for the time being. Many left-wing Western elitists, for instance the Webbs, have long seen in the Soviet Union an elitist society of a new kind – one based on the leadership of a scientific, technological elite rather than an elite of heredity or money.[62] In the Communist Party of the Soviet Union, there has clearly been the deliberate creation of such an elite, although in practice members of the CPSU are no doubt as corrupt as anyone else with a privileged position in an undemocratic and basically poor society.

So long as scientific and industrial development was to be the major aim of Soviet economic policy, this goal helped groups disproportionately better-educated and more highly urbanised, such as the Jews, and largely accounts for their over-representation in the state's leadership elite, especially within the intelligentsia.[63] Soviet Jews are almost entirely urban and are the most highly educated and best-trained of any ethnic group within Soviet society. This is true even now, even among younger age-groups who have borne the full force of recent anti-semitic moves.[64] Conversely, until now the Jews have made themselves invaluable to the Soviet regime.

Furthermore, the Soviet Union has adopted a nationality policy which – in theory – has attempted to put the Jews on an equal footing with other Soviet nationalities. This policy would 'solve' the Jewish question within the context of Marxism-Leninism by giving Jews an autonomous territorial existence accompanying their national identity. Such a solution would, in the long run, help the Jews, since many privileges have come, and will increasingly come, as the minority and 'backward' nationalities of the Soviet Union 'catch up' with those more urbanised and better educated, with nationalities possessing a coherent and autonomous territorial existence.[65] The centrepiece of Soviet attempts to 'normalise' the Jewish problem was the creation of the Jewish Autonomous Region, Biro-Bidzhan, in south-east Siberia on the Manchurian border. This project, seemingly motivated as much by fears of Japanese aggression as by philo-semitism, has been accounted a total failure by all Western observers.[66] Only a small percentage of Biro-Bidzhan's inhabitants are Jews; only an even smaller percentage of the Soviet Union's Jews – 14,000 in 1959 – live there.[67] Yet it seems that such Yiddish-language cultural life as the regime tolerates disproportionately emanates from there, and the Soviet government still publicises Biro-Bidzhan abroad as a Jewish showpiece.[68]

Had the Soviet regime been sincere in its policy of granting Jews the same status as other nationalities, this might have provided the constructive basis for *détente* between Soviet Jewry and their government. What is clear is that the Soviet state has had, since its origins, a history of anti-semitism which continues to this day. *Détente* between Russia's Jews and the Soviet government has, accordingly, proved impossible, and Soviet Jews are increasingly trapped. A revival of Jewish religious and cultural consciousness during the past ten years has not led to many second thoughts by the Soviet government but only to increased emigration which, while ensuring a new and better life for those who leave, cannot improve the lot of those who remain and possibly makes it worse.[69]

It is no exaggeration to say that, from 1917 until the present day, the lot of Soviet Jews has become progressively worse, regardless of the Soviet ruler in power. During the last five years of his life Stalin was extravagantly anti-semitic; yet, except for these 'black years' of 1948–53, Jews probably had more advantages in the Soviet Union than at present. The percentage of Jews among all Soviet scientific workers declined from 17.98 per cent in 1947 and 15.46 per cent in 1950 to 6.94 per cent in 1970,[70] while the number of Jewish university students has declined in absolute terms for the first time in Soviet history.[71] Totalling 111,900 in 1968–9 and 105,800 in 1970–1, their number dropped to 88,500 in 1972–3 and to only 66,900 in 1975–6.[72] Although this certainly reflects the very limited and declining number of Soviet Jews of an appropriate age,[73] there is general agreement that a new note of explicit anti-semitism has become evident in the recruitment of the Soviet Jewish intelligentsia. William Korey has recently reported that not a single Jewish student was admitted to the University of Moscow in 1977–8.[74] Many Western observers of the Soviet Jewish scene have pointed to the long-standing Soviet policy of ethnic quotas for admission to Soviet universities as, in the final analysis, responsible for much of the 'diminution in the Jewish proportion'. In William Korey's words,

Although quotas linked to the proportion of a given ethnic group in the population have governed admission to the universities in the Soviet Union for more than two decades, and although this system has always operated (in the words of one student of Soviet affairs) 'to the particularly severe disadvantage of the Jewish population', in the past few years it has begun to take a greater and greater toll.[75]

The main purpose of these quotas is not anti-semitic but to increase opportunities for the more backward Soviet nationalities which previously had virtually no access to university education. The great increase in the number of university places and positions in scientific research now available, for the first time, to the non-Russian nationalities of the Soviet Union is the major reason for the relative decline in the Jewish percentage in such positions. Given the spread of tertiary education to less developed parts of the Soviet Union, such a trend is inevitable.

Since, except in Biro-Bidzhan, Soviet Jews are not a nationality attached to a specific geographical area they are doubly disadvantaged by the well-documented tendency in all elite areas of Soviet society (for instance in party membership) for disproportionate increases to come increasingly from these geographically-specific nationalities through growth within their own national areas, especially among those groups which were previously most under-represented in the Soviet elite.[76] Jews are thus continuously 'squeezed' by the disproportionate growth in formerly 'backward' nationalities at the elite level on one hand, and by anti-semitism and demographic decline on the other. Yet for a long period they were disproportionately represented in the Soviet elite. The failure of the Soviet Union to 'normalise' the status of the Jews on a basis consistently equivalent to other minority nationalities of the Soviet Union has led directly to this state of affairs, entirely apart from the weight of Soviet anti-semitism.

Soviet policy towards minority and 'backward' nationalities has much in common with the policies of 'reverse discrimination' towards ethnic minorities which have taken hold in the United States over the past ten years. There are, obviously, many differences, but a socialist could well argue that the Soviet's policies are, in fact, better justified than are America's. For example, colleges and universities for blacks, some (like Howard University) of considerable distinction, have existed in the United States for some time, whereas higher education for the Soviet's more 'backward' minority nationalities in central Asia and Siberia is very recent. Both the nationality policies of the Soviet Union and the 'reverse discrimination' programmes of the American government, however, have this much in common: by direct intention or not, they threaten the Jews by decreasing Jewish membership in the 'large' and 'small' elites of their respective countries.

In the United States and other Western countries capitalism provides another escape route from government-inspired anti-semitism by permitting the creation of large personal fortunes and thus alternative sources of power and influence.

But there is also almost certainly no 'equivalent' economic source of Jewish power and influence within the Soviet elite. Because elite Soviet Jews are so disproportionately found in the intelligentsia, particularly in Moscow, Leningrad and Kiev, it is likely that they are under-represented among higher industrial managers, especially in the regions of heavy industry in the Soviet Union from which so significant a portion of the Kremlin's highest leadership has come for many years.[77] With the exception of machine and tool construction and the building industry, tertiary-educated Jewish 'specialists' do not number more than 11,000 in any purely industrial field.[78]

The creation of the State of Israel in 1948, though an inspiration to most Soviet Jews, may well have made life more difficult for them, as the existence of this object of Jewish hopes left them open to increased charges of 'cosmopolitanism'. Even the relatively friendly period of relations between the Soviet Union and Israel through the mid–1950s coincided with the worst excess of Stalin's last years. In the 1970s, as 'Zionism' has increasingly been regarded in the Soviet Union as akin to Nazism and a major arm of 'world imperialism', Soviet Jews are increasingly suspect. The preception of Israel as a mortal enemy of Soviet Communism precludes any philo-semitism among the Soviet elite of the type so common to the Western establishmwnt. Even should real peace come to the Middle East, it is unlikely that the legacy of Soviet antagonism to Israel will ever vanish.

The future for Soviet Jewry, while possibly not as bleak as many pessimists believe, certainly offers little room for hope. Since many religious and culturally conscious Jews have emigrated, those remaining will be less religious and less conscious of their culture; the demographic realities of Soviet Jewish life, as well as the

continuing 'squeeze' by national minorities – and open anti-
semitism – guarantee that Jews will be further reduced as a
proportion of the Soviet elite. It is clear that any *modus vivendi*
between Jewry and the Soviet state which would be regarded as
satisfactory to Western Jewish observers of the Soviet Union is
unlikely.

However, perhaps the conditions of Soviet Jewry will not
deteriorate as much as some might believe. In the words of one
recent Western observer, commenting on the continuing over-
representation of Jews in the Soviet Communist Party, 'Although
the regime may consider it inexpedient to ensure a fair Jewish
representation in local Soviets, it seems clear that it sees it as
expedient to have an over-representation of Jews in the Party.'[79]
Since this obviously is not due to philo-semitism, it must be a
consequence of the Soviet tradition of relatively open promotion of
the educated, urbanised strata to elite positions. The migration of
Soviet Jewish activists may in the long run improve their lot, as the
remaining Jews presumably are less suspect in their loyalties. A
general peace in the Middle East could transform the situation, as
would, of course, a real liberalisation of Soviet society – a prospect
which must, unfortunately, be accounted improbable in the
extreme. If there is a lesson for the Jews to be derived from the
history of Soviet Jewry, it is the folly of 'equality' and the virtual
impossibility of Jewish existence in a Marxist state.

Notes

1. Alexis Goldenweiser, 'Legal Status of Jews in Russia', in Jacob Frumkin, Gregor Aronson and Alexis Goldenweiser (eds.), *Russian Jewry 1860–1917* (New York, 1966), p. 85.
2. Ibid., p. 118.
3. Ibid., p. 96.
4. Ibid., p. 102.
5. Ibid. See also Ilya Trotsky, 'Jews in Russian Schools', in ibid., pp. 408–15. According to Trotsky, in 1909 the Jewish quota was raised to 15% within the Pale, 10% outside and 5% in the two largest cities (p. 412).
6. Ibid.
7. See ibid. and S.M. Dubnow, *History of the Jews in Russia and Poland from the Earliest Times until the Present Day* (originally 1920; reprinted with new material, 3 vols., New York, 1975). See also Joel Cang, *The Silent Millions* (New York, 1969), pp. 23–40.
8. Ibid., vol. III, *passim*.
9. Goldenweiser, 'Legal Status', especially pp. 92–3, 109–17.
10. Ibid., p. 116.

11. Ibid., p. 110.
12. On the Rubinsteins, see *Encyclopedia Judaica* (Jerusalem, 1972), vol. 14, p. 374.
13. Julia Namier, *Lewis Namier. A Biography* (London, 1971), p. 31.
14. Goldenweiser, 'Legal Status', p. 107.
15. Jacob G. Frumkin, 'Pages from the History of Russian Jewry (Recollections and Documentary Material)', in Frumkin, Aronson and Goldenweiser, *Russian Jewry*, pp. 47–8.
16. Ibid., p. 50.
17. Ibid., p. 51.
18. Ibid., pp. 53, 55.
19. Ibid., *passim*.
20. Goldenweiser, 'Legal Status', pp. 100, 104.
21. See I.M. Dijur, 'Jews in the Russian Economy', in Frumkin, Aronson and Goldenweiser, *Russian Jewry*, pp. 120–43.
22. Cited in ibid., pp. 142–3.
23. Ibid., *passim*.
24. Ibid., p. 134.
25. Ibid.
26. Ibid., p. 143.
27. Ibid., p. 142.
28. Trotsky, 'Jews in Russian Schools', p. 413. These figures seem impossible, given the quotas in force.
29. Ibid.
30. See Frumkin, 'Pages from the History', Goldenweiser 'Legal Status' and Dijur 'Jews in the Russian Economy', *passim*.
31. See A. Menes, 'Yeshivas in Russia', in Goldenweiser, 'Legal Status', pp. 382–407.
32. Ibid., p. 384.
33. Ibid., pp. 352.
34. The Soviet Union regards 'Jews' as a nationality, and hence official census figures are kept on the population of 'Jewish nationality'. The best recent discussions of Soviet Jewish population figures are U.O. Schmelz, 'New Evidence on Basic Issues in the Demography of Soviet Jews', *Jewish Journal of Sociology*, 16 (1974) and A. Nove and J.A. Newth, 'The Jewish Population: Demographic Trends and Occupational Patterns', in Lionel Kochan (ed.), *The Jews in Soviet Russia since 1917* (3rd edn, Oxford, 1978), pp. 132–67.
35. The *World Almanac, 1979* (p. 218) puts the figure at 2,678,000. (This figure is derived from the *American Jewish Year Book 1978*.) It is interesting to note that a number of observers place the 'real' Jewish population considerably higher. Roy Medvedev, the dissident historian who is half-Jewish, estimates the number of 'hidden' Jews at 'anywhere from one to *ten* million' (Hendrick Smith, *The Russians* (London, 1976), p. 576; author's italics). If anything like the latter figure is indeed correct, the Soviet Union still possesses the largest Jewish population in the world – though, of course, the meaningful Jewish identity of 'hidden' Jews may be doubted. In 1978, the largest Jewish urban concentrations were Moscow (285,000), Kiev (170,000) and Leningrad (165,000) (*World Almanac*). Again, some observers believe that these are underestimates.
36. Of the many works on Soviet Jewry, perhaps the most generally helpful and up to date is the volume of seventeen topical essays edited by Kochan, *The Jews in Soviet Russia Since 1917*. The Institute of Jewish Affairs in London annually produces half-a-dozen or more Research Reports on aspects of Soviet Jewish life; these are also extremely informative. Jewish magazines like *Commentary*, *Midstream* and the *Jewish Observer* regularly carry a considerable number of articles

and reports on Soviet Jewish life, as do Jewish newspapers like the *Jewish Chronicle*.

37.   Joshua Rothenberg, 'Jewish Religion in the Soviet Union', in Kochan, *The Jews in Soviet Russia*, p. 190.

38.   Ibid., pp. 190–1.

39.   Ibid., p. 191.

40.   On Soviet Jewish emigration see Lukasz Hirszowicz, 'The Soviet Jewish Problem: Internal and International Developments, 1972–1976', in Kochan, *The Jews in Soviet Russia*, pp. 366–409, and Smith, *The Russians*, pp. 573–92.

41.   Smith, *The Russians*, pp. 580–1.

42.   Archie Brown, 'Political Developments, 1975–1977', in Archie Brown and Michael Kaser (eds.), *The Soviet Union Since the Fall of Khruschchev* (2nd edn, London, 1978), p. 318.

43.   On these two trends see Lukasz Hirszowicz, 'New Data on Jews in the USSR', Institute of Jewish Affairs [IJA] Research Report, London, Nov. 1977, and his 'Less Noted Sides of Soviet Jewish Policies', IJA Research Report, April 1976, especially pp. 3–4, as well as his article in Kochan, *The Jews in Soviet Russia*, pp. 385–8.

44.   In Soviet terminology, 'academic workers' include professors, lecturers and academic research staff.

45.   Leon Shapiro, 'Outline of the History of Russian and Soviet Jewry 1912–1974', in Dubnow, *History of the Jews*, p. 466. Shapiro notes, 'It is obvious that some among the Soviet hierarchy were not happy to see so many Jews achieving enviable status in the arts and sciences or for that matter to see Jews still occupying responsible positions in industry and the various Soviet institutions'.

46.   Mordecai Altshuler, 'The Jew in the Scientific Elite of the Soviet Union', *Jewish Journal of Sociology*, XV (1973), p. 47.

47.   Ibid., p. 48.

48.   Statistics cited in S. Levenberg, 'Soviet Jewry: Some Problems and Perspectives', in Kochan, *The Jews in Soviet Russia*, p. 34.

49.   Hirszowicz, 'Soviet-Jewish Problem', in ibid., pp. 386, and Nove and Newth, 'The Jewish Population', especially pp. 160–1.

50.   Hirszowicz, 'Less Noted Sides of Soviet Jewish Policies', pp. 2–3.

51.   Ibid., p. 3.

52.   Ibid., p. 2.

53.   Ibid., p. 3.

54.   Ibid.

55.   Figures for 1961, 1965 and 1969 are from Zev Katz, 'After the Six-Day War', in Kochan, *The Jews in Soviet Russia*, p. 345, Table C, based on estimates by Professor T.H. Rigby. The 1976 percentage is derived from Table 2, 'CPSU: Ethnic Composition', in Robert G. Wesson, *Lenin's Legacy: The Story of the CPSU* (Stanford, California, 1978), p. 281. This table states that 294,744 members of the CPSU were Jews in 1976, out of a total party membership of 15,638,891. This result – a *rise* in the Jewish percentage of the CPSU at a time of increased anti-semitism and declining Jewish numbers – seems incredible, and may possibly reflect the differing sources used. (Professor Rigby has informed the author that his figures for Jewish membership in the CPSU during the 1960s may have been underestimates). See Everett M. Jacobs, 'Further Considerations on Jewish Representation in Local Soviets and in the CPSU', *Soviet Jewish Affairs*, 8 (1978). Jacobs notes that: 'The numbers of Jewish Party members apparently increased by about 25,000 between 1961 and 1976, and Jews have remained the most Party-saturated national group. In 1976, one out of every seven Soviet Jews, or possibly one out of five adult Jews, was a member of the CPSU' (p. 31). However, Jacobs concludes that 'the proportion of Jews in the CPSU has declined from year to year'.

56.   See, e.g., Mikhail Argusky, 'Russian Neo-Nazism – A Growing Threat',

Midstream, Feb. 1976.

57. We use this as a shorthand term; most minority Soviet nationalities have a long history of anti-semitism. Probably the worst anti-semitism in the Soviet Union at present is Ukrainian.

58. Rothenberg, 'Jewish Religion'.

59. See Kochan, *The Jews in Soviet Russia*, *passim*; Hirszowicz, 'Jewish Cultural Life in the USSR – A Survey', *Soviet Jewish Affairs*, 7 (1977) and Nora Levin, 'The Murder of Jewish Culture in the U.S.S.R.', *Jewish Frontier*, Oct. 1977.

60. Rothenberg, 'Jewish Religion', p. 191 and note 1.

61. For moving first-hand accounts of the life of individual Jews in Soviet Russia, see, for example, Elie Wiesel, *The Jews of Silence* (London, 1973) and Grigory Svirsky, *Hostages: The Personal Testimony of a Soviet Jew* (London, 1974).

62. See, for example, the Webbs' *Soviet Communism. A New Civilization?* (London, 1935).

63. This point has been made many times by writers on Soviet Jewry. See, for example, Jacobs, 'Further Considerations', p. 33.

64. See, for example, Michael Checinski, 'Soviet Jews and Higher Education', *Soviet Jewish Affairs*, 3 (1973).

65. Again, this point has often been made, though usually by writers who contend that the Jews are systematically disadvantaged by the failure of the Soviet's attempts. See Jacobs, 'Further Considerations', p. 30.

66. On Biro-Bidzhan, see C. Abramsky, 'The Biro-Bidzhan Project, 1927–1959', in Kochan, *The Jews in Soviet Russia*, pp. 64–77.

67. Ibid., p. 7.

68. See Hirszowicz in ibid., pp. 385ff. and his 'Biro-Bidzhan After Forty Years', *Soviet Jewish Affairs* 4 (1974); see also the publicity given to Biro-Bidzhan in, for example, *Moscow Weekly Sputnik*, and other English-language Soviet journals, *passim*.

69. See Smith, *The Russians*, pp. 584–5.

70. Altschuler, 'The Jew in the Scientific Elite', p. 47.

71. William Korey, 'Quotas and Soviet Jewry', *Commentary*, May 1974, p. 55.

72. Ibid; Jacobs, 'Further Considerations', p. 31.

73. See Schmelz, 'New Evidence', p. 210. But Hirszowicz ('New Data', p. 2), using 1970 demographic statistics, projected that in 1976 the number of Jewish tertiary students would be 'lower than 66,500, possibly nearer the 60,000 mark'. In terms of his estimate – and the further loss of Jewish numbers through emigration – the student population of 66,900 in 1975–6 could be accounted for entirely by natural demographic decrease, without resorting to anti-semitism as an explanation.

74. Jacobs, 'Further Considerations', p. 31, citing William Korey, 'Soviet Students – A Shock Report', *Jewish Chronicle*, 2 Dec. 1977.

75. Korey, 'Soviet Students', p. 55.

76. See, e.g., T.H. Rigby, *Communist Party Membership in the USSR* (Princeton, 1968), especially pp. 379–81.

77. See Brown (note 42), pp. 299–329. Dymshits, the highest-ranking Party Jew, is one of the few products of this milieu. (The author is grateful to Professor Rigby for pointing this out.)

78. Checinski, 'Soviet Jews', Table V, p. 15. Even so, Jews are over-represented in nearly all fields detailed in this table because of the low overall number of trained specialists.

79. 'Further Considerations', p. 34.

7 ISRAEL

As we have seen throughout this book, the continued existence of Israel is the central concern of diaspora Jewry, whose ability to influence national policy depends upon its continuing over-representation at the elite level and, ultimately, upon the capitalist structure of power which makes such an over-representation possible. In this chapter we shall discuss the relationship between Israel and diaspora Jewry as well as the possible future course of events in the Middle East.

However, we must make two caveats which particularly apply to this chapter. In the first place much has already been said and written on the Middle East, and in our analysis of the State of Israel and on the possible course to peace in the Middle East we cannot claim originality. Moreover, so rapid is the pace of change in that region, that this book is likely to be quickly overtaken by events.

Second, the author has often found himself divided between advocating a moderate, conciliatory approach to the Middle Eastern question and defending a stand by Israel in respect to the creation of a Palestinian 'homeland'. The result of this is that we must approach any discussion of the future of the Middle East with caution.

Perhaps the central point which can be made about the twin aims of world Jewry – the continuing existence of Israel and the continuing elite over-representation of diaspora Jewry – is that it is by no means clear that they are mutually compatible. This statement must be the starting-point of the discussion in this chapter.

The position of contemporary diaspora Jewry is, from a socio-economic perspective, abnormal. Jews are an ethnic elite, highly over-represented in the Western power structure and in the Western world's intelligentsia. Jews are to be found in the Western world almost totally in the upper middle class, with only a small minority remaining in the working class.

While Israel was founded for a variety of reasons, one of the most important was to normalise Jewish existence by creating a Jewish state. Entailed in the establishment of Israel is, then, a transformation of the Jewish social structure so that it resembles the structures of other nations. Israel was founded in no small part to right Borochov's 'inverted pyramid', to eliminate what the founders of Zionism perceived (wrongly) as the preponderance of Jewish businessmen and professionals in early twentieth-century Europe.

Ber Borochov was a Marxist who devoted himself to reconciling Zionism and Marxism.[1] In Laqueur's words:

> Borochov invested a great deal of analytical skill in justifying Zionism in Marxist terms. All other solutions he discarded by elimination: their anomalous social structure made it impossible for the masses of Jews to stay in the long run in eastern Europe. Nor would emigration to America or some other territory provide an answer because there was already no room for Jews in the basic branches of the national economy of these rapidly developing countries, and the new immigrants would again be reduced to a marginal, and therefore highly vulnerable existence in their new home . . . Borochov was convinced that by a correct Marxist analysis he had found the only practical solution: the Jewish middle class would be drawn by spontaneous forces to Palestine and gradually build up there the means of production. Expanding industry would attract the Jewish working masses to Palestine, and the industrial proletariat, pursuing a correct policy of class struggle, would establish itself as the vanguard of the national liberation movement.[2]

Ironically, there was little in Borochov's Marxist formulation of Zionism which conservative Zionists would not echo – at least up to the point when the Jewish proletariat was to establish itself as the 'vanguard' of the revolution. For to conservative Zionists the vision of a state where the Jewish people might comprise a nation like other nations was imperative. Theodor Herzl, the founder of modern Zionism,

> did not claim that the charges of anti-semites were altogether unjust: the ghetto, which had not been of their making, had bred in them certain asocial qualities: the Jews had come to embody the characteristics of men who had served long prison terms unjustly. Emancipation had been based on the illusion that men are made free when their rights are guaranteed on paper. The Jews had been liberated from the ghetto but basically, in their mental make-up, they had remained ghetto Jews . . . On one

occasion, in 1893, he suggested that half a dozen 'duels' would do a great deal to improve the situation of Jews in society.[3]

The urge for normality was thus implicit in conservative Zionism from its outset; this necessarily entailed the creation of a Jewish society in Palestine identical to that of other Western nations and which would doubtless include those social elements so strikingly absent from diaspora Jewry – a military, an aristocracy and a settled and important agricultural sector. Herzl, for example, 'preferred a democratic monarchy, or an aristocratic republic' in his ideal Jewish state; included in the elaborate plans he formulated for the Jewish state was 'a standing army (strength: one-tenth of the male population)'.[4] After a visit to the Paris Opera, Herzl wrote: 'We too shall have such resplendent lobbies – the men in full dress, the women altogether sumptuous.' And on another occasion: 'Circuses [games] as soon as possible: German theatre, international theatre, opera, musical comedy, café-concerts, cafés, Champs Elysées.'[5]

There were, of course, other motivating factors behind early Zionism. But most of these are akin to, and soon return to, the central factor of normality. Plainly, the primary reason for the establishment of Israel was to give Jews an ultimate place of refuge, a home to which they could flee should anti-semitism become intolerable in the country in which they dwelt. Entailed in this is a belief in the near-universality of anti-semitism. It was the Dreyfus Affair in France which stirred Herzl to publish *Der Judenstaat* in 1896, just as the revival of anti-semitism in other parts of Europe like Germany and Russia led other early Zionists away from a belief in full assimilation.[6] Given the history of Europe from 1897 to 1945, culminating in the Holocaust, they were undoubtedly correct. But beyond this belief was a profound conviction that Jewish life in Europe was abnormal and that this abnormality in itself *created* anti-semitism, by creating the ghetto Jew of caricature as well as the equally abnormal Jewish plutocrat.

A common theme – the impossibility of a 'normal life' for Jews in the diaspora – is at the back of the writings of the early theorists of Zionism. To Leo Pinsker, the author of the influential *Auto-Emancipation* (which appeared in 1882, over a decade before Herzl's *Judenstaat*), Jews

everywhere . . . were guests, nowhere at home. Thanks to their adaptability they had usually acquired the alien traits of the people among whom they dwelt. They had absorbed certain cosmopolitan tendencies and lost their own traditional individuality. They had deliberately renounced their own nationality, but nowhere had they succeeded in obtaining recognition from their neighbours as citizens of equal rank. All this was no accident or misfortune. No people . . . had any prediliction for foreigners. But the Jew was subject to this general law to an even greater degree than other foreigners precisely because he had no country of his own, because he was the stranger *par excellence*. Other foreigners had no need to be, or seem to be patriots. They could claim hospitality and repay it in the same coin in their own country. The Jew, having no country, could make no claim to hospitality. He was beggar rather than a guest.[7]

Zionism was from its outset a profoundly revolutionary doctrine, for it anticipated many of the central ideas of modern revolutionary movements. In particular, it anticipated the need to restore to the Jews the self-respect which had been lost through centuries of exile and servitude, and to overcome the 'mentality of the ghetto', the behaviour of ghetto Jews which in itself encouraged anti-semitism. The early Zionists repeatedly mentioned the 'new Jewish man' which settlement in Palestine would produce.[8] The early Zionists were generally socialists and men of peace, living in an age when statesman could still claim that 'the resources of civilisation had not been exhausted', and when holocausts of any sort were virtually inconceivable. But there is also within Zionism the seeds of Franz Fanon's doctrine of the liberating effects of violence upon captive and subjugated peoples. The practical form which the Jewish struggle in Palestine eventually took, first against the British and since 1948 against the Arabs was not, of course, foreseen by the pre–1917 Zionists, who hoped to establish themselves by legal means.

It is now over eighty years since Herzl first formulated his vision of a Jewish state and more than thirty years since Israel's foundation. Of the aims of the early Zionists, the theorists who wished to right the 'inverted pyramid' and create in Palestine a 'normal' Jewish society, we can say that they succeeded. It is this fact above all others which must be kept in mind in assessing Israel in the concept of contemporary Jewry.

Thirty-five years after its foundation the socio-economic and

demographic structure of Israel resembles that of any small or
middle-rank Western nation. On the criteria of *per capita* output
and income, Israel generally ranks towards the lower end of
performance among Western nations; in such areas as health care,
population longevity and education, it does rather better. To take
several important indices of measurement, Israel's *per capita*
income in 1976 was $3,831; by comparison, *per capita* income in
Italy was $2,758, in Belgium $5,851 and in New Zealand $3,969.[9] In
the United States it was $7,400. *Per capita* incomes in the
underdeveloped world range from $70 in Bangladesh to $4,758 in
Saudi Arabia (and an astonishing $11,431 in Kuwait); among
Israel's Arab neighbours, Egypt's *per capita* income was $263,
Jordan's $583, Syria's $747.[10] Israel's *per capita* energy
consumption in 1976 amounted to 1.9 tons of oil-equivalent; this
was above the figure for Spain and Greece, but considerably below
most other Western nations.[11] Israel's statistics for current life-
expectancy at birth – 70.3 years for males, 73.9 for females (1975) –
were among the highest in the world, but they are not so good as,
say, Norway's, where males could expect to live for 75 years,
females for 77.8 years.[12] Israel's occupational structure, though
distorted by a relatively large public sector, is also still recognisable
as fairly typical of any Western society. Of a total civilian labour
force of 1.2 million in 1976, the largest employer is the public sector,
with 370,000 wage-earners, then industry (280,000), commerce and
tourism (150,000), building (120,000), transport and communications (80,000) and agriculture (70,000).[13] The percentage of
the labour force employed in agriculture – about five per cent – is
similar to that in Britain, and has declined since the early 1960s
(128,000 were employed in the agricultural sector in 1960–1) as
productivity has increased.[14]

    Israel, in other words, has 'normalised' life for its Jewish citizens
to a remarkable extent. It has succeeded in fulfilling the aims of its
founders. This achievement should not be minimised, as Israel was
faced with monumental problems of moulding together a single
society out of human elements from all over the world. Of Israel's
population of 3.7 million (pre–1967 boundaries), 600,000 are Arabs
and their achievement can hardly be expected to equal those of the
populations of European or American origin. This also applies to
Israel's substantial population of Oriental Jews formerly living in
the Afro-Asian world, and now amounting to half the Jewish
population of Israel. Although the condition of Israel's Oriental

Jewish population has been the subject of much discussion – and has been viewed for ten years or more by radicals as a likely source of discontent within Israeli society – the rate at which the gap between European and Oriental Jews has closed is perhaps more striking than the remaining differences.[15] While the political leadership element in Israel continues to be derived very disproportionately from Jews of eastern European Ashkenazi stock, they were freely elected to their positions by a population with a very substantial percentage of Oriental Jewish voters. Certainly there is no evidence that Oriental Jews are markedly less 'patriotic' or more likely to support, or be sympathetic to, the demands of the Palestinians and radical Arabs. Oriental Jews were most migrants from the Arab world and would be the first to renounce Israel if it exploited them. Their refusal to consider leaving Israel, despite Arab invitations to return to their 'homeland' is an eloquent response to the widely held belief that Arab Jews were free and equal citizens of their former countries. In 1975, for example, the Iraqi government issued an invitation for all former Iraqi Jews (who numbered 125,000 in 1948, but only 300 today) to return 'home'. As far as is known, only one former Iraqi in Israel, Yusef Navi, accepted the invitation. After a year in Iraq, Navi re-emigrated to Israel.[16] In Iraq, one of the most radical and intransigent of all Arab states, nineteen Jewish 'spies' were sentenced to death by public hanging in January 1969.[17] Another eighteen Jews were hanged in secret between 1970 and 1972. Nazeim Kayzar, head of the secret police, ordered the murders of five members of one Jewish family in April 1973 in retaliation for the Israeli assassination of a Palestinian terrorist leader in Beirut on the previous day.

Israel's relatively successful settlement of its non-Westernised Oriental Jewish population points to the change which its existence, and in particular, its military success, has brought to its population of European Jews. A total of 1,221,000 Jews migrated from Europe and America between 1919 and 1977 (a further 799,000 came from Africa and Asia), of whom 337,000 – almost all survivors of the Holocaust – came in the three years 1948–51.[18] Therefore a very large percentage of the contemporary Israeli population knew the old pre-Holocaust *shtetl* world at first hand. They knew the continuous humiliation of Jewish life in a gentile world where anti-semitism was endemic. The necessity for military action to win Israel's independence, as well as the successive military victories of the Israeli army in the four Arab-Israeli wars, has entirely removed the *shtetl*'s legacy of humiliation. This has been a source of inspiration not only for Israel's Jews but for those of the entire world.

But Israel's real achievements, above all the restoration of self-respect to the world's Jews, have been accomplished at a high cost. This cost has not been accrued – as most left-wing critics of Israel allege – by the nature of Israel's ideology and social structure.[19] If there have been breaches of human rights in Israel – and there have been far fewer of these in Israel than in any other state in the Middle East – they have been the result of military and political necessity, and would cease if there were a genuine peace settlement. Rather, Israel's existence *as a nation*, and especially as one surrounded by perpetually hostile forces, has made it impossible for its Jews to participate with non-Jews in most civilian spheres of life.

Perhaps more seriously, much the same is true in the economic sphere. With the exception of citrus agriculture, the diamond trade and certain high-technology areas of military production, Israel is not among the world's leaders in any significant economic field. Israel – in the useful terminology of the historian Immanuel Wallerstein – is a 'semi-peripheral' state, at the fringes of the Western world, and is in no sense even close to the core of Western civilisation. This, it can be argued, constitutes the deviant nature of Israeli Jewry compared with diaspora Jewry.[20] These disadvantages are inherent in Israel's existence as a nation and one, moreover, geographically isolated from today's centres of Western life.

Left-wing critics of Israel frequently point out that Israel does, in fact, possess an elite, as well as an ethnically structured class society.[21] They claim that in Israel, the European (Ashkenazi) Jews form the elite and the Oriental Jews and Israeli Arabs are the working class. While this half-truth is accurate enough to be accepted by most radicals, it is just as pertinent to link such distinctions to the great cultural differences between those whose former home was Germany or the United States and those from the Yemen or Morocco. For many years to come Western migrants will be employed, in the main, in jobs of higher status and income. The difficulties in removing far smaller social differentials from the educational performance of American blacks is, of course, well known. Further, as Remba has pointed out, documentation of the social gap between 'Ashkenazi' and 'Oriental' Jews is based on statistics compiled by the geographical rather than the ethnic origin of those studied (Asia-African versus Europe-America). But

Sephardic (i.e. Oriental) Jews from southern Europe have higher incomes than Middle Eastern Jews. Bulgarian Jews, for instance, have a higher percentage of doctors and dentists than any other group in the population.[22]

The central point is that in the great majority of cases, Oriental Jews experienced a revolutionary *gain* in their living standards by migrating to Israel,[23] whereas the European Jews now living in Israel have certainly experienced a *decline* in their living standards compared with that which they would have known had they remained in the prosperous West. This argument is stronger for those Jews freely migrating from the United States and Western Europe since the 1950s than for those who came as destitute refugees, but it applies to almost all Western Jews. This cut in living standards is another facet of Israel's situation as a Western nation at the lower level of socio-economic performance.

However, one might argue that Israel's existence as a nation has affected the intellectual and cultural achievements of Israel's Jews at a more fundamental level. A number of studies have previously suggested that a characteristically Israeli Jewish personality has emerged in Israel, quite different from any stereotyped 'Jewish' personality of the diaspora.[24] Such studies have not, however, implied – as we shall imply – that the new Israeli personality has adversely affected the intellectual achievements of Israel's Jews. In some spheres, this decline must be due to some deep-seated and fundamental transformation in the Israeli psyche. For instance, the number of Israeli patents registered between 1958 and 1963 (the only period for which figures are available) totalled only two-fifths of the number registered in either Denmark or Norway, one-fifth of the number in the Netherlands and one-tenth of the number in Switzerland and Sweden in this period.[25] One could cite many other examples.

On the other hand, Israel's military triumphs have been a source of pride to every Jew. Israel's existence has, in a sense, 'redeemed' the Holocaust, giving a living centre of hope to hundreds of thousands of Jews who might otherwise be hopeless. The Israeli has helped to make the establishment right throughout the Western world philo-semitic rather than anti-semitic. And Israel has fulfilled what is perhaps the primary purpose of its existence: it has provided a place of refuge and a new and better life for hundreds of thousands of persecuted Jews. These achievements are inestimable. But, given the increasing dichotomy between the 'abnormal' life of diaspora Jewry and the 'normal' life of Israeli Jewry, even these achievements may not be enough.

This brings us to the important question of the political future of the Middle East, and to the possibilities of peace for that region. So inextricably linked is Israel's role *vis-à-vis* world Jewry and the future of the Middle East that no discussion of Israel can ignore its future relations with the Arabs.[26]

Despite all the disagreements about the future of the Middle East in their essence all future proposals can be broken down to three.

1. The radical Palestinian settlement. A 'secular, democratic state' in which Jews, Muslims and Christians would live in a bi-national or non-national state where each citizen would have equal rights and obligations. This solution would entail the return of large numbers of Palestinians to Israel, restoration of their property and 'dismantling' of the 'Zionist' features of the Israeli state – its army, religious establishment, the 'Law of Return', etc.

2. The UN Resolution 242 settlement:[27] evacuation of the West Bank and Gaza by Israel, followed by the creation of an independent Palestinian state in these areas (or one in confederation with Jordan), and the mutual recognition of Israel, within its 1949–67 boundaries, by the Arabs and of a Palestinian state by the Israelis. (This formulation leaves the vexed question of the future of Jerusalem unresolved; in all likelihood it would be redivided into Arab Jerusalem, under Palestinian or international Arab sovereignty, and Jewish Jerusalem, under Israeli sovereignty).

3. The radical Zionist settlement: the official incorporation of the West Bank ('Judea and Samaria') into Israel proper, probably by gradual steps, with Jordanian citizenship for most Palestinian Arabs living there; recognition of the fact that a Palestinian state already exists, in the Middle East, which is called Jordan, and that 'Palestinian' acknowledgement of this provides the best basis for a final settlement in the Middle East.

The second of these settlements provides not only the most hopeful and practical framework for real peace but perhaps the only chance for Israeli Jews to achieve in the Middle Eastern context the entrepreneurial and intellectual links which, in the diaspora, have given to Western Jews their singular achievement and disproportionate influence. However, if such a settlement is politically impossible, Israel's future could still be bright if its relationship with diaspora Jewry were re-examined and redefined in the light of what is really implied by a radical Zionist settlement.

The radical Palestinian solution outlined above may be dismissed by most Jews and by most Arabs. In the first place, it is politically impossible. Israel would fight to the last man to prevent a Palestinian-Arab invasion of its legitimate borders. It is unimaginable that any segment of Israeli society would ever accede to the radical Palestinian programme, which would presumably entail, in its most moderate form, the abolition of virtually all the traditional institutions of Israeli society, including the army, the Histadrut (the trade union federation), the Knesset, the Law of Return and the establishment of Judaism as the state religion. It would also entail the admission of hundreds of thousands of Palestinian refugees and presumably, the enforcesd acquisition by them of thousands of millions of dollars worth of Israeli property.

In the second place, the radical Palestinian solution is disingenuous and hypocritical, since the Palestinian Covenant calls not for the establishment of a 'secular democratic' state where all people now resident in Israel may live but for the establishment of an exclusively Arab Palestinian state where the only Jews permitted to live would be those whose ancestors were resident in Palestine prior to 1917. Article One of the corner-stone of Palestinian nationalism, the 1968 Palestinian National Covenant (*al-mīthāq*),[28] states that 'Palestine is the homeland of the Arab Palestinian people: it is an indivisible part of the Arab homeland, and the Palestinian people are an integral part of the Arab nation'. Article Five states 'The Palestinians are those Arab nationals who, until 1948 normally resided in Palestine regardless of whether they were evicted from it or have stayed there. Anyone born after that date of a Palestinian father – whether inside Palestine or outside it – is also a Palestinian'. Article Six, the key article in this case, states 'The Jews who had normally resided in Palestine until the beginning of the Zionist invasion will be considered Palestinians', while Article Fifteen states 'The liberation of Palestine, from an Arab viewpoint, is a national duty to drive the Zionist, imperialist invasion from the great Arab homeland and to purge the Zionist presence from Palestine'.[29] That 1917, or occasionally 1948, was the beginning of the 'Zionist invasion' has been stated repeatedly by Palestinian spokesmen.[30] Extremist Palestinian leaders have repeatedly and explicitly made plain their aim of sending the great majority of all Israeli Jews into exile. Nigula al-Dur, Deputy to the Chairman of the First Palestinian Congress, and later a member of the PLO Executive Committee and of the PLO's delegation to the Second Arab Summit Conference, wrote in 1963 that

> Permission to stay (in Palestine) should be granted to the Jews who shall declare that they are giving up the idea of the Jewish state and choose to stay in Palestine. Their number will be decided in the future *provided that it does not exceed the level of May 1948* and that priority be given to Jews from Arab lands. We do not have any obligation to keep a single Jew who entered Palestine after the end of World War I . . .[31]

It is difficult to know what to make of such statements as these. They are nothing less than the announcement of a second Holocaust, and would be treated as such by virtually all Israelis if the Palestinians were ever in a position to realise them. Indeed, their outrageousness suggests a third general objection to the radical Palestinian programme: the fact that most Arab leaders, including the leadership of the PLO, must know that a 'secular democratic state' is an impossibility. This idea, which first gained currency in March 1970[32] and was repeated by Yassir Arafat at the United Nations,[33] is itself a considerable toning down of the Palestinian Covenant, for it implies that all or most of Israeli Jewry would be permitted to stay in 'Palestine'. Arafat – apparently in direct contradiction to the Palestinian Covenant as it exists – stated in his November 1974 United Nations speech that 'In my formal capacity as chairman of the Palestine Liberation Organisation, I proclaim before you that when we speak of our common hopes for the Palestine of tomorrow we include in our perspective all Jews now living in Palestine who choose to live with us there in peace and without discrimination'. Moreover, there are many signs that the PLO has dropped even the idea of a 'secular democratic state' because of its evident impossibility, and is now prepared to concede to Israel the right to exist within its 1949–67 boundaries, in exchange for a sovereign Palestinian homeland on the West Bank and Gaza. Arafat often talks openly of the 'reality' of three million Israeli Jews, an ever-increasing number of whom are native-born; a distinguished Palestinian academic like Professor Khalidi of the

American University of Beirut can write a lengthy and constructive article on the shape such a West Bank-Gaza state might take.[34] If the official Palelstinian leadership is now prepared to abandon the concept of a 'secular democratic state' and accept a sovereign West Bank-Gaza state as the lasting settlement of the Palestinian question (subject to stringent guarantees for Israeli security), the whole Middle Eastern situation would be transformed overnight. Israel has always made the unconditional acceptance of its sovereignty and right to exist an absolute pre-condition for any negotiations with the Palestinian leadership. Palestinian willingness to accept this would isolate Israel further from its remaining friends, including the United States, should it still refuse to negotiate after such an announcement. Indeed, the fact that the Palestinian leaders have never made such a public acceptance of Israel's existence – suggesting that it is a 'final bargaining card' to be offered only at a general peace conference – implies that they still envisage the impossible 'secular democratic state', which Israel has rejected and will continue to reject unconditionally.

Fourth, the goal of a 'secular democratic state' throughout Mandate Palestine is unacceptable because it would be neither secular nor democratic, but predominantly Arab and Marxist-socialist. It would deny the Jews of Israel the right to self-determination and self-respect; the 'Palestine' envisaged is an Arab rather than a secular, multi-national society. Article One of the Palestinian Covenant states that 'Palestine is the homeland of the Arab Palestinian people: it is an indivisible part of the Arab homeland, and the Palestinian people are an integral part of the Arab nation'.[35] (This should, of course, be read in connection with Article Six, quoted above, which defines the great majority of Israeli Jews as 'invaders'.). There is no state in the Arab world which defines itself as 'secular'. *All* the Arab states, with the exception of Syria and Lebanon, define themselves in their constitutions as Muslim. Algerian leaders, who before independence had put forward the possibility of a 'secular Algerian Republic' in which Muslims and Christians would be equal citizens, immediately discarded any such hopes after independence, and the Sunni variant of Islam is, in fact, its state religion.[36] The Palestinian national movement must be seen in the context of a revived Islamic and Arab nationalism (though some of its most militant leaders are Arab Christians) which has generally proved intolerant of minorities and pluralism.

The second possible solution to the Middle Eastern question, which we have termed the 'UN Resolution 242' programme, has a wide body of support. In theory, it is favoured by all the great powers, including the Soviet Union, and perhaps the question concerning this programme is why it has not yet succeeded. There are, to be sure, formidable difficulties in its path. Israel must vacate the West Bank and Gaza, which she regards as vital to her security, and acquiesce in the establishment of a Palestinian state whose leadership would, at least initially, comprise the major PLO leaders, including Arafat. Israeli settlements in the West Bank would presumably not be permitted. The Palestinians in their turn would have to recognise Israel and give up their dreams of a secular democratic state. There is the problem, perhaps insoluble, of Jerusalem, and the matter of Jordan's former control of the West Bank. (In 1974, no fewer than 1,593,000 'Palestinians' were Jordanian citizens, including 670,000 living on the West Bank and 80,000 in Jerusalem.[37]). The establishment of such a Palestinian state would probably be the work of a general peace conference; this raises the question of participation at such a conference and the role of the Soviet Union. There are real doubts about the economic viability of a West Bank state. Any settlement would have to provide Israel with guarantees for its security.

However, the idea of a West Bank-Gaza state ideally remains the best possible solution to the Middle Eastern question. From the Israeli viewpoint, it would remove some of the necessity for the crushing military budget which had produced a 150 per cent inflation rate by 1980. It would allow the formation of a military alliance between the major moderate states of the area, especially between Israel, Egypt, Jordan and Saudi Arabia, which would provide the best guarantee against Soviet expansionism. Most of all, it would allow Israel to trade with the Arab states, to obtain their oil, to use Israeli brains and skills in combination with Arab money and manpower. With her skills and her links with the Western world and Western Jewry Israel would soon become a major economic power in the area. Israel's Jews might then begin to duplicate the entrepreneurial and intellectual success and leadership in the Arab world which diaspora Jewry has accomplished in the West.

Such a situation is not impossible. In the nineteenth and twentieth centuries up to the Second World War, Jews were to be found as disproportionately in the economic elites of many Arab countries, especially Iraq, Egypt and Morocco, as they were in France and Britain – indeed, much more so. In Iraq – where Sassoon Hisqail, a Jew, became that country's first Finance Minister – 95 per cent of the import trade was in Jewish hands prior to the Second World War, as were 90 per cent of government contracts and ten per cent of all exports.[38] It can be argued that the settlement of 750,000 Afro-Asian Jews in Israel following that state's establishment in 1948 ended successful native Jewish links with the Arab world precisely at a time when, because of oil and decolonialisation, its importance in the balance of world power was becoming far greater than before. Oriental Jews, most of whom came from Arab countries, might provide such a link between Israel and the Arab world, while remaining Israeli. There is some evidence that the Arab states, particularly the radical socialist Arab states, fear such an eventuality, or, at least, are well aware of the political possibilities inherent in genuine peace.[39]

There are, of course, formidable difficulties in the way of Israeli Jews becoming a major economic and social force in the Arab world. It is unlikely that the radical Arab states – Iraq, Libya, South Yemen and others – would give more than grudging acquiescence to any settlement which left Israel intact, and would, in all likelihood, provide money and weapons to Palestinian extremists also in opposition to such an agreement. The social and economic structures of most Arab states have changed greatly since 1948. Many are socialist of semi-socialist societies where entrepreneurs, whatever their origins, are no longer welcome. It would be generations before the legacy of bitterness felt against Israel passed. These difficulties, when added to the very real territorial sacrifices which Israel would be obliged to make and to the great political obstacles which exist, may simply be too great to make the programme a realistic one for any Israeli government.

The most basic Israeli objection to a small Palestinian state is that, if it were sovereign in any sense, it would be a base for terrorists as well as a Soviet satellite. This is indeed a major objection, as the West Bank splits the Israel of 1949–67 virtually in two, and an Arab army launching a surprise attack from the West Bank could cut Israel in half in a matter of hours. There would have to be the most stringent guarantees for Israeli security in any settlement. But the best defence for Israel would be the knowledge that moderate Arab leaders, moderate Palestinians and even radical Palestinians willing to assess realistically the dangers of military adventures against Israel would no longer have the desire for conflict as the main Arab grievance against Israel had been removed. Since Israel would still possess all the military resources it does at present – plus a fresh and plentiful injection of new armaments as the price of its evacuation of the West Bank – it would be the Palestinian state, rather than Israel, which would be at risk. As Professor Khalidi has put it, 'For how long would the Israeli brigadier generals be able to keep their hands off such a delectable sitting duck?'[40]

A West Bank-Gaza Palestinian state would be engaged for many years to come in the process of economic development and the reintegration of many of the Palestinian refugees in the new state. The full implications of this are perhaps lost on the opponents of such a state. Palestine would for many years be dependent for aid upon the other Arab states, especially Saudi Arabia and Kuwait; little of this could or would be diverted to military aggression against Israel. The removal of thousands of Palestinian refugees from southern Lebanon, Jordan and Syria would remove these sources of instability and camps of terrorism. In a Palestinian state, the technicians, businessmen, agronomists and administrators would – hopefully – quickly gain the upper hand over the radical elements. Indeed, it is quite possible that a freely elected government of Palestine might not even elect the Arafats and Habashes to influential positions. The divisions between the 1.2 million Palestinians living today in the West Bank and Gaza, the 700,000 in Jordan and half million or so living elsewhere in the Arab Middle East might prove a potent source of division and disunity. It is difficult to see such a state presenting a serious threat to Israel's existence.

Abroad, the creation of a Palestinian state would remove the major source of instability and radicalisation from the Arab and Muslim worlds, and would provide the best possible boost for Arab moderates. It would remove the international terrorism which operates with PLO assistance. It would weaken Soviet and strengthen American and Western influence in the Middle East. For Jews, it would remove the sense of isolation, the continuous anti-Zionist propaganda of the United Nations and similar bodies, and might, conceivably, benefit Soviet Jewry, since the Soviet government's hostility to its Jews stems in part from their association with 'reactionary' Zionism, the 'aggressor'. Most of all, it would bring the hope of peace to a corner of the world which has not known real peace in our time.

Many Israelis and Jews in other countries would still oppose such a settlement of the Palestinian question. To them, Judea and Samaria (the West Bank) are an integral part of the biblical land of the Jews and of Mandate Palestine, and hence an integral part of Israel. The West Bank was in Jordanian hands between 1948 and 1967 solely because a cease-fire was agreed in Palestine before the Israeli forces could conquer this area. The status in international law of the West Bank is unclear; the Jordanian incorporation of the West Bank into its territory in 1951 was illegal (and was not recognised by any Arab state). Israel has the right, both in international law and in morality, to establish new settlements there.[41] 'Palestine' is largely a fiction. There was no independent Palestine in the years between 1948 and 1967 when the West Bank was in Arab hands; the PLO is evidently an organisation dedicated to the destruction of Israel. The great majority of Palestinians (1.6 million out of 2.3 million in 1974, apart from Israeli Arabs) are Jordanian citizens and already possess a country and a homeland, which, though it is called Jordan, is in fact a state which was intended to be the Palestinian homeland by the British.[42] The interminable conflict in the Middle East began because the Arab states refused to accept the division of the Palestine Mandate into Arab and Jewish areas, which would have given them much more of this area than can now be formed into a Palestinian 'homeland'. The independent Arab states attacked Israel with the intention of destroying it. They were defeated and the Palestinians fled, and the Arab states have been unwilling to recognise the reality of Israel or to accommodate the Palestinian refugees.[43]

This viewpoint of non-recognition, the third of the basic positions of Middle East policy, is probably not given as much publicity as it merits.[44] Most observers of the Middle Eastern scene will conclude that it is the converse of the radical Palestinian position and ought to be rejected by moderates for many of the same reasons. Whether it ought ultimately to be rejected is an open question; that it is the converse of the secular democratic state proposed by radical Palestinians is much more arguable. The transformation of Israel into Palestine would see the world filled with twenty or more Arab states, including two Palestinian nations (Jordan and Palestine), but no Jewish state at all, while the annexation of the West Bank would still leave the Middle East with twenty Arab states, including one (Jordan) where Palestinians constitute the majority of the population. The official annexation of the West Bank would merely reunite the area of Mandate Palestine and complete the Zionist programme, and would leave the rest of the Middle East unaffected, while the collapse of Israel and its transformation into Palestine is integral to a revolutionary programme affecting the entire Arab world. The transformation of Israel into a 'secular democratic' Palestine is politically impossible, but the annexation of the West Bank is not merely possible, but apparently, the *de facto* policy of Begin's government.[45]

If Israel has a right to exist at all, proponents of the radical Zionist programme argue, then it surely has a right to Judea and Sumaria, territories which were part of the Jewish Holy Land in biblical times, part of the British Mandate and necessary (according to this argument) for Israeli security. There can be little point in examining here the merits of the radical Zionist case any further; what does need close inspection is the likely consequence of this programme for Israel and world Jewry.

Such a policy, if pursued single-mindedly, would isolate Israel to an even greater extent than at present. Israel could expect many decades of UN resolutions condemning her, innumerable terrorist incidents and even greater use of the oil weapon. Jews in the Western world could also expect to see the world's socialist parties become increasingly, and more explicitly, anti-Zionist, particularly if Israel attempts to carry out large-scale population transfers of the ever-increasing Palestinian percentage of enlarged Israel. Since Israel and world Jewry have now tolerated this for ten or fifteen years, these in themselves will not be new. What will have to alter, however, is the relationship between Israel and diaspora Jewry. The economic gap between the two will become more pronounced, and Israel will depend, as never before, on the largesse and influence of diaspora Jewry, particularly in the United States. This is an indefinite extension of the state of affairs at present. Both Israel and diaspora Jewry can live with this situation (though with ever more difficulty), and even profit from it. Israel may have abandoned for the forseeable future some of its links with diaspora Jewry in order to seek fulfilment of a territorial dream. Both the philosophy behind such a policy and the type of new Jewish man produced by the Jewish nation-state differ markedly from the typical philosophy and personality of previous diaspora Jewry. Yet, paradoxically, while eradicating the ghetto mentality typical of Jews in the Russian Pale and restoring to Jews their self-respect, the creation of a Jewish state, because it is Jewish, because it is a nation with a normal social structure and because it is a relatively poor and marginal Western state, has created a Jewish homeland which in some respects resembles the traditional Jewish ghetto of eastern Europe. Israel is Jewish, and the Jewish religion with its traditional institutions as well as Jewish culture, flourish there as nowhere else in the world. In this respect, it is like the Pale. Israel's occupational structure includes a working class of poor Jews, while the country as a whole is hardly rich and its inhabitants considerably less prosperous than if they lived in the richer Western countries. This, again, is like the Pale. Israeli Jews have been denied, and will apparently continue to deny themselves, the possibility of economic links in the Middle Eastern context, unlike the Jews of the Western world. This, too, is like the Pale.

This can be of benefit to the world's Jews because Israel has become, and would continue to be, the replica of the old rooted centre of Jewish life in eastern Europe, and the 'feeder', through diaspora Jewry, to a revived Jewish presence in the world. From Israel's *yeshivot*, its Talmudic academies, its Jewish religious schools and cultural institutions will come the future equivalent of the Jewish genius of the past hundred years. This implies a paradox which may not be acceptable to many Jews, nor easy to achieve in practice: the simultaneous existence of an essentially religious Israel with an increased presence in the secularised Western world.[46] It would entail a greater degree of symbiosis between Israeli and diaspora Jewry, and even a greater degree of migration, at least temporary, from Israel to the diaspora. For it is, historically, the post-*shtetl* generation breathing the first air of freedom, which has been the most productive of genius and achievement in the non-Jewish world. And, except for Israel, it is difficult to think of any place in the world where such a 'feeder' for Jewish achievement may any longer be found. Diaspora Jewry is everywhere faced with low birth rates, intermarriage and the disappearance of Jewish communal life on the one hand, and with the inevitable weakening of the vigour and creative abilities of all elites on the other. Unless Jewish life is to attenuate or disappear in the diaspora, some replacement must be found for the vanished Russian Pale. That replacement can only be Israel. But conversely, and paradoxically, a powerful and vigorous diaspora Jewry is absolutely necessary for Israel's survival.

The numerical importance of Israeli Jewry in the total world

Jewish population is certain to increase over the next decades. While the Jewish population of Israel will probably number 4.5–5 million by the year 2000, the Jewish population of the diaspora will, in all likelihood, decline; certainly it will not grow, and there will be ever-greater numbers of unaffiliated and assimilated Jews.[47] Israel's Jewish population may well form up to 50 per cent of the world's total Jewish population by the year 2000, instead of 20 per cent as today.[48] But large numbers of Israeli Jews leave Israel every year for the diaspora, unable to prosper in Israel and tired of the constant dangers of war. In America, they are an over-achieving and hard-working community, in the manner of all Jewish immigrants.

This possible future for Israel would not be intolerable, and may well revitalise both Israel and the diaspora. Unquestionably this scenario suffers from many serious faults in comparison with the future which might follow the creation of a West Bank state. The most important of these faults is demographic: it makes no allowance for the ever-growing number of Palestinians living within an expanded Israel. Already, the non-Jewish population of the Israel of 1949–67 amounts to 15 per cent of its total population.[49] The million or more Palestinians living in the occupied territories, added to the 500,000 living in Israel proper, means that one-third of the population of 'Palestine' is Palestinian. Given their high birth rate, even despite further Jewish migration to Israel, the Palestinian portion is bound to grow. These facts appear to play no part in Israel's policy-formulation, although the maintenance of an exclusively Jewish state is the *raison d'être* of Zionism, and of the expansionist Zionism which opposes a West Bank state of Palestine. It is difficult to see a way out of this without population transfers of the West Bank Palestinians, which could lead to an American boycott of Israel. Equally, it could lead to a new Middle Eastern war in which Israel would have few supporters. The alternative, to see the Palestinian population within Israel grow until it rivalled the Jewish population, would lead to the destruction of Israel and the establishment of a bi-national state which would not be primarily Jewish.

The most prudent course for Israel to take would be to accede to the establishment of a West Bank Palestinian state; although any supporter of Israel who states this must recognise the dangers and difficulties which such a recommendation entails. Such a solution would not preclude Israel's role as a 'feeder' for diaspora Jewry although, without the isolation from its neighbours such as Israel has experienced since 1948, it is natural to expect that it will reorientate itself towards the Arab world in a manner which is economically advantageous to itself, and which would cause a realignment of its cultural and intellectual links. This is not a panacea: indeed, the prospect of indefinite Israeli isolation from the Arab world, with resultant increased links to diaspora Jewry, is not unattractive given the demographic and social pressures which the continuation of a powerful Jewish community in the West will increasingly meet. The prospect of further hostility between Western Jewry and the socialist left, as a result of Israel's 'intransigence' and its treatment of the Palestinians, is also attractive.

Idealism aside, is such a course politically likely? Almost certainly not: the well-justified fears expressed by all Israeli leaders, even those of the left, and by nearly all recognised leaders of diaspora Jewry, against even negotiations with the PLO leaders, probably precludes such a course for the foreseeable future. So long as the PLO declines to change its Charter to recognise Israel's right to exist and to disavow terrorism, Israel will almost certainly continue to decline to take any step which can be construed as implying recognition of the PLO. It is Israel, and Jewry, which remembers the Holocaust and stands in danger of destruction through miscalculation. These memories, these fears, rather than stubbornness or 'imperialism', account for Israel's temper.

Notes

1. On Borochov, see, e.g., Walter Laqueur, *A History of Zionism* (New York, 1972), pp. 274–7.
2. Ibid., pp. 275. (Laqueur spells Borochov's name 'Borokhov'. This has been altered.)
3. Ibid., pp. 88.
4. Ibid., pp. 93, 94. It must also be noted that Herzl and most other early Zionists were socialists, advocating state or co-operative ownership of the means of production; obviously, the kibbutz and other examples of socialism in practice are also legacies of the pioneer Zionists.
5. Ibid., p. 94.
6. Ibid., pp. 3–39, 84–135.
7. Ibid., pp. 71–2.
8. Ibid., pp. 40–135.
9. These figures are in American dollars, and are derived from Jack S. Cohen, *Israel. The Facts* (New York, 1978), p. 5, and *The World Almanac 1979*. The Israeli data is for 1976; the other data for 1975.

10. Ibid.

11. 'Israel Energy Economy 1978', Israeli Government Ministry of Energy and Infrastructure, 1979.

12. *World Almanac 1979*.

13. *Facts About Israel* (Israel Information Centre, Jerusalem, 1979) pp. 171–2.

14. Ibid., p. 175. The number of agricultural employees has, however, remained steady in recent years.

15. See Yoram Ben-Porath, 'On East-West Differences in Occupational Structure in Israel', in Michald Curtis and Mordecai S. Chertoff, *Israel: Social Structure and Change* (New Brunswick, New Jersey, 1973), especially pp. 233–4.

16. *Myths and Facts 1978. A Concise Record of the Arab-Israeli Conflict* (Near East Reports, Washington, DC, 1978), p. 79.

17. Ibid., p. 81.

18. '32 years of Israeli Statehood in Statistics' Information Briefing, Israeli Information Centre, Jerusalem.

19. Left-wing criticisms of Israel and Zionism include Uri Davis, Andrew Mack and Nira Yuval-Davis (eds.), *Israel and the Palestinians* (London, 1975); A.W. Kayyali, *Zionism, Imperialism, and Racism*, (London, 1979); Moishe Menuhin, *The Depradation of Judaism in Our Time* (Beirut, 1969), and Gary V. Smith, *Zionism. The Dream and the Reality* (Melbourne, 1974).

20. Much the same is superficially true of Soviet Jewry, although the special circumstances of Soviet Communism mitigate against any sharing of power or influence, as was discussed in Chapter 6.

21. See, e.g., Uri Davis, *Israel: Utopia, Incorporated* (London, 1977); Section Seven, 'Oriental Jews in Israel', in Davis, Mack and Yuval-Davis, *Israel and the Palestinians*, pp. 243–72.

22. Oded Remba, 'Income Inequality in Israel: Ethnic Aspects', in Curtis and Chertoff, *Israel*, p. 201.

23. In some Afro-Asian countries (for instance, Iraq) many Jews were members of the economic elite. However, the majority of Jewry in these countries were living in poverty.

24. See, e.g., S.N. Hermann, *Israelis and Jews* (New York, 1970). An extreme pro-Palestinian statement of this new Israeli personality may be found in Sayed Yassin, 'Zionism as a Racist Ideology', in Kayyali, *Zionism*, pp. 87–105.

25. *Education and Science* (Israel Pocket Library, Jerusalem, 1974), p. 115.

26. No short bibliography could do justice to this complex issue. Among the most useful works on the subject are Irving Howe and Carl Gershman (eds.), *Israel, the Arabs, and the Middle East* (New York, 1972); Naday Safran, *Israel – The Embattled Ally* (Cambridge, Mass., 1976); Elias H. Tuma and Haim Darin-Drabkin, *The Economic Case for Palestine* (London, 1978); Y. Harkabi, *Palestinians and Israel* (Jerusalem, 1974); Shaul Mishal, *West Bank/East Bank: The Palestinians in Jordan 1949–1967* (New Haven, Conn., 1978); Harold Fisch, *The Zionist Revolution. A New Perspective* (London, 1978); Hillel Halkin, *Letters to An American Jewish Friend. A Zionist Polemic* (Philadelphia, 1977).

27. The author is aware, of course, that UN Resolution 242 does not specifically call for the creation of a Palestinian state or necessarily for the evacuation of *all* the territories occupied by Israel in 1967. However, it seems clear that virtually all foreign parties in agreement with UN Resolution 242 envisage an eventual settlement which would include the creation of a Palestinian state and mutual recognition (in some form) of Israel by the Arabs and of the Palestinians by Israel.

28. The best discussion of the various Palestinian National Covenants is found in Y. Harkabi, *The Palestinian Covenant and its Meaning* (London, 1979). See also Y. Harkabi, *Myths and Facts 1978*, (London 1978), and 'Information Briefing 29, Aspects of the Palestinian Problem' (Israel Information Centre, Jerusalem, Sep.

1974).

29. Harkabi, *Palestinian Covenant*, pp. 28–43; 'Information Briefing 29', p. 31.

30. Harkabi, *Palestinian Covenant*, pp. 43–50.

31. Ibid., p. 46. The Jewish population of Palestine was about 600,000 in May 1948.

32. 'Information Briefing 29', p. 13. See also Peter Hellyer, 'The Palestinian Resistance, 1964–1975', in Davis, Mack and Yuval-Davis, *Israel and the Palestinians*, especially pp. 130ff.

33. 'Address by Yasser Arafat to the United Nations General Assembly, November 13, 1974' (text published by the Lebanese Association for Information on Palestine), p. 21.

34. Walid Khalidi, 'Thinking the Unthinkable: A Sovereign Palestinian State', *Foreign Affairs*, June 1978. This article was reprinted as 'A Palestinian State. What it Might Mean in Practice' (Eurabia, Paris, 1978).

35. Harkabi, *Palestinian Covenant*, p. 28.

36. 'Information Briefing 29', pp. 13–14; *World Almanac 1979*, p. 513.

37. 'Information Briefing 29', p. 4.

38. Walid Khadduri, 'The Jews of Iraq in the Nineteenth century: A Case study of Social Harmony', in Kayyali, *Zionism*, p. 206, citing Joseph Schecteman of the Jewish Agency.

39. See, e.g., Paul Eidelberg, *Sadat's Strategy* (Dollard des Ormeaux, Quebec, 1979), p. 154.

40. Khalidi, 'Thinking the Unthinkable', p. 11.

41. Interview with Professor Eugene Rostow (former Under-secretary of State and Professor of Law and Public Affairs at Yale University) in *Foreign Policy Perspectives* (1978) and reprinted in *Canadian Jewish Herald* November 1978, pp. 3ff. On the legal position of the West Bank, argued by a scholar from the Israeli point of view, see Allan Gerson, *Israel, The West Bank and International Law* (London, 1978).

42. 'Information Briefing 29', p. 4.

43. See Harkabi, *Myths and Facts 1978*, especially pp. 1–17.

44. Such a concept is strongly associated with the Revisionist Zionist movement founded by Vladimir Jabotinsky (*d.* 1940) and now led by his political heir, Menachem Begin.

45. See the full text of the twenty-six-point plan submitted by Prime Minister Begin to President Sadat in December 1977, conferring a limited degree of home rule on the West Bank Arabs.

46. Something of this sort seems to be implied in the interesting work of Hillel Halkin, *Letters to an American Jewish Friend* (Philadelphia, 1977), Halkin's realistic presentation of the demographic implications of diaspora Jewish life in the context of a religio-cultural argument for Zionism is compelling. See also the illuminating work by Fisch, *The Zionist Revolution*.

47. See Halkin, *Letters*, pp. 70–1.

48. See *Facts about Israel* (Jerusalem, 1978), p. 5, and Roberto Bachi, *The Population of Israel* (Jerusalem, 1974).

49. Ibid.

8 CONCLUSIONS

There can be little doubt that the prevalent mood of both diaspora and Israeli Jewry is one of pessimism. More than at any time since 1948, the facts seem to justify this. Already the period of Jewish history between 1948 and 1973 seems to many as a lost golden age, an era of optimism and real gains which cannot be maintained in today's conditions.

The roots of the problem, the energy crisis and the weakening of America's political and economic strength, have already had many adverse consequences for Western Jewry. Many observers have perceived American Jewry as a sacrificial lamb for the failures of the American economy since the Vietnam war. In a perceptive article in *Midstream* (May 1978), for example, Michael Kort, an official of the American Jewish Committee, has linked the widespread use of affirmative action and racial quota schemes in the United States to the continual crisis in America's economy:

> American Jewry for the first time is in danger of being forced into an historically familiar and potentially disastrous squeeze, in which its interests are sacrificed in order to satisfy the rising expectations of a previously repressed or underdeveloped indigenous caste. What is so worrisome is that a look at the Jewish experience throughout history reveals that solutions adapted for similar situations in other societies made Jewish life untenable . . .
>
> America's capitalist economy is caught in a syndrome that is producing very familiar tensions. The economy has stagnated. Plagued by chronic high unemployment and inflation, burdened by a developing energy shortage and enormous oil importation costs, and pressured by foreign competition in a vast range of commodities, American capitalism lacks its earlier dynamism. It is not providing enough jobs for those already in the market place, and at its very moment of crisis it is faced with a large group of new practitioners – mainly women and blacks – who are not only demanding jobs but demanding access to the most desirable areas of the economy where jobs are scarcest. Beyond that, the increasing numbers of young people with college

education among all groups has further intensified the imbalance between available professional openings and qualified applicants.

Unable to mobilise and drastically expand the number of jobs, Washington has turned instead to a policy of selective redistribution in order to mollify at ·least a portion of those constituencies now aggressively entering the job market for the first time. The agent of implementation is the quota.[1]

According to Kort, the fact of Jewish 'over-representation' in the free professions – itself on historical product of anti-semitic discrimination in other areas of the economy – and the limited opportunities for further employment in these fields make it 'inevitable that the new so-called "benign" quota system will exclude Jews as efficiently' as yesterday's open anti-semitism. This 'will not only deny [Jews] access to certain jobs, it will gradually drive them out of sectors upon which a large part of the Jewish economy is dependent'. Jews are a '"non-minority" minority' who are penalised for forming a part of the majority, while they also continue to be penalised by the majority as Jews. The author concludes:

This dilemma is not accidental or transitory. It reflects a deep-seated crisis within American capitalism, and the fundamental elements of the crisis – a saturated job market and a rising, impatient, previously under-developed indigenous caste demanding access to the market – have worked havoc on Jewish communities before.

Beyond this, perhaps the most worrying aspect of the economic uncertainties of the past decade is the danger posed to Israel by the new-found political power of the Arab states. Every year seems to bring more gains in recognition and legitimacy to the PLO, without any movement on its part, even a symbolic one, towards recognition of Israel's right to exist. Moved in large part by the need to secure Middle Eastern oil and by the increasing importance of Middle Eastern trade, Western Europe has become progressively more explicit in its friendliness towards the PLO. The unremitting hostility of the Soviet Union, and of much of the Third World, continues as before. Even the elements of improvement on the other side – the Camp David agreement and peace with Egypt, the bitter and intractable divisions with the Arab world, the continuing support of the United States – have done little or nothing to alter the prevalent mood.

Nor are Jews troubled only by external factors. There are many trends within the Jewish community which bode ill for the future. The most basic and disturbing of these is the very low Jewish birth rate, which some observers believe will virtually exterminate the Jewish people in less than a century. This birth rate in most Western countries is now below the replacement level; unless there are mass conversions to Judaism – as some American Jewish spokesmen have actually suggested – the Jewish population of the Western world will, inevitably, fall in absolute terms and will certainly fall sharply in relative terms. Such a prospect is compounded by increasing rates of intermarriage and by the decline in religious observance. Only a minority of people who describe themselves as Jews know more than the minimal facts about their religious, historical or cultural heritage.[2] There is, in short, a pervasive fear throughout Western Jewry that the unparalleled success enjoyed by Jews since the Second World War is undergoing a systematic disintegration, and that the wheel of history is about to roll again, returning Jewry to the unfavourable position of the inter-war period or before.

It is easy to speak of the period since 1973 as marking yet another homegeneous era in modern Jewish history, a fifth stage of the model described in Chapter 1. The characteristics of this fifth stage appear to be not so much an alteration in the nature of the Jewish elite or 'masses' but a change in the relative power of the Western world itself, and especially of the Western core in the United States and Western Europe. Weakened by inflation, the energy crisis, rising unemployment, military inferiority and a decline in productivity and innovation, as well as by a prevalent mood of pessimism, lowered expectations and increased doubts about technology and consumerism, the West has undergone a relative and perceptible decline *vis-à-vis* both the Soviet Union and its empire, the oil-rich Arab world and the dynamic economies of eastern Asia. Although Jewry has apparently continued to enjoy elite socio-economic status within the Western world, it is particularly vulnerable in the current geopolitical structure of the world: Israel is the Arab world's prime enemy, while the Soviet Union's pervasive anti-semitism and anti-Zionism have increased as Soviet power has grown.

Even within the Western world many trends are now weighing against continuing Jewish success: not only is the West less important in the world's power structure than twenty years ago, but the elite position of the Jews is also threatened. The rise in the United States of reverse discrimination measures, though without real parallel elsewhere, is only one among many such disturbing tendencies which bode ill for the future. 'Today American Jewry remains relatively well off, suffering no more than most groups from the current tight job market. The real danger lies in the future – ten or fifteen years hence – when corrosive percent formulas will have eroded opportunities open to Jews', Kort has also noted.[3] In other Western nations perhaps the most worrying prospect for the Jews and their disproportionate representation at the elite level is the danger of socialism, with its programme of nationalisation and redistribution. In Britain, it seems inevitable that a future Labour government will be dominated by its extreme left and will attempt to enact far-reaching schemes of nationalisation and measures of wealth and income redistribution. This will be harmful to all disproportionately successful elites, including the most vulnerable, the Jews. Such left-wing governments, equally inevitably, would be inherently less sympathetic to the United States and more sympathetic to Third World revolutionary movements, including the PLO. Coincidental with the rise of a rejuvenated socialist left throughout the Western world, a revived neo-Nazi movement, openly anti-semitic and ready to engage in acts of anti-Jewish terrorism and violence, has appeared and grown in strength in the wake of the current recession and the antagonism towards Israel by the extreme left.

This is indeed a picture of increasing plausibility. There can be few Jews who are as optimistic about the future today as ten or even five years ago. It seems clear that the post-1945 period has not seen the end of anti-semitism or of threats to the Jews' untroubled existence. However, although the future may well be darker than the extraordinary period of gain and prosperity following the Second World War, the facts do not yet warrant extreme pessimism.

As to Jewish fears of a substantial reduction in their numbers over the coming generations, the most sensible tentative conclusion is that they are exaggerated, although some absolute reduction in size is perhaps invitable, except in Israel.[4] But a reduction in Jewish numbers as the result of low birthrate reflects a trend throughout the Western world. This means that the decline in the Jewish *percentage* of the West's population will not be so marked as one might suppose. Nor is there any reason why the Jewish birth rate might not begin to move upwards again. Among Jews the increasing importance of Orthodox sects – who do not practise birth control – as well as the rising proportion of Oriental Jews in Israel, whose demographic profile is more like that of the Arabs than of European Jews, gives some hope for rising numbers. Similarly, intermarriage may lead, paradoxically, to more rather than fewer people who consider themselves Jewish.[5] Also Jews are today in an unprecedently strong position because of their gains at the elite level of Western societies in the post-war period. So far, there is little evidence of a decrease in their numbers, and so long as Jews are able to compensate for their small size by their elite positions and so long as the establishment right remains philo-semitic, the worst aspects of anti-semitism may be avoided.

Apart from the strategic advantages enjoyed by Jews in today's world are certain tactical advantages which are less obvious, though no less significant. First, the struggle in the Western world is not between Jew and Arab or even Jew and Palestinian, but between Jew and gentile anti-Zionist. This hostile group must always remain small, and contains few adherents to whom the Middle East is truly central. Given the ease with which anti-Zionism degenerates into anti-semitism it is likely that many radicals would be reluctant to embrace it wholeheartedly. There remain significant sectors of the moderate left which support Israel with enthusiasm and conviction. In contrast, for many thousands of Jews around the world, the continuing existence and welfare of Israel is a matter central to their political and personal existence.

Second, it should not be forgotten that there can be no real or permanent alliance between right-wing anti-semitism and left-wing anti-Zionism. So long as this remains true, it is unlikely that the remaining anti-semites of the extreme right and the new anti-Zionists of the extreme left will ever openly join forces; indeed, they are at great pains to distinguish their own beliefs from those of the other extreme. The continuing attack by the British National Front and its sister movements on Israel and the 'international Zionist conspiracy' is strongly reminiscent of much of the extreme left and its rhetoric. Despite this, the ideology of each precludes a working alliance with the others. We have seen as well how the ultra-right and ultra-left have evolved conflicting distortions and myths about the Holocaust, each attributing wickedness to the 'Zionists' for contradictory reasons.

Such points are tactically advantageous. Equally, however, they are not central to the continuing erosion of strength among Israel's supporters, and the growth of anti-Zionism, especially among socialists, will rise in years to come as the radical ideologies of the Vietnam generation come to occupy increasing positions of authority in the Western world's left parties, and as the revival of explicitly Marxist thought, which has been evident among Western Marxists for twenty years, makes Marxism more acceptable and widely known. In the long run a continuing economic recession will make this process more likely still. So, ironically, will another generation of predominantly conservative electoral victories. Unless there is a genuine and universally accepted peace treaty in the Middle East, and should the stalemate there continue, most mainstream socialist parties in the Western world will have adopted explicitly anti-Zionist platforms by 1990.

Let us conclude the political discussion in this book by returning to the matter raised at the very beginning: the gap between Jewish numbers and their achievement, above all their grossly disproportionate membership in the 'small' and 'large' elites. Our contention has been that this greatly enhanced Jewish influence and power on the issues which Jews regard as vital, above all the survival of Israel. We believe that this gap can exist only under capitalism because capitalism is inegalitarian, while under capitalism there are centres of power besides the government. Capitalism makes irrelevant the two great problems faced by the Jews, their very small numbers and the persistence of anti-semitism, by magnifying the Jewish presence at the elite, decision-making level, and by permitting the Jews to establish centres of power. Socialism and egalitarian doctrines close these options and generally entail support for radical anti-Zionism.

What the socialist and egalitarian fail to understand is that for the Jews, equality is not enough, so strong and so pervasive is the historical burden of anti-semitism. At present, given the weight of numbers which prevails among the Third World and Communist bloc countries against Israel, the Jews are greatly outnumbered. This is the central issue to which the socialist seeking *rapprochement* with the Jews must address himself.

Many left–liberal Jews may believe that it is the mission of Jewry to be 'a kingdom of priests and a holy people', and that this demands of the Jew some higher standards of morality which preclude self-interest and looks to the redemptive, prophetic role of the House of Israel in the larger world. However, Jews cannot formulate universal political ideologies and remain within the Jewish religious tradition and framework. Christians (and adherents of other religions like Islam and Buddhism) *can* legitimately do this and still remain true to their underlying faith. Since such a position is impossible for Jews, those who wish to formulate a universalistic ideology cannot do so within the framework of Judaism. This has produced the long line of those whom Deutscher has termed the 'non-Jewish Jew'[6] – those men and women of Jewish origin who found Judaism totally inadequate for world reformation and advocated a universalistic, secular faith in its place. Deutscher's own list of 'non-Jewish Jews' is Spinoza, Heine, Marx, Rosa Luxemburg, Trotsky and Freud. One may dispute some of his choices: Spinoza lived before the age of ideology and revolution; Freud's enterprise was scientific and he never quarrelled with his Jewish identity, as most of the others did. All, according to Deutscher, were similar in important respects:

> like Marx, Rosa Luxemburg and Trotsky strove . . . for the universal as against the particularist, and for the internationalist, as against the nationalist, solutions to the problems of their time . . . All these thinkers and revolutionaries have had certain philosophical principles in common. Although their philosophies vary, of course, from century to century and from generation to generation, they are all, from Spinoza to Freud, determinists, they all hold that the universe is ruled by laws inherent in it . . . All these thinkers agree on the relativity of moral standards . . . all these men, from Spinoza to Freud, believed in the ultimate solidarity of man; and this was implicit in their attitudes towards Jewry . . . These 'non-Jewish Jews' were essentially optimists, and their optimism reached heights which it is not easy to ascend in our times.

The harm which this thinking has done, especially to other Jews, is very great. The essential problem with the radical 'non-Jewish Jew' is not his misplaced and naïve idealism but his failure to understand power and to be ruthless enough to carry out a revolution. Consequently, the Jewish radical, usually one of the makers of revolution, is invariably among its first victims.

The 'non-Jewish Jew' with his idealism, has gone only one step beyond the liberal Jewish intellectual who, in his belief that Jews ought to become 'a kingdom of priests and a holy people', asks the Jews to 'be good', to behave in a way which puts them at risk or helps to diminish the few protections which Jews possess. He, too, attempts to make of Judaism a universalistic sect, idealistic rather than realistic.

Some pessimism and realism, then, are only valid options open to the Jew. Even Deutscher admitted this frankly:

> It is an indubitable fact that the Nazi massacre of six million European Jews has not made any deep impression on the nations of Europe . . . Was then the optimistic belief in humanity voiced by the great Jewish revolutionaries justified? Can we still share their faith in the future of civilization?
>
> I admit that if one were to try to answer these questions from an exclusively Jewish standpoint, it would be hard, perhaps impossible, to give a positive answer.[7]

Deutscher goes on to give the only answer open to socialists, and demonstrates how little even the greatest of historians had learned from history:

> As for myself, I cannot approach the issue from an exclusively Jewish standpoint; and my answer is: Yes, then faith was justified. It was justified at any rate, in so far as the belief in the ultimate solidarity of mankind is itself one of the conditions necessary for the preservation of humanity and for the cleansing of our civilization of the dregs of barbarity that are still present in it and still poison it.

Liberal Jews, while not going this far, would surely agree with Deutscher's overall optimism, his belief in the 'ultimate solidarity of mankind' and the necessity of 'cleansing the dregs of barbarity', though their definition of these might well differ from the socialists. In this they go beyond what Jews may infer from his religious faith, and come close to copying the most dangerous naïvités of the 'non-Jewish Jew'. The best features of Judaism and the Jewish experience is its sense that tragedy is never far away.

Many liberal Jews, not yet persuaded by such arguments, would reply that, in the final analysis, Jews have 'natural affinity' for the

political left, which is the biggest fallacy of all. The political stance
of a variegated ethnic group is the product of the set of historical
and economic circumstances which that group meets. The left–
liberalism of many Western Jews is the product of a special set of
historical circumstances which existed from about the third or
fourth quarter of the nineteenth century to about the third quarter
of the twentieth. Jews were not notable as revolutionaries or
radicals until the time of Marx. As late as 1834, as E.J. Hobsbawm
has pointed out, of forty-six prominent Galician revolutionaries
arrested by the Austrian authorities only one was a Jew.[8] The
radicalism of Western Jewry in the period 1850–1950 has been a
specific response to political and social exclusion, to right-wing anti-
semitism and to the chronic poverty of the Pale and later urban
ghettoes. Other nations have included a majority who were
chronically poor but those nations possessed a conservative faction
more prominent and numerically greater than Western Jewry in this
period. Probably the main reason for this has been the abnormal
social structure of Jewry compared with all other settled peoples
who possessed an aristocracy, a priesthood enjoying legal
establishment and an agricultural sector. Even so, the left–
liberalism of Jewry at this time can perhaps be exaggerated.[9]

Certainly, as the causes of the Jewish affinity for the left have
passed, so, too, will Jewish commitment to such a position. This has
occurred throughout the Western world and is not inconsistent with
any religious tenet of Judaism. Such a mood of realism, of very
guarded optimism for the future amidst a background of historical
tragedy, seems best suited to today's world.

Notes

1. Michael Kort, 'Quotas and Jewish History', *Midstream*, May 1978, pp. 50–1.
2. Many of these points are made in, e.g., Hillel Halkin, *Letters to An American Jewish Friend. A Zionist Polemic* (Philadelphia, 1977).
3. Kort, 'Quotas', p. 51.
4. Samuel S. Lieberman and Morton Weinfeld, 'Demoghaphic Trends and Jewish Survival', *Midstream* (Nov. 1978).
5. Ibid.
6. Isaac Deutscher, 'The Non-Jewish Jew', in his *The Non-Jewish Jew and Other Essays* (Oxford, 1968).
7. Ibid., pp. 37–8.

8. E.J. Hobsbawm, *The Age of Revolutions, 1789–1848* (London, 1962), p. 234.

9. On inter-war eastern Europe, for instance, see Bela Vago, 'The Attitude Toward the Jews as a Criterion of the Left–Right Concept', in Bela Vago and George L. Mosse (eds.), *Jews and Non-Jews in Eastern Europe, 1918–1945* (New York, 1974).

INDEX

academics, Jewish 63–4, 122–4
Alderman, Geoffrey 17, 118–19, 154
anti-semitism: in America 22–3, 138,
    149; in Australia 164, 169, 173; in
    Britain 14–17, 161–3; in
    contemporary world 78–93, 226;
    in France 33–4; in Germany 25 ff;
    in Russia 180–5, 187–8, 190–6;
    realignment of 77–114; types of
    78–9
anti-Zionism: 65–6, 67–8, 69, 102,
    104–14, 130, 151, 226–7; in
    Australia 167–71; in Britain
    160–3; in the Soviet Union 195–6
anti-Zionists and the Holocaust
    108–14
Arafat, Yasser 113, 210
Ashkenazi Jews: in Britain 19–20; rise
    in America 25–6
Australia, Jews in 58–60, 62, 104,
    113–14, 119–20, 128, 163–173
Australian Labour Party 165–8, 170–3

Balfour Declaration 12
Baruch, Bernard 20, 23
Bevin, Ernest 18
Biro-Bidzhan 192–3, 194
blacks (US) and Jews 139–40, 144–5
Borochov, Ber 52–3, 201
Brandeis, Louis 23
Britain, Jews in 152–63; con-
    temporary rise 58, 104; history of
    12–19; voting statistics 118–19

capitalism: in Britain 13, 15–16; in
    France 33–7; in Germany 29–32;
    in Russia 163–5; in the United
    States 20–2
Carmichael, Joel 126
Carter, Jimmy 98–9, 145–7
Churchill, Sir Winston 16, 95
City of London 13, 15
civil rights (in US) 50, 139–42, 144–5
Commentary 48, 125–7, 130
conservatives, contemporary, and
    Jews 80–6, 153–6
Conservative Party (UK) 16–19,
    95–6, 152–60, 161–3
'Cousinhood' 13–17

De Gaulle, Charles 37
Democratic Party (US) 120–1, 139,
    146–8
Deutscher, Isaac 226–8
Disraeli, Benjamin 13
Dreyfus Affair 14, 34

East End (London) 17
Einstein, Albert 52
elites: definition 11, 43–9; in Russia
    183–5, 188–90, 193; Jewish
    participation in 31–2, 50–64
elitism 43
Encounter 48, 126
Establishment, Western, and Jews
    93–6

Fascism 79
France, Jews in 33–8
Fraser, Malcolm 114, 172–3
Friedman, Milton 125

German Jewish history 27–32

Herzl, Theodor 34, 201–2
Himmelfarb, Milton 125
history, modern Jewish, model of
    11–12, 222–5
Hitler, Adolph 34
Hollywood 26, 142
Holocaust 51, 79–80, 86–9, 108–12,
    142, 165, 205; American reaction
    to 23–5; and extreme left 108–12;
    and neo-Nazis 86–9; British
    reaction to 16–17; in Germany 27,
    31–2

immigration, Jewish: in Britain 14,
    17; in France 35–6; in Germany
    32; in the United States 22–3, 56
intelligentsia, contemporary 48, 63–4;
    Jews in 63–4, 121–9
Isaacs, Sir Isaac 164
Israel: and contemporary
    conservatives 93–7; and
    contemporary geo-politics 81,
    94–5, 224–5; and social demo-
    crats 112–14; and the extreme left
    107–12; and the Soviet Union

232